Summer of '77

Beaches, bars and boogie nights in Ibiza

Robert Fear

Contents

Author's Note 7

1 Leaving England 9

2 Barcelona to Ibiza 13

3 Back in Es Cana 17

4 Looking for a room 21

5 Finding work 25

6 Monday morning feeling 29

7 Work and play 33

8 Night of pleasure 38

9 Mixed emotions 42

10 News from home 47

11 Afternoon cycle ride 52

12 Tootsies opening party 56

13 Back to work 61

14 Meeting Kim 65

15 Night out with Kim 69

16 More news from home 74

17 Leaving work 78

18 Time off 83

19 Trip to Majorca 87

20 Finding my friends 91

21 Meeting up at last 95

22 Back home in Ibiza 99

23 Catching up 103

24 Bletchingley lads 107

25 Starting at Tootsies 111

26 Struggling at work 116

27 Election day 121

28 Meeting Helen 124

29 Trouble at Tootsies 128

30 Change of plan 133

31 Spending time with Helen 137

32 Sad farewell 142

33 Meeting Alice 146

34 More trouble at Tootsies 151

35 Getting to know Alice 155

36 Handing out flyers 160

37 Bletchingley lads arrive 164

38 Feeling homesick 169

39 Finding another job 174

40 Fresh start 178

41 Enjoying work 182

42 Letters from Alice 186

43 Friday night in Grannies 190

44 Welcome day off 194

45 More letters from Alice 198

46 Payday arrives 202

47 Funky moped 206

48 Anxious wait 209

49 Days fly by 213

50 Meeting Angie 216

51 Fight night 221

52 Bundle of letters 225

53 Back to work again 230

54 Number plate incident 234

55 Meeting Penny 239

56 Stormy weather 243

57 Finishing work 248

58 Letters from Penny 253

59 Last days in Es Cana 259

60 Leaving Ibiza 265

What happened next? 271

Contact the Author 275

More about the Author 277

Other books published by Robert Fear 279

Acknowledgements 285

Author's Note

I sometimes have problems remembering what I did yesterday, let alone last year.

So what am I doing writing a memoir about something that happened over forty years ago when I was 21?

My secret is that I hoard things. In this case, letters I received in Ibiza during the summer of 1977, while working the season there. Without them, I would have had no chance of recalling events from so long ago. With them, I have been able to trigger long lost memories.

Although I no longer have any contact with the characters in this story, apart from my family, some names have been changed to protect identities. There are also people whose names I have forgotten where I have used fictional ones.

I cannot guarantee every element of this memoir is accurate. Conversations are reconstructed while recollections may have been distorted through the telescope of time. The letters, however, are true reflections from that amazing summer.

Enjoy reading about the six months that changed my life.

1

Leaving England

Had I made the right decision?

It was such an easy one to make nine months ago as the four of us flew home from Ibiza after a magical two-week holiday. We vowed to return for the next summer season.

Now here I was, alone, as the bus headed out of Victoria Coach Station into the gloom of a rainy mid-April morning in London. As I peered through the window, I could just make out the outline of Sarah as she walked back towards the train station.

* * *

In July 1976 I had spent two weeks in Es Cana, Ibiza, with three mates. Our holiday ended too fast, and we aimed to return for the start of the 1977 season. Circumstances changed and one by one, Mutts, Sam and Siv postponed their departure until later in the summer. I remained determined.

I had started work at Williams & Glyn's bank in the City of London after leaving Reigate Grammar School. It was my intention to work there for a year, before going to university. Money altered that, and I had stayed with the bank instead.

My choice to go abroad for six months shocked my parents. They worried it would impact my future career. Siblings Christine (16) and Alastair (19) thought I was mad. Both had questions about what their 21-year-old brother intended to do.

This decision to leave became more complicated as I grew close to Sarah. We had met in the autumn and soon got very involved. Our social life together was great as we enjoyed ourselves at parties, pubs and discos. Favourite memories were of the Monday mornings I took time off work and sneaked round to Sarah's house after her mum left. Sarah opened the front door in her dressing gown, and we went straight up to bed where we kissed and cuddled the morning away. One Monday, we were making love in the front room when a key clicked in the door. We scrambled for our clothes, but it was obvious to Sarah's mum, as she walked in, what we had been doing. After a while she forgave us.

It was difficult to save money. I netted £120 a month at the bank but also worked behind the bar at the Station Hotel to earn extra cash. The Station was the only pub in the village of South Nutfield where we lived.

When I left there was enough in my money-belt to keep me solvent for the first few weeks in Ibiza. I had £400 in travellers' cheques (the equivalent of £2400 or $3000 today) plus 40 French Francs (£5) and 5400 Spanish Pesetas (£45).

* * *

On the morning of April 12th, 1977, Sarah accompanied me for the hour-long train journey to London. Few words passed our lips. We held each other close. Bouts of sadness swept over us. There was a sudden realisation of how much our lives would change.

We walked to the coach station, and the pain became intense. After an emotional farewell embrace, Sarah waved me off. The coach made its way through the traffic of central London. I tried to make myself comfortable, but the turmoil in my stomach and unease in my head got worse. My eyes gazed at the grey city scenes outside as we travelled around the outskirts of London.

The enormity of my actions enveloped me for a long time. The bus picked up speed. As we neared the port of Dover, my mood changed. A huge weight lifted from my shoulders. I was on my way.

* * *

The ferry edged away. In the early evening light, the clouds cleared, and the sun appeared on the horizon for a moment. Through the descending gloom, I glimpsed the famous white cliffs of Dover as we left the shores of England.

The seas were choppy, and the wind icy as we sailed across the channel. I put on a jumper and buttoned up my denim jacket. Determined to stay on deck, I enjoyed the chill that blew against my face and through my hair. A surge of elation swept over me as I realised my dream was coming true.

Deep in my own thoughts, I did not hear her approach. It took a few seconds to realise someone had spoken.

'Hi, where are you heading?' she repeated.

Taller than me and several years older, long blonde hair wrapped around her shoulders, and pale blue eyes glistened.

I averted my gaze for a moment, before replying, 'Hi, sorry I didn't notice you there. I'm travelling to Barcelona by coach, and then getting a ferry across to Ibiza.'

'What are you planning to do there?'

I beamed a smile at her. 'I'm hoping to work for the season in a place called Es Cana.'

Her eyes looked deep into mine. 'Is this the first time you've worked abroad?'

'Yes, I've just finished at a bank in London. Where are you heading to? Sorry, what's your name?'

'Everyone calls me Micky, but my real name is Michelle. I'm off to Barcelona and we're on the same coach. I saw you earlier, and thought, as you are on your own, you'd appreciate the company. I'm an English teacher returning to the school where I work, after an Easter break at home in Bristol.'

Micky edged closer as if to get protection against the biting wind. 'And what's your name?'

'Most people call me Fred.'

'Is that a nickname then?'

'Yes, I got it at school, and it's stuck ever since. My friends know me as Fred although my real name is Robert.'

Her eyes widened. 'You seem more like a Fred than a Robert.'

I gave her a wide grin. 'How long have you worked in Barcelona?'

'Just under a year. I finished Teacher Training College not long after Franco died in November 1975. Spain always interested me. When I saw an advert in the paper for a teaching position there, I jumped at the chance.'

'Are you enjoying it?'

'On the whole, yes. Spain is changing fast after forty years of dictatorship, but people's attitudes will take longer to change. Life for a woman is still difficult. I'm lucky they look after me while at the school, but things can be awkward outside sometimes.'

'Do you ever regret doing it?'

'No, not at all. Travel gives you a new outlook on life. You'll discover that for yourself this summer. Provided you don't weaken, and I doubt you will, Fred.'

'Thanks, Micky. That's nice of you.'

The loud sound of the ship's siren broke the atmosphere. The ferry had arrived at the port of Calais.

Micky gave me a peck on the cheek and winked. 'I'll see you back on the bus, take care.'

'Yes, great to meet you.'

What a lovely surprise, I thought, as I smoked a quick roll-up, before returning to the coach.

* * *

We were among the first to drive off the ship.

Two officers boarded and gave our passports a cursory glance. Things had become easier since the UK entered the Common Market (later the European Union) in 1973.

After a brief stop on the outskirts of Calais, to pick up another six passengers, we sped off into the night. As there were still free seats, Micky joined me at the back of the coach.

It felt good to have company. We chatted away for ages as the bus headed south through rural France. Then the coach entered the first toll booth and the motorway network. Midnight passed, and we snuggled together to keep warm.

The night flew by as we snoozed and held each other tight. There were several stops at service stations, one where we changed drivers. Other passengers took refreshment breaks. We were so relaxed and comfortable we stayed on the bus.

As the sun rose, we stopped at a little French village. This time we joined the others and sat outside a small restaurant in the early morning sunshine. There was a refreshing breeze. Micky and I enjoyed our breakfast of black coffee and croissants.

It was mid-morning when we arrived at the French/Spanish border post of La Junquera.

Spain was not a member of the Common Market, and the controls were strict. We had to disembark to walk through customs and have our passports checked.

2

Barcelona to Ibiza

After negotiating the Spanish border, the rest of our coach trip passed fast.

I slept most of the way and missed much of the coast road experience Micky raved about.

It was early afternoon when we arrived in Barcelona. The sun blazed from blue skies. Micky and I had a farewell hug before we went our separate ways. We swapped addresses and promised to keep in touch. That was the last time I saw her, although she crossed my mind often.

I had several hours to kill before the evening ferry left for Ibiza. Most of the afternoon I spent watching the world go by from various vantage points on Las Ramblas as I made my way down the long avenue towards the port. I drank three beers and finished the sandwiches from home.

Micky had advised me to take a taxi to the Ferry Terminal, as it was easy to get lost in the industrial area with its fences, blocked streets and lack of signposts. I arrived in good time and passed two backpackers struggling on foot towards the port.

I bought my ticket, which was excellent value at 334 pesetas (£2.85). A cabin would have cost treble that. After boarding the ferry, I bagged a seat on the upper deck.

There was frantic activity on the dockside as the last of the trucks drove across the ramp. The nine-hour trip to Ibiza was soon underway.

On deck, I leaned over the railings. The twinkling lights of Barcelona faded into the distance. A crescent moon reflected off the dark ocean as the ferry sailed through the calm waters of the Mediterranean. There was a gentle breeze, but it was still warm. Waves lapped against the sides of the boat as it ploughed onwards.

I smelt the saltiness of the water and the clean sea air. Along with the faint whiff of diesel from the ship's engines, another familiar smell drifted over. I recognised it from various parties at home. It was the sweet aroma of hashish and came from my left. I turned in that direction and saw a young couple smoking a joint.

I had tried hash twice, but it had done nothing for me. Several of my friends swore by it and recommended the relaxing effects it had on them. I preferred beer.

The guy saw I was looking over and beckoned me to join them. He was tall, with long greasy black hair, and a knowing look on his face. She was shorter with plaited brown hair. Her hazel eyes twinkled in the moonlight as she smiled in my direction.

His husky Scottish voice whispered, 'Did you want to try some my friend? It's nice stuff.'

With a shake of the head, I changed the subject. 'Hi, my name's Fred. It's a lovely evening, isn't it? Have you been to Ibiza before?'

They both chuckled as if they shared a secret. 'I'm Alex, and this is my girlfriend Sharon. We've lived in Ibiza for four years now and have just been to Barcelona on a shopping trip. Where are you headed?'

'Es Cana. I spent a two-week holiday last year with three of my mates. We all planned to come back again for the season, but I'm the only one who made it. My plan is to spend the summer there and get work, maybe in a bar.'

They looked at me through glazed eyes.

Sharon's voice was soft with a noticeable Nordic accent, 'Yes, we know Es Cana well. We have a stall at the Hippy Market there every Wednesday during the tourist season.'

My eyebrows raised. 'What type of things do you sell?'

'Necklaces, wristbands and clothing we make ourselves. Alex is good at caricatures and makes money doing those. We go to different places during the week, such as Ibiza Town, San Antonio and Santa Eulalia. The Hippy Market at Punta Arabi in Es Cana is our most profitable though.'

'Fascinating. Where do you live?'

She drew on the remnants of the joint. 'We are part of a small commune in a remote area to the north of the island, three kilometres from the old fishing village of Portinatx. It is a lovely place. We rent a 300-year-old *finca* from a local couple who have retired to Ibiza Town. The setup is basic with no electricity or running water, but we find the surroundings suit our lifestyle.'

Alex sparked up another joint and took several deep drags before exhaling the smoke. A smile crossed his face as he offered it. 'Have you ever indulged, Fred?'

'I've tried it twice in England, but it never agreed with me.'

'You should try this, it's the finest Moroccan hashish. We've just picked up a consignment in Barcelona. It gives you a clean high and is the best gear I've come across.'

I thought before shaking my head. 'No, you're OK. When the time is right I will, but I want to keep a clear head for the moment.'

Both looked at me in amazement.

Sharon's brow furrowed. 'Don't leave it too long, I'm sure you'd enjoy it if you tried it. We know from experience it gives you a new perspective on life.'

I felt uneasy but still resisted. Our conversation became more difficult as they floated off into their own worlds.

Alex smirked. 'We'll be here all night, so if you change your mind come and find us.'

'Yes, will do. Thanks for your company. I'm going to buy a drink. Did either of you want anything?'

They shook their heads in unison.

I walked down the metal staircase and found a small bar. The barman was standing around looking bored.

He turned to face me. 'What can I get you, mate?'

I had expected to try out my Spanish, but the distinctive Australian twang threw me.

'I'll have a large vodka and orange juice, please.'

His eyebrows shot up. 'They're all large in Spain, mate.'

15

He put ice cubes into the glass and poured vodka until the ice floated. Then he added the mixer to the remaining third.

He passed it over the bar. I handed him the correct change and pulled up a seat. As I sipped my drink, the taste of vodka was strong. I fell into conversation with the barman, Aaron, who had been working on the ferry for several weeks. With long fair hair tied back in a ponytail, he looked tired.

I flashed him a grin. 'How did you end up getting a job here?'

'I travelled around Europe for six months, but my money was running low. A Spanish friend of mine put in a good word, and I landed this little number. It's not well paid but keeps me going.'

'How much time do you spend on the ferry then?'

'It's almost non-stop. The only chance I get to take a nap is when we dock. Even then I stay on the boat in my cabin.'

'No wonder you look so tired.'

'Yes, it's a lot of work but I'm due a week's break after this trip. So, I hope to catch up on sleep and explore Barcelona then. I've not had the opportunity yet.'

I ordered another vodka and orange just as a group of Spanish lorry drivers came into the bar. Their loud conversation and raucous laughter grated with me, so I said goodnight to Aaron and headed upstairs.

Settled in the deck chair, I pulled my sleeping bag up around me against the cooler breeze of the night and sipped on my drink. The effects of the vodka soon sent me to sleep.

It was after 7 am when I awoke. The screeching of birds around the boat meant we were nearing land. I watched in awe as the coast of the island came into view, and the sun rose over the horizon. Everything looked so peaceful as we passed tree-covered hills fringed with sandy beaches.

A small group of fishing boats headed in the opposite direction. The stone walls of Ibiza Town appeared as the ferry manoeuvred past the rocky outcrops towards the harbour. Within minutes, we had docked and disembarked.

I set my mind on getting breakfast, before finding the bus station and making my way across the island to Es Cana.

3

Back in Es Cana

As I walked from the bus stop towards the seafront that morning with my black duffel bag, the streets of Es Cana were quiet compared to the previous July. I saw a few locals and just the occasional tourist.

In the middle of an elevated row of shops, I came across the closed front entrance of Grannies Bar. I peered through the bars of the gate and down the steps. There were empty glasses on the outside tables. I saw a scrawled notice: *Open from 8 pm*. I aimed to come back later to catch up with Mick and Pat, the bar's owners.

Further down the road, I arrived at the Restaurante Es Cana. It overlooked the curving beach which formed the seafront. I took a seat at a table on the veranda.

Life slowed as I soaked up the warm spring sunshine. I gazed out at the blue waters of the Mediterranean Sea. There were several people scattered along the clean sandy strip, a sharp contrast to the packed beach I remembered.

The waiter came across. During the winter months, I had tried to learn Spanish from a Berlitz book and tape recording. Now was my chance to test it out.

He greeted me, *'Bon dia senyor, com estàs?'*

I struggled with the accent but assumed he had welcomed me and asked how I was.

With a slight stutter, I answered, *'Muy bien gracias y ¿usted?'*

This was a phrase I had learned – Very well thanks, and you?

The waiter replied, *'Molt bé, així que gràcies.'*

I did not understand a word. This was not the Spanish I tried so hard to learn. As I stared at him, he asked another question, *'Vol alguna cosa de menjar o beure?'*

I recognised the words for eating and drinking, so I replied, *'Puedo tomar una cerveza frio por favor.'* – Can I have a cold beer, please?

The waiter bowed. *'Si senyor, cervesa embotellada o cervesa de barril?'* This time I understood. Did I want bottled or draft beer?

I stuttered again, *'Una botella de San Miguel por favor.'* – A bottle of San Miguel, please.

San Miguel had been my favourite beer the summer before, although it got warm in the July heat. I assumed it would stay cool for longer in the more temperate April sunshine.

Within minutes the waiter returned with a chilled San Miguel. *'¡Salud!'*

'¡Salud!' – Cheers.

I lifted the bottle to my lips and sipped on the tangy, refreshing beer. It tasted fantastic. I relaxed more and more with each sip.

As I sat and chilled out, my thoughts turned to the Spanish I had tried so hard to learn.

At school, I had been hopeless at languages. I studied Latin for two years, and French for five, but failed my exams. I was so bad I only got 10% in my French mock O (Ordinary) Level. They didn't even allow me to sit the final exam.

My motivation during the winter was different. I wanted to learn the language, so I tried to memorise a lot of Spanish phrases. This was the real world though, and I had already encountered problems understanding the waiter. It would take me a few weeks to learn that the locals in Ibiza speak a Catalan dialect, different from Castilian Spanish. No wonder I was confused.

For an hour, I watched the world go by. It dawned on me I had made it. The hard work over the winter months had been worthwhile. My dream was coming true.

After a *bocadillo de jamon* (ham roll) and another San Miguel, I settled the bill and headed for the sand.

I tucked my bag behind rocks at the end of the beach, before taking off my shoes and socks and rolling up my jeans. The water was cold as I paddled along the edge. The gentle swell of the sea washed against my bare legs.

* * *

I strolled along the alleyway leading to the Red Lion Bar.

This had been a familiar watering hole the previous year, and we'd got to know Tich behind the bar well. Despite his nickname, he was not that small. Two inches shorter than me (5 ft 6 ins), he had neat blond hair and blue eyes.

Tich was a livewire. Like a few of the English locals, he came from Leicester. This was a connection for me because I was born there, although I remembered little about the place as my family moved away when I was 11.

Everything was quiet as I popped my head around the door to confirm whether the Red Lion was open. There did not appear to be anyone there.

'Fred, how the hell are you?'

I spun around.

Tich smiled over at me as he rolled a barrel of beer along the floor, and then pushed it behind the bar.

A wide smile spread across my face. 'I'm fine, mate. How about you?'

'It's all good here. Getting ready for another season of madness. Roger and Margaret are still in England, so I have to get everything sorted on my own.'

'Need a hand?'

'No, you're OK. Do you fancy a beer?'

'Please. San Miguel?'

Tich reached into the fridge and pulled out two bottles. He opened them and passed me one.

He raised his bottle. *'¡Salud!'*

I clicked my bottle against his. *'¡Salud!'*

'So, you made it back, Fred. What happened to your mates?'

'Yes, I kept my word, but Mutts, Sam and Siv won't be here until later in the season. They didn't save enough money over the winter.'

'So many holidaymakers say they'll come back, but few make it. So, well done. Do you think you'll be here for the season?'

'I hope so, provided I can get a place to stay and some work.'

'You've come early enough to bag yourself somewhere to stay. Tony's Bar is your best chance. He has rooms in the basement that are basic but cheap. To be honest, you only need a place to sleep and tidy up.'

'Sounds good.'

'They're open, so I'd suggest you head over there to ask whether he still has rooms available.'

'Thanks, Tich. That's a great help. What about work, do you know of anything?'

'That's a tough one. It's too early for bar work, and those who come back each year have jobs lined up. You might find something come May or June time though. Tootsies and Grannies get busy in the high season and they always need help.'

My smile widened. 'I remember they were both hectic last July. Anything apart from bar jobs for now?'

'There's building work, but it doesn't pay well. When you see Mick and Pat from Grannies, you could ask them. Pat's dad, Jim, has retired here and owns his own villa, but he still works to keep his hand in. You might get labouring work with him. Be warned though, he never stops talking.'

'Brilliant. Thanks for your help.'

'No problem, I'm sure everything will work out for you. Sorry, I need to get on and sort a few more things out in the bar and cellar. Why don't you head over to Tony's? Do you know where it is?'

'It's across the wasteland from the El Cortijo disco isn't it?'

'Yes, if you get to the back entrance of Grannies then you've walked too far.'

'Thanks, Tich.' I shook his hand. 'I'll see you later.'

'Take care, and best of luck, Fred. I'm sure we'll see plenty of each other during the summer.'

I downed the rest of my beer, grabbed my bag, and headed off towards Tony's Bar.

4

Looking for a room

It took five minutes to walk to Tony's.

I opened the door to an empty restaurant, but there were several people sitting at the small bar in the far corner. As I walked over, Pat saw me. She jumped off her stool and threw her arms around me. 'Great to see you, Fred. Are you on your own?'

Before I could speak, Tony came from behind the bar and shook my hand. 'I knew you'd be back. What happened to your friends?'

'They plan to come out later when they have more money. I wanted to come back now, even if it meant returning on my own.'

'Well done my friend, do you fancy a drink?'

'Could I have a San Miguel, Tony?'

'Make yourself at home. You remember my girlfriend, Sue, don't you? This is Pedro and Roberto. They'll help with the restaurant this year.'

Sue smiled across, and the boys greeted me, *'Buenas tardes, Fred, ¿cómo estás?'* – Good afternoon, Fred, how are you?

I beamed back at them. *'Muy bien, gracias.'* – Very well, thanks.

Tony, whose real name was Antonio, was a little taller than me, with short black hair and striking blue eyes. Born in Barcelona, he came to Ibiza in search of work in his early twenties. They took him on as a waiter and then as a chef at a hotel in San Antonio, on the western coast of the island. With this experience behind him, Tony branched out on his own. His building was one of many constructed over the past few years to cater for the booming tourist trade in Es Cana. The increased number of charter flights from the UK and Europe meant opportunities to profit from hungry and thirsty holidaymakers.

His girlfriend, Sue, was from Somerset and had come to Ibiza on holiday in 1974. She fell in love with Tony, the sunshine and the lifestyle. After a brief period back in England, she gave up her job as a receptionist and returned to help run Tony's Bar.

We sat perched on stools at the bar and sipped our drinks.

Pat swivelled on her stool. 'So, what are your plans, Fred?'

I'd met Pat and Mick in Grannies. They were from my home city of Leicester and had moved to Ibiza five years ago.

My eyebrows furrowed. 'Well, I need to get somewhere to stay, and then I hope to find work. Although I saved money in England, it won't last more than a few weeks.'

A smile creased Pat's face. 'You've arrived early in the season, so should be in with a good chance.'

She turned to Tony. 'Do you still have any rooms free in the basement?'

He looked in my direction. 'Yes, I have, would you be interested? There are six single rooms with a bed and washbasin in each, shared bathroom and toilet. Most of the rooms are occupied, but I have one available at the far end which might suit you.'

'Sounds great, Tony. If it has a bed, somewhere to store my things, and a place to wash, that'll be fine. How much?'

'We'll worry about that later, but I'll charge you a fair price. When you've finished your drink, I can show you the room.'

I nodded in agreement and shook his hand. *'Muchas gracias.'* – Thank you very much.

His lips parted in a grin. *'De nada.'* – You are welcome.

So, my room was sorted. I wouldn't need the small tent I'd brought.

Pat grinned at me and took a long drink of her gin and tonic. After a moment's thought, she turned towards me. 'My dad, Jim, needs help with his building work. It's not well paid, but I'll ask him if he can take you on as a labourer.'

'That's kind of you, Pat. I've got no experience but I'm a quick learner.'

I finished my drink, and Tony took me down a flight of steps at the side of the building, and along the basement corridor to the end. My new home was a whitewashed concrete room with small windows high up the walls at ground level. It contained a washbasin, wardrobe, chair and a bed. There was no lock on the door, so I had to be careful with my passport and money.

Tony left me to settle in and unpack. It was a relief to have a roof over my head. I made myself comfortable, had a siesta and a bath.

* * *

Early the next morning I sat at a table on the veranda outside Tony's Bar after a breakfast of fried eggs on toast and a strong mug of tea. The gentle warmth of April sunshine contrasted with the rain I had left behind in England. A hint of pine drifted over from the nearby trees and the birds were singing. Contentment swept over me.

'Can I get you anything else to drink?' asked Sue.

'No, thanks. I'm fine. How much do I owe you?'

'Oh, don't worry. You're part of the family now. I'll start a tab for you. Just settle up when you pay your rent.'

I set off towards the seafront. The previous evening, I'd visited places I remembered from the year before. Today I wanted to venture further afield. I walked around the sandy bay where a few scattered bodies lay soaking up the rays. Beyond the beach, a small winding path undulated along the coastline. I followed it and soon found myself up on a headland with spectacular views across the sparkling blue sea. Straight in front of me was a rocky island, a few hundred yards offshore. On either side were several smaller ones. Fishing and leisure boats weaved through channels between the islands. Birds and insect life added a background chorus to the wonderful scene.

After sitting for a while, I continued walking. The path curved around the rocky headland. I peered over the steep cliffs, careful not to slip, and brushed against the thorny bushes that encroached over the dusty track. The long trousers and plimsolls I wore gave me good protection. As the sunshine beat down, it released the smells of surrounding vegetation and pine trees. I breathed it all in. Soon, the coastline levelled out again, and the path headed downwards. I spotted a small cove with a strip of beach in the distance.

Scrambling down the hillside, I arrived at a deserted sandy area. The temptation was too much. I stripped off my clothes, looked around to make sure no-one was watching, and waded out into the clear, cold water.

I swam for a while, and then floated on my back soaking up the sun. Time passed, and I could have stayed there for ages. Out of the corner of my eye, I spotted an older couple making their way to the cove. I was a long way from my pile of clothes but swam in that direction. To my horror, they were headed for the same place.

Relief flooded over me as I saw they had stripped off and lay on their towels naked. As I climbed out of the water, trying to cover myself, they waved. I smiled and sat on a rock to dry.

The walk back was more difficult. I hadn't realised how far I'd come. My limbs ached from the exertion, and the sun burned my shoulders. What had been a pleasant stroll became a struggle. I was relieved to see the beach of Es Cana once more.

By then it was mid-afternoon. I was hungry and thirsty. On the veranda of Restaurante Es Cana, I ordered a San Miguel and a dish of *Arroz de Matanza*, a typical local meal of rice, pork and herbs, with a tasty sauce. It proved to be filling and satisfying. The restaurant sold postcards, so I picked out two with island scenes. With a ballpoint pen borrowed from the waiter, I wrote one to Mother and another to Sarah. My writing was small, so I crammed in lots of news about my arrival, and how I had settled into life abroad.

I also told them where they could reply – c/o Red Lion, Apartado 90, Santa Eulalia, Ibiza.

Tich had suggested I use the Red Lion's address and pick up letters whenever I dropped in to see him. There was no Post Office, so I bought stamps at a local shop and left the cards with them to include with their outgoing mail. Tired but happy, I returned to my room for a late siesta.

5

Finding work

After a long sleep, I freshened up and made my way to see Tich in the Red Lion.

As I strolled into the bar he grinned. 'Hiya, mate. How's it going? Are you settling in OK?'

As I told him about my walk, Tich took out two bottles of San Miguel from the fridge and uncapped them. 'Great to hear. It's a fantastic place, isn't it? Shame I don't have much time to get out during the summer. That's why I enjoy winter. No tourists, the weather is mild, and I can relax.'

'Are there many who live here during the winter?'

'Only a couple of us in Es Cana, apart from the locals. There are others who stay year-round in Santa Eulalia. If I want company, I sometimes head over there.'

Four Scottish lads came in and asked for the Red Lion speciality cocktails. I sat back and watched Tich as he worked his magic. He shouted across the sound of the cocktail shaker, 'I ran into Pat earlier. She said Jim wanted to talk to you about the job. If you're in Grannies later, you can catch up with her.'

'Brilliant. Cheers, mate.'

'No problem. It looks like things are coming together for you. That's one advantage of being here early in the season.'

* * *

Grannies was busy, which surprised me. Mick and Pat were working with Graham, a friend of theirs from Leicester who I knew from the previous year. They served groups of thirsty customers. The weekend had arrived, and there were plenty of tourists to liven up the place.

Mick spotted me, poured a glass of Estrella, and passed it over.

I gave him a thumbs-up and made my way to the outside terrace.

There was a table with only one guy sitting at it, filling out paperwork in a ring-bound folder.

I interrupted him, 'Would it disturb you if I sat here?'

'No, lad. Take a seat. I'll join you in a minute.' I recognised the Liverpool accent.

Five minutes later, he closed the folder and slammed it on the table. 'Right, that's done. Fancy another drink?'

He strode off to the packed bar and returned with two beers.

He raised his glass. *'¡Salud!'*

I clinked mine against his. *'¡Salud!'*

'My name's Bill, what's yours?'

'I'm Fred, good to meet you. Thanks for the drink.'

'You're welcome, you here on holiday?'

'I came here for two weeks in July last year and loved the place so much I've come back for the summer.'

'That's fantastic. This is my third year here. I'm a rep for Cosmos. What are you hoping to do?'

'I plan to work on a building site. Later in the season, I hope to get a bar job.'

Bill ran his fingers through cropped brown hair. 'Hope it goes well for you Fred. You must excuse me. The Cosmos gang just came in, so I'd better circulate. Can't neglect my customers, can I? I'm sure we'll see each other around.'

I gave him a warm handshake. He was a tall, thin, good-looking guy, with a healthy tan. I was sure he had girls lined up to go out with him.

Back at the bar, I asked Pat for another Estrella.

'Here you are, Fred. Sorry, we've been so busy, I haven't had time to catch up with you.'

'Cheers, Pat. How much do I owe you? Mick gave me a beer earlier, and I had two yesterday.'

'Don't worry. We'll run a tab. You can pay at the end of the month.'

'Great. Thanks. Tich said you had news for me.'

'Yes, I almost forgot. Jim wants to talk to you about the labouring job if you are still interested. He'll be here at midday tomorrow.'

'I'll make sure I'm here, Pat. Thanks for putting a good word in for me.'

'No problem, Fred.' She pecked me on the cheek.

After another two beers, I retired for the night. It was 1:30 am.

* * *

Saturday morning, after breakfast at Tony's, I headed back to Grannies. Mick and Graham were hard at work, stocking up the shelves and fridges.

I called over to Mick, 'Can I help with anything?'

'No, you're fine, Fred. Do you want a drink while you wait for Jim?'

'Black coffee, please.'

I took a seat at the bar.

Grannies was larger than I remembered. Stone steps led down to the terrace. Parasols shielded customers from the sun during the day. In the pub itself, the wooden bar was twenty yards long, stools placed along it at regular intervals. Tables and chairs lined the shutters separating the bar from the terrace. The shutters were opened during the summer months. At the far end was a spacious standing area for drinkers to congregate and play pub games. A separate room ran behind the whole length of the bar. You entered through a door at the far end, but there was no direct access to get served. It contained pinball machines and comfy couches.

Background music came from an eight-track tape player on a shelf in the small kitchen at the entrance end of the bar. There were two speakers placed high on the walls, and two more in the back room.

Mick brought my coffee. The same height as me, he had short brown hair and brown eyes.

A touch of mischief crossed his face as he spoke, 'Here you go, Fred. Jim should be here soon.'

Minutes later, Jim arrived. He had a deep tan. A short shock of silver hair topped his wrinkled face.

A faint smile appeared as he came across and shook my hand. 'You must be Fred. I've heard a lot about you from Patricia. Shall we sit outside and have a chat?' I nodded and followed him. 'Sorry, my time is limited, so let's talk business. Have you done any building work before?'

'No, Jim. I've had two summer jobs helping on a farm, which included lifting and carrying. What will this job involve?'

'Well, the project I'm working on is a two-storey house in the grounds of a villa, that belongs to the Bee Gees. As a labourer, I expect you to do the hard graft, transporting buckets of bricks and cement for the bricklayers. There is a more experienced guy there, Chris, who can show you the ropes.'

'The Bee Gees. Wow, that's amazing. I didn't realise they had a place in Ibiza.'

'Yes, it's a few kilometres from here. They're not there often, and you're unlikely to see them. The villa's hidden by trees from the main road, and they have security guards. The house we're working on is for guests, accessed by a separate track.' Jim paused for a moment. 'Could you cope with the work do you think?'

'I'll give it my best shot.'

'Good, can you start on Monday morning? Pay's not brilliant, 50 pesetas (42p) an hour, but should keep you going. You're staying at Tony's, aren't you? Be ready by 7 am. I'll come and meet you. Make sure you bring enough food and drink for the whole day. There's a supermarket near here where you can buy supplies. Have you got any boots?'

'No, sorry.'

'What shoe size are you?'

'I'm an 8.'

'The same as me then. There's a spare pair in the car that should fit. I'll get them for you.'

We shook hands and he rushed up the steps. Within two minutes, he returned with the boots. They were on the large side, but I had thick socks to pad them out.

Jim called over his shoulder, 'See you Monday morning. Look forward to working with you, Fred.'

'Me too, Jim.'

6

Monday morning feeling

Jim's voice boomed through the open window of my room, 'Wakey, wakey, rise and shine.'

I shot up from my slumbers and almost fell off the bed. What was happening? With a jolt, I remembered. It was Monday morning.

'Come on, Fred. Get yourself together and be up here in five minutes.'

I scrabbled around and pulled on jeans, a t-shirt, socks and the pair of boots Jim had lent me. In the wardrobe was a small paper bag with two bottles of orange drink, a tin of sardines, and bread I had bought on Saturday. A quick splash of water on my face and brush of my teeth later, I grabbed the bag, headed along the corridor, and up the stairs.

My head throbbed from the drinking excesses of the night before. Unprepared for the day ahead on a building site, I regretted saying I would start so soon. After meeting Jim on Saturday, the weekend became a haze. I enjoyed a swim and a meal before I moved from bar to bar and orientated myself in my new hometown. Sunday continued in the same vein and I hadn't got to bed until 2:30.

'Morning, how are you doing, Fred? Are you ready for a hard day's work?'

'A bit rough around the edges, but I'll be fine,' I grimaced.

I jumped into the front passenger seat of Jim's Seat 500. He crunched the gears as we sped away. Jim started talking and did not stop during the thirty minutes it took to drive to the building site.

He told me about his life back in England, the different work he had done, and the people he had met. It sounded like he missed home. I asked, 'Do you ever regret leaving Leicester and moving out here?'

He glanced over with a frown. 'No, not most of the time anyhow. I love the warm climate, but I get homesick sometimes. My wife is here, and my daughter, Patricia, but most of the family is still in England. They try to come out for holidays and stay at my villa while they're here, but it's not the same.'

'Would you ever move back?'

'No. We've been here for five years and are settled. I have to keep busy though. That's the main reason I do this building work. I don't need the money but want to remain active. Mind you, I'm fitter at 70 than I've been for a long time, so it must do me good.'

We left Santa Eulalia and headed out on a rougher road through the countryside. Jim resumed his rambling. My thoughts turned to the challenge of the day. I dreaded the hard work ahead. My head still throbbed, and my throat was dry. I sipped on a bottle of orange.

The car bounced along between the potholes. After a while, we swung off up a small track, to the rear of the grand three-story villa belonging to the Bee Gees. I caught glimpses of the vast white building through the pine trees, with a large swimming pool at the back. Several people worked in the spacious garden.

We arrived at the half-built two-storey house behind. Chris came over to greet us. He was a stocky middle-aged guy. A cap protected his bald head from the sun. Although my hair was long, it occurred to me I might need protection too. We got out of the car, and Jim introduced us.

'I'll leave you in Chris's capable hands, Fred. He'll show you the ropes.'

Chris guided me towards the front of the house. 'We've got a busy day ahead, so let's get cracking. Here's the plan. I'll be here on the mixer. There's a rope pulley to lift the buckets of bricks and cement to the roof. When I've loaded them, I'll haul them up to you. You can then carry them to the bricklayers on the far side. They're two local guys who speak no English.'

'OK, Chris. How do I get up there?'

'There are stairs inside but take care as there are no side rails yet. Also, be careful as you walk across the top of the house. There are still gaps in places.'

Once up there, I looked around. It was 8 am, and the sun edged above the trees. Long shadows fell over the assault course that made up the roof. Chris hauled up two buckets full of bricks and shouted, 'Fred, I'll mix the first batch of cement. Take those bricks to the far side and unload them. Once you get back, I'll have the next load ready for you.'

I heard the mixer as it fired into action. One bucket of bricks was all I could manage at a time. I struggled over the rooftop and handed them to the two Spanish lads.

They greeted me and unloaded the bricks, passing the empty buckets back.

Next came the cement. Chris hauled up two more buckets. I set them down before lowering the empty ones. Another shout came from ground level, 'Be as quick as you can, Fred. It's best if you take both loads with you as I'll have two more done soon.'

With a huge effort, I lifted both buckets and made my way across the roof, avoiding all the obstacles and trying not to trip over or spill the contents.

So, it continued. More cement and bricks at regular intervals. Weary arms, tired legs, and blistered hands added to my discomfort as I struggled to keep up with the constant supply. The sun beat down and sweat poured out of me. I finished the last of the orange drinks.

A quick glance at my watch showed it was only 10 am. It seemed more like midday.

After another half an hour, Chris called me for a break. We sat in the shade. I tried not to show my exhaustion. Jim came to join us. He had been working inside on the ground floor.

He gave me a concerned look. 'How's it going?'

'Not too bad, thanks. I'm keeping up, but it's hard work.'

Chris interjected, 'You'll soon get used to it. Do you want some tea?'

'Yes, please,' I replied through parched lips.

He poured me a cup from his large flask, and we sat around sipping on refreshing, sweet tea. I broke off two chunks of bread and scooped sardines from the tin to make a sandwich. The others ate biscuits.

Our break was over before I knew it, and I was soon back on the roof. The sun beat down even stronger. My arms stretched from their sockets, and my legs ached from the effort. The hangover was worse than ever. I swore to stay off the booze in future when I worked.

At 1 pm we took another break. It was siesta time. I finished my bread and sardines and was thankful to Chris for the spare bottle of water he gave me. We lay in the shade and relaxed. I couldn't sleep but appreciated the two-hour rest and being out of the scorching sun. Chris and Jim dozed. I assumed the Spanish lads were doing the same.

We worked for another three hours in the afternoon. By the end of the day, I found it difficult to walk, and any strength in my arms had gone. I stumbled and tripped over obstacles as I made my way across the roof with the last loads of cement.

Jim dropped me off at 6:30 pm. He had talked the entire journey, but I was too tired to take anything in. As he drove off, his parting words rang in my ears, 'See you in the morning, Fred. Get a good night's sleep. Make sure you buy plenty of food and drink for tomorrow.'

I waved at him, unable to utter a word.

As I stumbled down the stairs, someone was in the bathroom, so the bath had to wait. In my room, I stripped off and lay on the bed for a rest.

Two hours later I woke with a start. Every muscle in my body ached. I hobbled along the corridor with a towel around my waist and ran a bath. With relief, I sat in it as the hot water rose, reflecting on the day as my muscles relaxed. I washed my matted locks, which were thick with dust.

With a fresh t-shirt, shorts and flip-flops, I felt more refreshed and made my way upstairs for something to eat. I had missed the supermarket, as it closed at 8 pm. I'd have to ask Tony or Sue about supplies for the next day.

The place was quiet. Tony was behind the bar and Roberto in the kitchen.

'Hola, Fred. I hear you started work with Jim today. How did it go?'

'Well, but I'm knackered.'

'Do you want a beer? It looks like you need it.'

'Please, Tony, and something to eat. An omelette would be great if that's possible.'

'No problem, my friend.'

He opened a bottle of San Miguel and asked Roberto to cook a Spanish omelette for me.

I sipped the beer and asked about water, bread and ham for the next day.

'Why not ask Sue first thing in the morning, before you go? The restaurant doesn't open until seven, but she will be here from six.'

'Great. Cheers, mate.'

After two beers and the omelette, tiredness overwhelmed me.

I struggled down the stairs. A quick brush of my teeth and I was in bed, asleep before I knew it.

7

Work and play

It was still dark when I woke the next morning, in the same position I had fallen asleep.

Aches and pains racked my body as I struggled out of bed. I checked my watch. It was 6:15 am, so there was time to see Sue before Jim arrived.

Even walking up one flight of stairs from the basement was a struggle. As I rounded the corner of the building, I spotted Sue putting the rubbish out at the back.

I walked towards her. 'Morning, Sue. How's it going?'

She turned and smiled. 'Good, Fred, what about you? Tony mentioned you started work with Jim and looked exhausted yesterday evening.'

'It's tough going, and I'm feeling it today. I hope it will get easier soon.'

She came over and gave me a hug. 'You'll be fine, I'm sure. The restaurant isn't open, but I could get you a mug of tea and a round of toast. Tony said you needed supplies.'

'Tea and toast would be great. I'll need water for today. Maybe bread and ham too, if that's all right.'

'No problem. Sit on the veranda and I'll bring everything over.'

She swept back her long brown hair and sauntered to the kitchen.

As I looked out over the wasteland, glimmers of daylight appeared. Birds sang to greet the morning light, and a gentle smell of pine drifted from nearby trees.

It occurred to me it was a week since I had left England. What a contrast between the rainy gloom there, and the glorious weather in Ibiza.

Sue brought over a mug of tea with toast, butter and marmalade.

She fetched a large straw shoulder bag and handed it over. 'A tourist gave me this as a present. I thought you could use it for carrying things. I've put in three bottles of water, along with ham and cheese rolls. There's also a tube of suntan lotion, as I noticed you caught the sun yesterday.'

'That's kind of you, Sue. Thank you so much.'

'I could do the same every workday morning and add it to your tab.'

I grinned at her. 'If you don't mind, I'll take you up on that.'

Her green eyes twinkled. 'I put an alarm clock in your bag. Someone left it here last year, and I thought you might find it useful.'

'Fantastic. I meant to bring one with me but forgot.'

Sue continued preparations for opening the restaurant. At 7 am the first locals waited outside for their breakfast. With a wave to Sue, I hitched the straw bag over my right shoulder and hobbled out to meet Jim, who had just arrived.

He beckoned from his car. 'Morning, Fred. How are you today?'

I eased myself into the front seat. 'Aching all over, but it should get easier soon.'

Jim gave me a reassuring nod. 'I'm sure it will. I love your handbag, where did you get it?'

'Sue gave it to me and filled it with food and water.'

He shot me a roguish grin. 'She's great, isn't she?'

We were on our way again. Non-stop talking from Jim ensued once more, but I let it wash over me as I took in the surroundings on the journey to work. The sun edged over the horizon. Fresh morning light bathed the countryside.

Before I knew it, we had bounced along the country lanes and up the track to the house. Chris waved across as we got out of the car.

He burst out laughing when he saw the straw bag. 'You look like a local, Fred, but you're the first man I've seen with one of those. Women use them to carry their shopping.'

I smirked. 'Well, I'm not proud. It will come in handy.'

Chris suggested we start straight away. I rubbed suntan lotion onto my arms and face, before a painful climb up the stairs. The first buckets were the most difficult, and I stumbled several times crossing the roof. After that, it got easier as my body loosened up.

The morning passed faster than the previous day. I soon got into a rhythm transporting the bricks and then cement to the bricklayers. Rather than concentrate on the tasks at hand, as I had done on Monday, my mind wandered and took me away from the physical effort.

I recalled events leading up to this trip: the daily routine of commuting to the bank in London, working evenings and weekends at the Station Hotel, and the friends I had left behind.

The mid-morning break came and went. My body still struggled with the hard work but adjusted to my more positive outlook as I transported the heavy buckets in the midday heat.

At lunchtime, I finished the delicious rolls Sue had prepared and drank the water. This time I joined the others and slept during siesta. Jim had to wake me up at 3 pm, but I was soon back in the routine again.

As the week progressed my muscles strengthened, blisters hardened, and a noticeable tan developed on my arms and face. Tiredness became less of a problem. I ventured out more in the evenings, although I limited myself to two or three beers, and was in bed by 11 pm.

* * *

Friday night was different though. I could relax and enjoy myself.

Jim paid me 2000 pesetas (£17) for the week, and I was in a mood to celebrate. I had spent little of the money from home as I was running tabs in most of the bars I visited.

After a meal of ham, egg and chips at Tony's, I headed over to the Red Lion.

Roger and Margaret had returned from their winter break in England. They didn't recognise me straight away. As I ordered a beer from Margaret and explained there was a tab in the name of Fred, a look of recognition crossed her face.

She gave me a sweet smile and brushed back her fair hair. 'Fred, how are you? Tich said you were back. I hear you're working with Jim.'

'Yes, it's going well. How are you and Roger?'

Her light green eyes sparkled. 'We're glad to be back. England is too cold and rainy for my liking these days. We spent most of the winter with my brother in Manchester. Roger worked on a building site. I helped in a pub. We're not making enough here yet, so we needed to raise funds.'

They were in their late thirties and moved to Es Cana in 1975 to rent the Red Lion. Prior to that they had regular holidays in Ibiza and fell in love with the island. Roger came over and shook my hand with a vice-like grip. He was taller than I remembered, with wavy brown hair and brown eyes. 'Good to see you, Fred. Your mates didn't make it then?'

35

'No, they hadn't saved enough money, but they want to come out later in the season.'

'Hope it works out for you. I'm sure it will. I'd better get on as it's getting busy. Tich is off this evening, so you might catch him around town later.'

'Cheers, Roger. It's great to see you both again.'

After two bottles of San Miguel, I walked to Grannies. It was not as busy as the Friday before.

Pat poured me an Estrella. 'How's work with my dad? He seems happy enough with what you are doing.'

'Great to hear. I struggled to start with but am more used to it now.'

There was a hint of laughter in her voice as she passed me my beer. 'He hasn't talked you to death yet then?'

'No, but he loves talking, doesn't he?'

She giggled. 'Don't I know it.'

Pat moved away to serve the next customer.

I spotted a spare place at a table on the terrace. There were three girls sitting there.

I hovered beside them. 'Hi, is it OK if I join you?'

An attractive blonde girl looked me up and down. 'Yes, why not, take a seat.'

She patted the bench next to her. 'Make yourself comfortable.'

As I sat, I glimpsed her mini skirt and slim long legs.

She introduced me to her two friends, Monica and Janine.

They leant across and gave me a peck on each cheek. As they did, wafts of perfume drew me in, and I caught sight of more bare legs and short skirts. Both girls were good-looking, with dark hair and hazel eyes.

They spoke in unison, 'Nice to meet you.'

'Are you sisters?' I enquired.

A small grin stole across Monica's face. 'Yes, how did you guess? We are twins, although not identical.'

I turned to the blonde girl next to me and gazed into her blue eyes.

There was a moment's silence before she gave my arm a squeeze. 'Hi, I'm Cathy. We're student nurses from Leeds on a week's break, but we go back tomorrow afternoon. There are four of us, but we haven't seen Ann much since the second day. She copped off with a Spanish fella and has been spending her time with him. Are you on holiday as well?'

I beamed at them and told my story.

Cathy edged closer. 'Have you found work?'

'Yeah, I got a room straight away, and started work on a building site last Monday.'

I noticed the girls' glasses were empty. 'Can I get anyone a drink?'

Monica and Janine asked for gin and tonics, while Cathy wanted vodka and orange.

As I walked to the bar, I wondered what the evening had in store for me.

8

Night of pleasure

Graham grinned as I asked for the round of drinks. 'Looks like you've pulled. The blonde one can't keep her eyes off you.'

It was his third year working at Grannies. He was a handsome, muscular guy, taller than me, with short fair hair, and bright blue eyes.

My eyebrows rose. 'I'm not sure, they're student nurses, and maybe too classy for me.'

Graham winked. 'Don't run yourself down, mate. I know from experience how easy it is to pick up girls here. You're the type they want. No strings, no commitments, just fun for the night.'

'We'll see,' I replied with doubt in my voice.

I picked up the tray and carried it to the table.

After handing the drinks round, we clinked glasses. 'Cheers, girls. Good health.'

They thanked me. I had joined Cathy in drinking vodka and orange, as a change from beer.

We fell into conversation and talked about their experiences as student nurses. They were partway through their third year and appeared to love the lifestyle, despite the hard work involved.

Cathy looked serious for a moment. 'We enjoy the challenge of looking after people. The night shifts can be tough, and the studying is difficult, but it's worthwhile.'

Janine glanced at me. 'What did you do in England, Fred?'

'I worked at a bank in the City of London for two-and-a-half years, commuting from Surrey. My plan was to work there for a year, before going to university. The money was tempting though, and I figured a career in banking would suit me. Then we came on holiday last year, and everything changed.'

The girls smiled as I continued, 'Friends found it difficult to understand why I wanted to give up such a good career and risk it all by coming here. My parents tried to dissuade me, but my mother supported me, once she knew I had my heart set on it. It confused my younger brother and sister, though, and most of my friends.'

Cathy gushed, 'It's a brilliant thing to do.'

I sensed her sexy body close to mine and became aroused.

Monica looked at her empty glass. 'Anyone want another drink?'

We nodded in agreement. Monica and Janine made their way to the crowded bar for refills.

Cathy whispered in my ear, 'I hope you don't think I'm being forward, but it's my last night, and I'd love to spend it with you. The other two are heading off to the disco in a while. My roommate, Ann, is with her Spanish fella, so we can have the room to ourselves. Are you up for it?'

My eyes widened. I stuttered, 'Sounds fantastic.'

She placed her hand on my thigh. I got even more turned on as she put her other arm around my shoulder and gave me a passionate kiss.

Monica and Janine came back. They exchanged knowing looks as they sat on the bench opposite.

There was more small talk as we sipped our drinks. The atmosphere became strained. Before long, the other two headed off to the disco and wished us a fun time.

Cathy and I left soon afterwards. We held each other's hands tight as we made our unsteady way across the wasteland towards the Hotel Caribe. It was the same place I had stayed at in 1976.

I could not believe such a beautiful young woman wanted to spend the night with me. The anticipation of our time together overwhelmed me. I was nervous I would fail her.

There was a crowd of guests asking questions at the reception desk, so I got past without being noticed. We made our way up the circular stone stairway to the second floor and Cathy's room.

She turned the key and pulled me inside. 'There's vodka on the side and ice in the fridge. Could you make us drinks while I slip into something more comfortable?'

She grabbed a bag and headed into the bathroom.

I walked into the main room. It was like the one I had stayed in the year before. Siv and I shared one, while Mutts and Sam had another on the same floor.

After making the drinks, I stepped outside onto the balcony to breathe in the night air and calm my nerves.

A few minutes later, I sensed movement behind me. As I turned around, I could not believe what I saw.

Cathy looked gorgeous in a nurse's outfit, with her blonde hair tied back in a bun. I fantasised about women in uniform and this was a dream come true.

She made her way towards me and gazed deep into my eyes. My pulse raced and butterflies flew in my stomach.

I passed her a drink. My hands were shaking.

She whispered, 'What do you think?'

My eyes widened. 'You look amazing,'

With my hand round her belted waist, I drew her close. We locked in a passionate embrace and became lost in our own world.

A few minutes later, Cathy pulled away and guided me into the room. With a chuckle, she pushed me on to the bed. As I lay there, she took my pulse and checked the watch hanging from her uniform.

Stroking my forehead, she exclaimed, 'You'd better be careful with your blood pressure, Fred. Why don't you lie back and relax while I entertain you?'

She flicked the switch on a cassette recorder and swayed to the uplifting music of George Benson. With flowing hand movements, she caressed her body and pulled up the front of her skirt to reveal suspenders at the top of wonderful stockinged legs.

As she continued to gyrate, Cathy slipped out of her uniform in slow, sensual moves. I got the first glimpse of her ample bosom through a lacy bra. She kicked off her shoes, undid the suspender belt, and peeled down her stockings. All the time she did not take her sparkling blue eyes off me.

She came close and pressed my head against her stomach. I kissed her all over and breathed in the perfume of her skin. My hands massaged her legs, before moving up to her breasts, and undoing the bra. She removed her knickers and revealed shaved pubic hair.

I moved back and took in the beauty of her naked body. As I did so, she undid the bun and let her long blonde hair hang free.

She lifted me to my feet. 'Now it's your turn, Fred.'

though? Did she have a boyfriend at home? Who else had she been with on her holiday? These were questions I could never answer.

Once again, an overwhelming sadness swept over me. She was gone, for good.

Sadness turned to guilt as Sarah sprang to mind. Did I feel the same about her as when I left only eleven days ago? I remembered the times we enjoyed over the winter and my declared love for her. Did she still miss me? Would she find someone else? I could not expect her to stay loyal while I had the time of my life, could I?

With these thoughts racing through my head, I fell into a deep sleep.

* * *

The sun had set when I woke again after some mixed-up dreams. I could only remember one.

I was with a girl in the back seat of a cinema watching a film. We smooched and fondled each other. I remembered being turned on as her hand massaged my crotch. Everyone there, even the characters in the film, stared at us and booed. As the boos became louder and louder, we raced outside. Once on the pavement, there was a strange sense of movement. The street we were on tilted upwards, and it felt as though we were taking off. I grabbed the girl's hand to halt her slide. But it was too late. She slipped from my grasp. I lost my grip, and fell as well, but woke with a start, before I hit the ground.

With a towel wrapped around me, I walked along the corridor. The bathroom was free, so I soaked in a warm bath, before dressing again in a fresh t-shirt, jeans and plimsolls.

I took a slow walk around the bay. The skies darkened with threatening clouds, which blotted out the moon and stars. Since my arrival, I had seen two or three showers, but they never came to much. This looked like a real storm. I quickened my step as large drops fell. By the time I reached Grannies the heavy rain had drenched me.

Customers from the terrace sheltered inside. I weaved my way through the packed bar. I spotted Bill, the Cosmos rep. He sat on a stool next to a guy in a kilt. They were both chatting to Graham, who spotted me.

'Hey, Fred, come over here. Bill, Alan, this is Fred, have you been introduced yet?'

Bill shook my hand. 'Yes, we met last weekend, and I saw you this morning with one of the student nurses, didn't I?'

My face reddened. 'You mean Cathy? Where did you spot me with her?'

'I was on the coach and watched you kissing each other goodbye. She belonged to the Cosmos group I escorted back to the airport. I overheard her saying what a great night she'd had.'

Graham realised I was embarrassed and lightened the mood as he passed me a glass of Estrella. 'So, you scored, Fred? Was it the blonde girl who couldn't take her eyes off you? I said you were in with a chance. Is that your first since you arrived?'

'Yes, and one I'll remember for a long time.'

'Don't worry, mate. There will be plenty more during the season. Alan and I had a competition last year. How many, Alan?'

His mouth twisted into a grin. 'I think it was 25, and if I remember right you made it to 16.'

Graham growled, 'Yes, but working in Cortijo's, you get to pick up the stragglers at the end of the night when the disco finishes. Your dress always attracts them, doesn't it?'

Alan looked serious for a moment, but then laughed at Graham's jibe.

About the same height as me, he had brown eyes, shoulder-length dark hair, and spoke with a soft Scottish lilt.

He turned with a smile. 'So, it looks like you're settling in, Fred. Graham said you came on holiday last year with your mates. I don't remember seeing you. It was my first season here, but I worked at Cortijo's all summer. Did you ever go?'

'Yes, twice, but didn't stay long as it was packed to the rafters. Good to meet you now though.'

I offered my hand.

Alan shook it with enthusiasm. 'I start work in half an hour. Why don't you come over later? I'll get you a drink, and introduce you to John, the English guy who runs it?'

'Will do. Thanks.'

The heavy rain subsided, and customers ventured out onto the terrace again.

Mick and Pat were at the other end of the pub. An argument erupted between them. Customers looked on in amazement. Graham dashed the length of the bar and bundled them into the small kitchen area.

A few curt words later, he turned to the waiting punters. 'Sorry about that, what can I get you?'

Then Pat stormed out. Streams of tears ran down her face as she sobbed. Mascara streaked her cheeks and her mouth was fixed in a hysterical grin. She tripped as she clambered up the steps. I had never seen her in such a state.

Mick chased after her, but returned five minutes later, and shrugged his shoulders in our direction. He resumed work behind the bar and poured himself a vodka and orange, which he downed in two gulps.

Once Bill and Alan had gone, I pulled Graham to one side as he collected glasses. 'What was that all about, mate?'

'Oh, it happens now and then. I'm used to it. Pat had a few gin and tonics this afternoon with friends. She arrived at work half-cut and carried on drinking. Mick, who should know better, had a go at her. Her jealous streak kicked in, and she accused Mick of sleeping with a customer. Then the shouting started. That's when I broke it up.'

I gave him a sympathetic smile. 'I don't remember this sort of thing happening last year.'

'They've always been like it, but there are periods of peace between them.'

Graham dived behind the bar and served customers again with a gloomy faced Mick.

After another beer, I decided to go to Cortijo's and take Alan up on his offer.

I raised my voice, 'Mick, Graham, I'm heading off now, catch you later.'

Graham gave me a thumbs-up and Mick nodded in response.

The storm had subsided, but large puddles across the wasteland were difficult to see in the dark.

El Cortijo was one of two discotheques in Es Cana. It livened up after 11 pm and had a permit until 4 am. At the entrance desk, I spotted Alan. He beckoned me in and disappeared behind the bar.

He called over as I approached, 'What do you fancy, Fred?'

'I'll have a vodka and orange, please.'

As he poured my drink, I took in the surroundings. It was still early and the disco was empty, very different from the packed place I remembered. Down a few steps in front of me was the large circular dance floor bathed in flashing lights from the disco ball which hung from the ceiling. Comfy seats and tables surrounded two-thirds of the dance floor at a higher level.

Alan placed my drink on the bar top. 'Here you go. *'¡Salud!'*

I grinned and took a sip. 'Cheers, Alan.'

'John will be here later, so I'll introduce you then if I get a chance. Excuse me for now.'

He turned to serve a group of tourists who had just arrived.

As the disco filled up, the volume of the music increased. The disc jockey pumped out popular songs from Abba, Queen, Status Quo, Rod Stewart, David Bowie, and many more. Soon the dance floor was full of excited lads and lasses cavorting to their favourite tunes. There was one special song, *Boogie Nights* by Heatwave, that got everyone singing along.

I stood near the bar and watched the action around me as I drank another two vodka and oranges. A wave of sadness swept over me as I re-lived the previous night in my head. I missed Cathy's company and wished she was still with me.

I waved goodbye to Alan and mouthed, 'Catch you later.'

He glanced my way and shouted, 'Take care, see you soon.'

Back in the room, I lay on my bed. Loneliness overtook me for a long time before I drifted off to sleep.

10

News from home

On Sunday, I woke in a depressed mood that I found difficult to shake all day.

Most of the afternoon I spent at the Panorama pool near the seafront, where I swam, sunbathed and read a book, to try and lift my spirits. After a meal and three beers at Restaurante Es Cana in the evening, I retired to bed early.

Monday perked me up as I returned to the routine of the building site. It meant I needed to concentrate on the tasks at hand and devote my energy to carrying countless buckets across the roof again.

After work on Wednesday, I took a bath before heading upstairs to Tony's for something to eat.

Sue was behind the bar and opened a San Miguel for me. 'Hiya, Fred, how's it going?'

'Good, thanks. Work's still tough, but I'm getting used to it.'

She passed my beer, then reached under the counter, and handed me two letters. 'Tich came in earlier and asked me to give you these. They arrived this morning at the Red Lion.'

I glanced at them. One was from Mother. The other from Sarah. Postmarks were from the previous Friday and Saturday.

Excited, I walked out to the veranda, sat in the dusky light, and opened them. I read both several times.

My dear Robert,

Your card arrived this morning and Sarah just phoned to say she received one too. We had a chat. Chris has arranged an evening together with her.

The only post is from Williams and Glyn's which included another of the magazines with your picture in it. There is a note of appreciation for your help in producing it, and two copies of the photo. I have enclosed one of them with this letter.

Chris thinks Alastair finishes his first year at Stirling University in a month. So far, he has been unsuccessful in finding a job for the summer.

I think of you each morning at 7:30 am, at getting up time. Other times as well, but that moment remains fixed in my mind. We miss you and we're glad to have your card.

Father spent four days in Nottingham last week at a conference. So, we were "two", just the two womenfolk.

How is the weather at present? It is cool here. The blackthorn is in bloom and they call this the blackthorn winter. I have planted a few potatoes and broad bean seeds.

We send our fond love to you and best wishes.

Your loving,

Mother

Dear Fred,

Thank you for your postcard. I received it yesterday. I hope you have found a job. I miss you very much. Sharon and Co. have stopped ribbing me now, but they carried on for a few days. I have been looking for a new job, but not found anything suitable.

I hope you are keeping well and having a great time. As you have got an apartment, you won't need to use your tent.

I rang your mum last night. I am going over on Sunday to see her, cut Christine's hair, and then go out in the evening.

There was a party on Monday down the Station Pub, at 1 in the morning. Someone gave Bob £15 to strip on the pool table. He did that, and it ended up with everyone taking their clothes off and dancing to the jukebox. Jerry and Sylvana almost had it away over the pool table. Carol told me this on Tuesday as Tish was there when it happened. He joined in.

I didn't mean our parting to be so tough. There was so much I wanted to say, but when the time came, I couldn't say anything. The journey home went well as I caught a train as soon as I got to the station.

Evenings have been quiet, although I have been to the Station once or twice. My diet is going well. I have lost five pounds so far.

My parents send their regards.

Lots of Love,

Sarah

Home seemed so distant, but the letters cheered me up.

The photo from the bank amused me. They had a strict "no hair below the collar" rule for male employees but I got away with it. They turned it to their advantage when they used my image and an interview as recruiting material aimed at university graduates.

Sarah's story from the Station pub did not surprise me. I had heard rumours of the landlord and landlady's antics when I worked there in the evenings and at weekends. It was the gossip of the village. Jerry and Sylvana were an odd couple.

I missed my family and Sarah, but I had made my decision and would stick to it.

* * *

The sun shone all week and it was hot up on the roof.

I discarded my t-shirt and wore shorts rather than long trousers. My strength increased day by day. Blisters continued to harden, and I developed more of a tan. By Friday afternoon, I had survived two weeks of building work, and another 2000 pesetas were in my pocket to help pay off my tabs at the weekend. I needed to get to a bank in Santa Eulalia the next week to change travellers' cheques. Sue had advised me not to use the hotels or *cambios* in Es Cana because they offered poor exchange rates and charged a high commission.

In May, the season ramped up a gear. Sunday, May 1st would be the opening day party for Tootsies. We had visited Tootsies Bar several times in 1976. It was a pub in Punta Arabi, near to the Hippy Market, with a large outdoor garden. It took fifteen minutes to walk there from Es Cana, and longer on the way back in the dark after a few drinks.

* * *

On Friday evening, after an omelette at Tony's, I headed over to the Red Lion.

The bar was busy, and I had to wait for a drink. A group of English lads played darts at the far end and customers lined the counter. The jukebox pumped out music and the air was thick with cigarette smoke.

Tich shouted above the noise of waiting punters, 'Did you get your letters OK, Fred?'

'Yes, thanks for dropping them off, Tich.'

He handed me a San Miguel and grinned. 'No problem, I was passing anyway.'

I walked over to watch the darts.

It reminded me of Monday nights at the Prince Albert in Bletchingley. It was there I got to know the locals, including Mutts, Sam and Siv, who'd come to Ibiza with me. The Prince Albert ran a darts team, which took part in a Monday night league. I was never any good at darts, although they gave me an occasional game. What I proved good at was scoring. I had a talent for adding and subtracting numbers. Because of that, I often ended up chalking scores for the league games.

I chatted to two of the dart players and found out they were from Brighton. They invited me to join in and wrote my name on the board. It was a game of 501, to start and finish on a double. The winner stayed on. Loser paid for the winner's drink, which had to be drunk before the next game.

When my turn came up an hour later, I had drunk several beers and felt more confident. First, I chalked a game. It was over before I knew it. Brian, the winner of six games in succession, whitewashed the challenger. This meant he finished before his opponent had even started the game.

My first dart hit double 20 at the top of the board, stayed there for a moment, and fell out. The second missed the board. The third slipped from my fingers and landed in double 3, at the bottom. I was away.

Brian downed his latest beer. He threw three erratic darts, missing a double each time. Then the miracle happened. My first dart landed in treble 20, as did the second. I took a deep breath and threw my third. It contrived to hit treble 20. Excited shouts of "180" came from the on watchers. I had never hit 180 before and stood amazed at my success.

I took another three turns before there was double 8 left. By then Brian was close behind and I needed to finish. The first dart landed at least an inch outside the target, but the second ended up in the middle of the bed. I had won.

My next opponent was Mark. He waited while I downed the bottle of San Miguel Brian had bought me. He missed a double on his first turn, as did I. The longest game of darts I can remember followed. Neither of us could hit a double. Spectators lost interest and the watching crowd thinned.

Ten minutes later, Mark hit double 16. I then got a start with a wayward throw which hit double 7. Soon Mark was on double 19, which he missed. I had 76 left. My first dart hit 20, as did my second. I concentrated hard to steady my arm. The final dart found its way into double 18. My second victory.

The third game, against Paul this time, started after I had downed another beer. My luck ran out as he whitewashed me. I bought Paul his victory drink.

By then the Brighton lads had lost interest in the darts and talked about where to go next. After much discussion, they decided on Snoopy's, the other disco in Es Cana. I joined them for several beers, but by 2 am I needed to sleep.

I weaved an unsteady path back to my room.

11

Afternoon cycle ride

Sunlight drenched my bed as I woke late on Saturday morning, groggy after the beer I'd drunk. It had been a great evening though with the Brighton lads.

My stomach churned, so I settled for tea and toast in Tony's. Pedro served behind the bar and Roberto was in the kitchen.

I was feeling brighter after breakfast and hired a bike for the afternoon. A shop on the main street lent them for 25 pesetas an hour.

At first, I cycled along the streets of Es Cana and enjoyed looking at them from another viewpoint. The pavements were busy with pale-faced holidaymakers exploring their new surroundings. I almost collided with a couple who looked the wrong way before they crossed the street.

The bike was a boneshaker. As I headed out to the west, the road surface was uneven. The ride became tougher as I swerved to avoid the potholes. Shocks vibrated through the handlebars, and I lost my grip twice. Despite this, it was good to have the breeze in my face, and the sun on my back, as I cycled along.

The roads twisted and turned, as I followed the coast around Punta Arabi and through the villages of S'Argamassa and Cala Pada. I passed pine-fringed beaches and caught glimpses of the sea. A few new tourist developments dotted the coastline, in between the traditional houses, shops and bars.

After a while, I came to the main road which ran from the north of Es Cana to Santa Eulalia. I followed it south-westwards towards Santa Eulalia. Soon I found myself in the square where I had changed buses when I arrived from Ibiza Town.

My thirst led me in search of a drink. I spotted Fred's Bar and decided it was an appropriate place. With my bike propped against the outside wall, I walked into the gloomy interior and blinked after the bright sunshine.

I strolled over to the counter and ordered a draught beer. As I stood and sipped it, I glanced around and saw groups of men sat at the wooden tables. I realised English was the main language being spoken, and the newspapers were days-old copies of *The Sun* and *Daily Mirror*. I felt out of place amongst the rustling of papers and whispered conversations.

Chalked on a blackboard was a small menu of English food. I ordered shepherd's pie with my next beer.

A gruff Yorkshire voice boomed from behind the bar, 'Tek a seat at that corner table an' ah'll bring it over in a few minutes.'

I assumed that was Fred.

Seated on the hard, wooden chair, I placed my drink on the table.

I glanced up and saw a man limping from the bar with a large glass of whisky and ice in his hand. He shouted greetings, in a distinct American accent, to others in the room before sitting down in the seat opposite.

My food arrived. I dug into it with vigour. The cycle ride had given me a good appetite. As I polished off the plate, my table companion burped and glanced towards me.

I smiled at him and he grinned. 'Looked like you enjoyed that.'

'Yes, it was great, have you tried it?'

He pointed at his drink and slurred, 'No man, I'm not into food much, I prefer this stuff.'

He pulled out a pack of Camel cigarettes, flipped back the top and offered me one.

I took it and gave him a light. We both sucked on the smooth taste and exhaled plumes of smoke. He moved closer and I could make out a mass of scars on his face and arms.

I turned to him. 'Do you live in Santa Eulalia? You seem to know lots of people here.'

'Yeah man, been here ages now. Came to Ibiza in '73 and loved it, so I stayed. I've got a small apartment just outside town, overlooking the sea.'

I looked at him with curiosity. 'So, you work here then?'

He threw back his head and laughed.

All eyes turned in his direction as the raucous laugh subsided into chuckles. 'No man, I'm pensioned off from the Army. I served in Vietnam and during my second tour, I got blown to smithereens. I was lucky to survive. They shipped me to the States, filled my body with metal, and stitched me up again. They kept me in hospital for ages, and I still go there every few months for check-ups.'

My jaw dropped. I looked at him with new respect.

He continued, 'The climate here helps my aching bones, and the booze is cheap. I've made friends, although most of them think I'm crazy. I suppose I am sometimes.'

To break the momentary silence, I asked, 'Do you want another drink?'

'A bourbon, with water, and ice would be great. Thanks, man.'

Back at the table, I clinked my glass against his. *'¡Salud!'*

We chatted a while longer and I told him what I was doing in Es Cana. His eyes glazed over. He nodded as I talked, but I sensed his mind was elsewhere.

I stood up and offered my hand. 'I have to go now.'

He gave me a firm handshake from his seated position. 'Nice talking to you man, take care and hope to see you again.'

'Yes, me too, my name's Fred.'

'I'm Michael, or Mike, known as Mad Mike to my friends. Have a safe journey back to Es Cana.'

He waved over as I headed out of the door.

The bike had fallen over, but it was still there. It had not occurred to me to secure it when I walked into the bar. I figured it was all right, being opposite the police station.

With a slight wobble, I set off towards Es Cana along the main road. A car came straight at me and I had to swerve. I realised I was on the left-hand side of the road and switched to the right with a yank on the handlebars. That could have been nasty.

The return ride took thirty minutes, and I dropped the bike off as dark descended. Grannies was close by, so I popped in for a drink. Mick and Pat were both there. They seemed on better terms than the previous Saturday. Pat handed me an Estrella. She stroked back her shoulder-length brown hair, and her amber eyes sparkled.

'Evening, Fred. How's it going?'

'Good, thanks. I've just been out for a bike ride to Santa Eulalia. It was fun.'

'You should have said. We have spare bikes in the back room. You could have borrowed one of those.'

'Oh, I didn't realise. I'll bear that in mind for next time.'

Mick came over and shook my hand. 'Great to see you, Fred, your tan's coming on, isn't it?'

I gave him a broad grin. 'Must be all the work outside. Did you want me to settle my tab? I've got cash with me.'

'No rush. You can pay it later.'

He left to serve a group of girls.

My body ached from the day's exertions. I was about to leave when Alan walked in with a tall, silver-haired guy.

They joined me at the bar. Alan grinned. 'You didn't meet John the other night, did you? John, this is Fred. Fred, this is John.'

I shook their hands. 'Cheers, Alan. Good to meet you, John.'

John bought us a beer and we moved out to the terrace as it was cooler there.

We chatted for a while before they left to open the disco.

John smiled. 'Might see you later, Fred.'

'Maybe. I'm knackered from this afternoon's bike ride.'

'OK, if not, are you going to Tootsies opening party tomorrow?'

'Yes, I'm planning to.'

At the bar, I ordered a goodnight drink of vodka and orange and paid my tab. It came to 2325 pesetas, which seemed reasonable.

12

Tootsies opening party

Sunday dawned.

Tony's was open but not busy, so I sat on the veranda. I soaked up the warmth of the morning sunlight.

Sue's cheery voice came from behind me, 'Morning, Fred. You're up bright and early for a weekend.'

I told her about my bike ride and meeting Mad Mike.

Sue tilted her head. 'Oh, yes, everyone knows of him. He's a nutter but has great stories to tell, if you have time to listen to his ramblings. Anyway, can I get you breakfast?'

After devouring my full English and mug of tea, I planned a morning at the Panorama pool. I gave Sue a hug as I left.

'Thanks for looking after me. I don't know what I'd have done without your help in the mornings before work.'

'No problem, Fred. I enjoy helping others. I remember how difficult it was for me when I first came here.'

She pecked me on the cheek.

In my room, I threw a beach towel, swimming trunks, a book and suntan lotion, into my straw bag, and walked to the pool for a relaxed morning surrounded by pale tourists on their first weekend in Es Cana.

* * *

Tootsies was already packed when I arrived at 3 pm. Their opening parties had gained a reputation for being the best in Es Cana.

I recognised a few people: Mick, Pat and Graham, Sue and Tony, and Roger, Margaret and Tich. They had all taken time away from work. Grannies and the Red Lion were closed for the afternoon. John and Alan from Cortijo's came along later.

Ray and Gordon organised proceedings. This was their fourth year at Tootsies. They were both from a military background and had served for twenty years before retiring from the forces. Ray was a tall, imposing man with short red hair, freckled skin and green eyes. Gordon was shorter, muscular and stocky, with curly brown hair. Neither of them smiled much.

They had arranged the wooden tables, shaded by large parasols, around the garden area behind the main bar and building. Raised circular tables stood in between them, protected by straw shades.

A variety of cooking was underway. A huge circular pan of paella simmered, burgers and sausages sizzled on a barbecue, and potatoes baked in a small oven. Trays of salads and accompaniments were arranged on either side. Bottles of beer and soft drinks stayed chilled in buckets of ice. Two barrels of beer sat shaded under another table, with pumps clamped above them. Spirits and jugs of sangria were also available. On a separate table were a few bottles of the local speciality, Hierbas Ibicencas, an aniseed-based, herb-flavoured green liqueur. As I discovered the year before, it was easy to drink, but its effects were lethal in the hot weather. I avoided it this time.

Each guest paid 500 pesetas, which covered as much food and drink as you could manage. The sun streamed down, and the skies were a deep blue. Locals and tourists mingled. A great atmosphere prevailed.

I collected a beer and a plate of paella: chorizo, chicken, peas, squid, mussels and prawns cooked with rice. I found a spare place on a table and sat shaded from the sun by a parasol. The meal was delicious, and I returned for seconds then grabbed another beer and wandered around to talk to people.

I spotted Gordon on a break as he smoked a cigarette, congratulated him on a successful event and introduced myself.

He responded with a firm handshake. 'Thought I recognised the face, but we see so many tourists come through during the summer, it's difficult to remember everybody. I was talking to Mick and Pat earlier and they mentioned your name. They said you might be interested in bar work later in the season.'

'That's what I was hoping. I'm labouring on a building site with Pat's dad, Jim, for now. Although good experience, it's not well paid, and I only plan to do it for a few weeks at most.'

Gordon scratched his head. 'We might have something for you at the start of June. It gets busier then and we'll need a bar waiter to collect orders from the customers outside, pick up drinks from the bar then take them to the tables. Do you remember Robbie from last year? That's the job he was doing.'

I gave a slow nod. 'Robbie, yes. Scottish, a very talkative guy, with short curly black hair?'

'Yes, that's him. He was with us for two years. When he left in September, he said he wouldn't be back. A real shame as he was superb at his job.'

Gordon offered me a Ducados cigarette from a pale blue and white packet. 'I notice you smoke roll-ups, have you tried these? They're only 7 pesetas for 20.'

I took one and lit his, before lighting my own. It had a strong taste and there was no filter, but I enjoyed the smoke. I beamed a smile at him. 'Cheers, Gordon. They're not bad. My supply of Old Holborn is almost finished, so I might try these.'

He nodded and looked at me through narrowed eyes. 'So, what do you think about working as a bar waiter, Fred?'

'I'd be interested, Gordon. Is there anything else I should know about the job?'

'Well, Pat said you had bar experience from England. That's a start. It gets very busy here, so you have to work fast. The ability to remember orders and add prices in your head is essential. You also need to socialise and encourage customers to buy more.'

'I worked in a bank, so I've got a good head for numbers.'

'OK, that helps. I'll have to check with Ray, my partner, but we might give you a trial. We'd get you a work permit as we run everything by the book here. The pay is 100 pesetas an hour, but you can earn good tips if customers like you.'

'Brilliant, Gordon. When will you let me know? I'd have to give Jim at least a week's notice.'

'Leave it with me. I'll get a message to you within the next week or two. Sorry, I need to go back to work as the queue is building. I hope we can sort something out for you.'

He threw the stub of his Ducados to the floor and ground it out with his boot. We shook hands.

I lined up for another beer. As I sipped it, I felt elated at the thought of getting a job at Tootsies. It was better paid and would be a relief from the monotony of lugging buckets of cement and bricks across that roof.

* * *

The sun had set as I walked along the dusty road to Es Cana in the twilight.

During the afternoon, I had drunk seven or eight beers, and I knew it. With work the next day, I needed to sleep. Before going to my room, I popped into Tony's. The restaurant was quiet, but there were a few customers around the bar. Tony was serving.

I leant against the counter.

'Evening, Fred. It was fun, wasn't it? Do you want a beer?'

'No, thanks. I'm still bloated from the party. Could I have a vodka and orange, please?'

'No problem.'

Tony scooped ice into the glass, poured a generous measure of spirit, and topped it with orange juice. 'Here you go. Enjoy. I've got your tab here.'

He gave me a scribbled scrap of paper. I read it: Rent – 17x90 = 1530, meals & drinks – 1275, work supplies – 9x120 = 1080, Total = 3885. I unzipped my money-belt and counted out the notes and change. There was only just enough there. It left me with 475 pesetas.

I handed it over. 'Tony, here's the cash, you'd better check it.'

He counted it, folded the notes, and put them in his wallet. The change went into his pocket.

Tony smiled at me. 'Thanks, Fred. Did you want any laundry done? We have a neighbour who does ours. If you drop it off tomorrow evening, they'll return it by Thursday or Friday.'

I nodded in agreement. 'That would be great, I'll sort out my washing and drop it in. Do you have spare sheets I could use while they clean the others?'

'They'll be ready for you tomorrow.'

I sat at the bar and sipped my drink. Tony's charges were reasonable, as he had promised. Even so, my two weeks of wages had only just covered the total bill.

When Jim picked me up in the morning, I'd ask him if we could go to a bank at lunchtime to change travellers' cheques. Banks in Ibiza were not open at weekends and only opened from 10:30 am to 2:30 pm on weekdays.

Tony was deep in conversation when I left.

I waved goodbye. 'Enjoy the rest of your evening. See you tomorrow, Tony.'

'*Buenas noches,* good night, Fred. Sleep well.'

As I lay in bed, anxious thoughts played on my mind. I needed to get a better-paid job in order to survive the summer and hoped my chat with Gordon would lead to something.

It took me a while to drop off to sleep.

13

Back to work

My alarm clock woke me at 6 am on Monday, after a night disturbed by strange dreams.

Sue caught my mood as I sat for tea and toast. 'You OK, Fred? You don't seem your normal cheerful self.'

I attempted a smile. 'Sorry, Sue, just feeling down this morning. I'm sure I'll be all right once I get going. Did you enjoy the opening party yesterday?'

'Yes, it was a great afternoon, wasn't it?'

'The atmosphere was brilliant. They make a real effort, don't they?'

She gave me a broad grin. 'You're right, although I'm sure they made good money. I saw you chatting with Gordon, and I can imagine what it was about. I know Robbie left at the end of last season and said he wasn't coming back. Did he offer you a job?'

I looked at her, surprised. 'He needs to talk to Ray first, but that was the idea. If it works out, I'd start in June.'

'Just be careful with those two. They expect a lot from their employees. I've known others who haven't lived up to their expectations.'

'Thanks. I'll try to take care but would prefer that to being on building sites for the rest of the summer.'

She placed her hands on my shoulders and gave them a gentle massage. 'I'm sure you'll be fine, whatever you do. I'll get your supplies. Jim's just arrived.'

'Cheers, you've been a great help, as always.'

Taking my rolls and bottles of water, I put them in my straw bag, before giving Sue a quick hug.

* * *

Jim agreed to take me to Santa Eulalia at lunchtime. He had financial matters to sort out too. It was 12:30 pm when he dropped me off at the Banco De Credito Balear.

Over the next two hours, I had a lesson in patience as I learned how Spanish banking worked. I queued to have my documents checked. An elderly cashier took away my three £20 travellers' cheques and passport for review. After an eternity, he returned with my passport and a signed slip. Then I joined another long queue to collect my cash. There was almost a carnival mood among the waiting crowds.

I walked out with 6950 pesetas at a rate of 117 to the pound, after a small deduction for the commission.

Jim and I drove back to the Bee Gees' villa, having missed our siesta.

* * *

In my room, tired after another hard day of graft, I stripped my bed and sorted out clothes for laundry. I took the bundle up to Tony and returned with fresh bedding.

I still felt down and wasn't hungry. I headed to the Red Lion to see how much I owed there.

There was no music from the jukebox and only three customers at the bar. Tich worked alone.

He waved as I approached. 'Hi, mate. How's it going?'

'Feeling a bit down today. It's quiet in here isn't it?'

Tich reached across to shake my hand. 'Yes, I know. Most Mondays are busier than this. I think Cosmos and Club 18-30 have started their party nights. We might see stragglers later. Anyway, what can I get you?'

'Could I try one of your cocktails to cheer me up?'

'OK, what about my favourite, "A Slow and Comfortable Screw Against the Wall"?'

I burst out laughing. 'Sounds interesting. I'd love one of those.'

I watched fascinated as he put a generous measure of vodka, a shot of Southern Comfort and some orange juice, with crushed ice, into his cocktail shaker. After a vigorous shake, he poured the contents into a cold glass and added measures of sloe gin and Galliano.

Adding a slice of orange and a straw, he passed it over. 'That should do the trick, Fred. Enjoy.'

'¡Salud!'

I sipped the drink and my spirits rose by the minute. 'Great choice, Tich. How much do I owe on my tab?'

He pulled out a small notebook, found my page, and added it up. 'It comes to 950 pesetas. Do you want to carry it over to this month or pay it now?'

'I'll pay now.'

I pulled out a 1000 peseta note from my money-belt. Tich gave me the change and reached behind the bar for a letter.

He smiled as he handed it to me. 'This arrived for you this morning.'

It was from Sarah. I ripped it open and read it several times as I sat sipping my cocktail.

Dear Fred,

Your letter arrived yesterday. I hope you are keeping well, and the job is not too much hard work for you.

On Sunday I went around to your house. Your father picked me up, and he seemed very pleased to see me. Chris's boyfriend, Alan, was there. In the evening, we visited The Crown. That is when I missed you most, as I had never been in there without you. Bob, the landlord, asked me how you were.

I went to Sharon and Carol's party on Saturday. In the beginning, I felt very lonely until Sharon introduced me to friends of hers, and then I had a laugh. Carol and I danced, trying to sweat our fat off. It was funny you not being with me. It was the first time I had been out with them on my own. Still, it gave me a chance to wear my long dress.

I am going to a Post Office Disco on Saturday, so I shall find out what Kevin has got in store for me. He still will not stop chasing me. You know I told him I was pregnant. Well, he said he would marry me if you didn't want me. I just laughed at him.

I hope our good times will continue when you come home (your sister thinks they will). I really am missing you. In fact, I don't know what to do with myself. I am finding little jobs to keep me busy. Last week I was lucky everyone wanted their hair cut.

I must finish now, but I will write again soon. Take care of yourself.

All my love,

Sarah

P.S. I miss you, so please be careful.

It was great to hear from Sarah. The letter reminded me of how much I missed her.

I could not imagine how it must be for her, as she had so many reminders of me at home. My thoughts turned to whether our relationship could survive the time apart.

I had written to her the previous week and would write again soon. In addition, I had written to Mother and a few of my friends. Post arrived fast this early in the year. Tich had said at the height of the season, letters took up to three weeks to arrive.

* * *

The rest of the week dragged.

I was stronger and more used to the physical side of the labouring, but the monotony got to me more and more. It was a relief when Jim told me they planned to finish the brickwork the following week. I could then move indoors to help him and Chris with interior work.

Four weeks had passed since I left England, and so much had happened. I realised it was going to be hard to survive until the end of the season. In my planning, I dreamed of the sun, sea and sex, but never considered how work would impinge on that. It was all tougher than I imagined, and I had to be careful with my money to make it last until October.

On Friday night, I visited Grannies and sat at the bar drinking, first beer and later vodka and orange. I chatted to Mick, Pat and Graham when they had time. The Club 18-30 crowd were in and it got raucous as they took part in various boozing games, encouraged by their rep, Liz. On her break, I talked with her about life as a rep. It sounded a stressful job, although well paid as wages came from England. She took a few of her party to Cortijo's in the early hours, the ones who could still stand up. I joined them for a while and had several more vodkas.

Everything became a haze.

14

Meeting Kim

On Saturday morning in Tony's Bar, I was feeling sorry for myself.

The English Breakfast I ordered had not gone down well. At Sue's suggestion, I tried a Bloody Mary, which helped relieve my hangover.

A man's voice came from nearby, 'Are you OK, buddy?'

I turned and saw a man with two women at the next table.

I gave the guy a weak smile. 'Yes, thanks. Just suffering from last night.'

A smile lit his face. 'I've been there. Are you here on holiday?'

I studied him for a moment. He was middle-aged and had an American twang to his voice. Next to him sat a well-dressed woman, who I assumed to be his wife. Opposite them was a young lady whose stunning looks caught my attention. Red plaited hair framed her pale freckled face.

After a pause, I replied, 'Hi, I'm Fred. No, I'm working here. After a two-week holiday last year, I came back for the season.'

He shook my hand. 'I'm Gary. This is my wife, Lorna and our daughter, Kim.' I smiled across and could not keep my eyes off Kim. 'We're travelling around Europe for six months and staying here at Tony's for a few days. He rented us an apartment on the top floor. Where are you living?'

'I have a small room in the basement.'

Three sets of eyes looked at me with interest.

'Where are you from?' I asked.

The flicker of a smile passed Lorna's lips as she swept back her auburn hair. 'We live in San Francisco – Gary's a doctor and I'm a teacher – but we've taken a sabbatical to tour Europe with Kim before she goes to college in the fall.'

I joined them at their table. 'Sounds amazing. Where have you been so far?'

Gary swept a hand across his tanned forehead. 'We started in the Canary Islands in February. After a week touring Lanzarote, and five days on Tenerife, we visited the island of La Gomera and fell in love with it. After four weeks there, we returned to Tenerife and flew to the Algarve in Portugal.'

He took a sip of coffee, before continuing, 'Three weeks later we hired a car and spent ten days driving up the west coast to Porto. Then we flew to Barcelona and stayed a week. While there we found out about Ibiza and got the ferry here on Tuesday night.'

My hangover forgotten, I smiled back. 'Fascinating. I've heard of La Gomera and plan to go there one day. How long are you staying here?'

'Only until tomorrow, we have a flight booked to Paris in the afternoon.'

As I looked towards Kim, she gave me the sweetest of smiles. Although innocent looking, she had a mischievous twinkle in her deep green eyes.

Her soft voice broke the silence, 'What are your plans for today, Fred?'

'Nothing planned, Kim. What are you doing?'

Her face lit up. 'We've hired a car and want to visit Ibiza Town this afternoon. Do you have any recommendations for places to visit while we're there?'

'No, sorry. I only passed through when I arrived, although I've heard the Old Town is interesting.'

Gary flashed me a grin. 'Why don't you join us? I'm sure Kim would appreciate the company of someone nearer her own age.'

I glanced at Kim. She nodded in agreement.

* * *

It was early afternoon as we made our way through the Old Town.

We walked upwards along the narrow, winding cobbled streets towards Dalt Vila (Upper Town). Gary and Lorna led the way, while Kim and I talked non-stop and became engrossed in each other's company.

From the high ramparts, there were fabulous views over the town and out to sea. We came to a drawbridge which led to a large entranceway. Once through the huge wooden doors, we walked across a courtyard and then the main square. The weather was hot, so we took a break. We were all relaxed and enjoying ourselves. I was glad I had accepted Gary's invitation.

We climbed further, stopping off at gift shops and art galleries on the way to the cathedral. After an hour, we found ourselves on the battlements. Our eyes surveyed the panoramic views of the surrounding castle, an old church and the huddle of buildings that made up the town. Further out was the harbour, and we saw fishing boats docking.

Kim stood next to me. The same height, she was in tight denim jeans and a revealing blouse. She had a fantastic figure, and I enjoyed her company. Those sparkling eyes and infectious smile relaxed me. I loved her Californian accent. It sounded so sexy.

Kim squeezed my hand. It seemed she enjoyed my company too.

Gary and Lorna looked contented as smiles lit their faces. They soaked up the late afternoon sun and admired the stunning views. Lorna had a small Kodak camera and took a few shots. She had one of the four of us taken by a fellow tourist, against the backdrop of the Old Town.

* * *

Back in Ibiza Town, we sat outside a restaurant with views across the harbour.

The street was bustling, and we watched the world go by while drinking glasses of sangria. We were hungry after our exertions. The waiter suggested *tapas* and we agreed.

Within ten minutes, he returned with a colleague and laid out an amazing collection of dishes, explaining what they were in both Spanish and a heavy accented English, '*Patatas bravas* (Fried potato dices), *Gambas* (Sautéed prawns), *Aceitunas (*Olives), *Carcamusa* (Beef stew with vegetables), *Setas al Ajillo* (Mushrooms with garlic), *Albóndigas (*Meatballs with sauce*), Tortilla Española* (Spanish omelette), *Chorizo a la sidra* (Chorizo sausage cooked in cider).'

We marvelled at the choices.

I turned to the waiter. '*Muchas gracias, señor.*'

He cracked a grin. 'You are welcome. Enjoy your *tapas.*'

I gave him a thumbs-up as we started to transfer the food to our plates.

An hour later, with stomachs full, and another sangria jug empty, Gary signalled to the waiter he wanted to pay.

It was 9 pm when we got back to Es Cana. Kim and I had spent the journey snuggled up together in the back seat, and Gary and Lorna invited me for a good night drink. We made our way up the three sets of stairs to their apartment. Kim held my hand tight as we climbed.

Compared to my room, it was luxurious. At the corner of the top floor, it had two outside balconies with great views over the resort. There was a large reception room, a small kitchen, a spacious bathroom, and two bedrooms.

Gary confided they were paying 3000 pesetas a night, enough to cover my rent for more than a month. This was where Tony made his money, I thought. We sat out on the balcony with drinks. Relaxed, we soaked up the atmosphere, but I could sense Kim was restless.

Gary sprang to his feet. 'Lorna and I will go to bed soon. Why don't you two young things head out and enjoy the rest of the night?'

He pressed a bundle of notes into my hand and whispered, 'This should cover a few drinks and entrance to the disco.'

Kim came over to her dad and gave him a hug. Lorna gave us her blessing.

I shook both their hands. 'It's been a fabulous day, thank you so much. I promise I'll take care of Kim.'

There were smiles all round as we headed for the door.

Kim skipped down the stairs. 'This is great, Freddy. My dad must trust you. He is always so protective. I don't know what's come over him.'

I caught her up and put my arm around her shoulders. 'Where shall we go then? What about Grannies first, and then Cortijo's?'

'Sounds good to me, lead the way.'

She gave me a cuddle and a kiss on the lips.

Grannies was buzzing as we walked down the steps to the terrace. I found us a place to sit, before going inside to get a gin and tonic for Kim, and vodka and orange for me. Graham's eagle eyes had spotted Kim.

'Wow, she's a cracker, Fred,' he exclaimed as he poured the drinks, 'where did you find her?'

'She's staying at Tony's with her mum and dad. They're from California and I've spent the day with them. They've allowed me to take her out for the night.'

Graham winked. 'Take good care of her then.'

15

Night out with Kim

We sat opposite each other and sipped our drinks.

I gazed into Kim's eyes. 'It's great to be with you tonight, I wasn't expecting this to happen.'

'You don't know how surprised I am, Freddy. This is so unlike my dad. How did you manage that?'

'No idea, but I'm so glad he let you come out with me. I've loved your company today and didn't want it to end so early.'

We held hands across the table and Kim's foot stroked my leg.

I tilted my head to one side. 'Your mum said you were going to college in the autumn?'

'I have a place at San Francisco State University studying for a degree in Biology, Marine Biology and Chemistry. It's near to our home, so I don't have to move. Not yet anyway. I'll see how things work out.'

'Wow, you must have a real talent for sciences. I was hopeless with them at school. I was better at the arts – English Literature, British Government & Politics, History.'

She beamed at me. 'Everyone has their different talents. The subjects I chose excite me, although I'm still unsure what I'll do after college. Didn't you want to go to university?'

'I had a place at Loughborough to study Economics but took a year out to get work experience instead. One year turned into three as I liked the money and started a career in banking. After last year's holiday, my priorities changed again. I threw it all in, and now I'm here.'

Kim looked concerned. 'Do you have any regrets?'

'No, but it's tougher than I imagined because of the physical work I am doing.'

Graham passed by with a stack of empty glasses. 'Can I fetch you lovebirds another drink?'

I nodded. 'That would be fantastic, mate. Thanks.'

'I'll bring them over.'

He made his way to the bar with a column of glasses which stretched way above his head. It looked dangerous, but Graham assured me he had never broken a glass collecting them that way.

After he had placed our drinks on the table, I introduced him to Kim. They shook hands.

Graham's smile widened. 'Great to meet you, Kim. I'm sure Fred will take good care of you tonight. If you want anything else, just shout.'

I gave his arm a playful punch. 'Cheers, mate.'

The drinks tasted stronger than the first round and helped relax us further.

I squeezed Kim's hand. 'So, whose idea was this trip?'

A smile lit up her face. 'It was a dream of mine. I wanted to travel alone but even though I'm 18, my parents wouldn't consider it, so they took a break from work to come with me. We've had a fantastic time, although they smother me sometimes. That's why it's so refreshing to be out on my own with you.'

'Why are they so protective of you, are you an only child?'

She tugged at her earlobe. 'I am now. I had an older brother, Scott, who died in a motorcycle accident two years ago. It's been a traumatic time as I was close to him, and he always looked out for me. We were distraught when it happened. It wasn't his fault. A drunk truck driver took him out as he rode along the Pacific Coast Highway.'

'That's awful, Kim. I'm so sorry. It must have been tough. Now I understand why your dad doesn't want to let you out of his sight.'

I held her hands tight as tears welled up in her eyes.

Kim took a gulp of her drink and changed the subject, 'How do your parents feel about this adventure of yours?'

'They think I threw away a great opportunity at the bank. My mother is more understanding, but my father didn't speak to me before I left. Mind you, we haven't seen eye to eye for a long time. He's a religious man, and I rebelled against him and his beliefs. In his eyes, I've let them down as their eldest son.'

'That's where I'm lucky. I'm close to my mum and dad, more so since we lost Scott.'

Graham had noticed our glasses were empty and bought us another round. It was past midnight. Time flew as Kim and I continued our conversation.

Kim explained she had a boyfriend at home, but their relationship was on hold while she was away. I said the same applied to myself and Sarah. We spoke about other relationships we had been in, and the fact neither of us wanted to settle yet.

I stroked her arm. 'Do you still want to go to the disco?'

Kim glanced down. 'Would you mind if we didn't, Freddy? We won't be able to hear each other. I'd prefer if we went somewhere quieter.'

'Fine with me. Why don't we take a walk along the seafront?'

'Great idea.'

* * *

There was a cool breeze as we walked hand in hand by the shoreline.

We removed our shoes. Gentle waves lapped against our feet. We enjoyed the crisp coolness of the water as we waded to the far side of the bay. Reflections glistened on the undulating sea from the third-quarter moon high in the sky.

We found a small secluded cove and sat on the sand. Away from the lights of Es Cana, the stars were bright, and we stared at them, enthralled.

Kim enthused, 'This is amazing, just what I needed.'

She snuggled closer in the slight chill of the night. Peace and tranquillity pervaded the atmosphere. We drifted off in our own thoughts, comfortable in each other's company. Although our time together was short, we did not want to rush things.

After a while, Kim turned and gave me a gentle kiss on the lips and held me tight. I responded. Hands roamed, and we undressed each other until we lay naked, protected against the sand by our discarded clothes.

I gazed at Kim's stunning, well-proportioned body, in admiration. Aroused, our fingers explored each other, and we came close to climaxing.

Kim pulled back for a moment. 'I'm not on the pill, Freddy, so can we enjoy ourselves without going the whole way?'

'No problem, darling. I'm enjoying this so much and don't want to spoil it.'

Our exploration of each other's bodies became more intense, and we climaxed in an explosion of pure joy and excitement.

I held her tight. 'That was amazing, Kim.'

She smiled as her fingers stroked my chest and strayed below again. I reciprocated, and we soon lost ourselves in another fervent embrace. The sensuality between us was like nothing I had ever experienced.

* * *

Dressed once more, we sat on the sand.

Kim was in a reflective mood. 'Do you believe in God?'

My eyebrows shot up. 'Why do you ask, darling?'

She gazed up at the star-laden sky. 'Well, although I'm excited by science, and it provides answers, I always think something or somebody else is out there.'

'Yes, you're right. There must be a greater force we can't comprehend. I became disillusioned with religion a few years ago. It causes so much hurt and pain in this world. Because of that, I lost any belief God exists. How could he, when his followers have been responsible for so much suffering, death and destruction?'

'I know, my love, that's how I feel. My parents were never religious, and I don't have the same background as you, but Scott's death destroyed any flicker of belief I had. The world is so unfair. How could an all-seeing God allow such things to happen?'

We held each other and wanted the night to go on forever. The stars had faded though, and there were hints of daylight on the horizon.

With pain in my heart, I turned to her. 'I suppose we'd better get you back. Your mum and dad will be worrying.'

'Yes, I know, you're right. Time has gone too fast, but it's been magical. Thank you for the love and care you've shown me. I'll never forget tonight.'

* * *

We sat on the balcony of the third-floor apartment at Tony's.

It was 6:30 am. Kim and I drank cups of tea she had made. The sun rose above the horizon, the birds twittered close by, and the gentle aroma of pine drifted across. We held each other's hands and kissed.

Her parents appeared in their dressing gowns.

Gary turned in our direction. 'I thought I heard voices. Did you have a good night?'

A huge grin lit up Kim's face. 'Yes, it's been great.'

'That's reassuring to know. We got worried when you didn't come back after the disco closed but knew we could trust you.'

I gave Gary and Lorna a concerned look. 'Sorry, we're later than planned. After Grannies, we decided the disco would be too loud. Instead, we took a long walk along the beach and enjoyed each other's company so much, we didn't notice the time.'

Lorna smiled. 'That's OK, we're just glad you had a good time. It's a shame we're leaving today. You could always come and visit us in the States one day.'

'I'd love that Lorna. Thanks for the offer.'

Kim wrote out the address and phone number of their place in San Francisco and pressed it into my hands.

I scribbled the Red Lion details along with my home address and passed them to her. 'Maybe you can send me a postcard or two from places you visit during the rest of your trip.'

Kim grinned and gave me a hug. 'Yes, I'll try to do that.'

We all had breakfast together, less than twenty-four hours after we had first met. It seemed such a long time ago.

I said my farewells to Gary and Lorna. They both hugged me, before heading upstairs to pack.

Kim and I had a last, fond, farewell kiss.

16

More news from home

After work the next Wednesday, I stopped off at Tony's.

There were two messages for me. Gordon had asked that I stop by to discuss the job with him and Ray. There was also some post at the Red Lion.

I finished my meal and walked to Tootsies. I ordered a beer from the young lady behind the bar and asked whether Gordon and Ray were there. She told me they would be back at 8 pm. That was only a quarter of an hour away, so I sat outside and waited for them.

They arrived a few minutes later.

Gordon boomed, 'Hi, Fred, I don't think you've met my partner yet. Ray, this is Fred. Fred, this is Ray.'

I stood up and shook his hand. He towered above me.

A fleeting smile crossed his face. 'Good to meet you, Fred.' They sat down and Ray continued, 'Gordon tells me you're interested in working for us as a bar waiter. We've discussed it and would like to offer you the job. Could you start on the first Monday in June, the 6th?'

I beamed at them both. 'Fantastic news. Thank you. That gives me time to give Jim plenty of notice. Is there anything else I need to do before then? Gordon mentioned about getting a work permit.'

'Don't worry, I'll pick you up at 8 am on the Monday and take you into Santa Eulalia to get that done first. It takes two or three hours. Once we complete your application process, you can start.'

'What hours will I be working?'

Gordon smoothed his moustache. 'Most days will be from 10 am until 7 pm, although you get breaks during the day when it quietens down. If it's busy, you may need to stay on longer, but we'll pay you whatever hours you work.'

Ray added, 'From the second week you'll get Mondays off. How does that sound?'

'That sounds great.'

We stood and shook hands to seal the deal.

Ray took a step back. 'I'll see you on Monday the 6th, make sure you're ready.'

Roger was alone behind the bar in the Red Lion and didn't have time to stop and talk. He gave me a San Miguel along with two letters. They were from Sarah and Mother. I sat at a small table outside in the alley and took my time reading them.

Dear Fred,

Thank you for your letter which I received yesterday. The Station got your postcard too. It is now up in the bar.

I hope you are keeping well. How is your suntan coming along? The weather here is terrific: rain, sun, and more rain. I heard today from one of our clients that the girls in Ibiza go topless on the beach. Sharon said she doesn't mind you liking it out there, provided you don't expect us to do the same.

I'd love to come out to see you. On Saturday, I went to the disco and really missed you being there.

People keep asking me when you will be back. I say I don't know. My mum sends you her best wishes.

Have you done much touring and visiting places, or haven't you had enough time? Have you cut down on your drinking, or do you still drink as much as you used to?

Well, I had better finish now.

Lots of Love,

Sarah

My dear Rob,

Thank you so much for your letter and your latest news. We are glad you have got both a room and a job. I am sure the aching muscles will soon become strong. When you said the villa belonged to the Bee Gees, I thought you meant someone whose initials were B.G. But Father said it was the musical group.

Yes, thank you, we are keeping well. Chris is enjoying her job and is glad to be in regular work. I will pass your message on to Alastair, although he may be busy winding up the end of his university year. He finishes in May.

Perhaps you will get to know a little about the local life and colour before many tourists arrive. Father and I enjoyed Majorca when we were there. How warm is it this time of year?

Last Sunday, Chris and Sarah spent the evening together. They met here and then Sarah's father came to meet her afterwards.

We are wondering if you needed to take the tent, but maybe it will be useful later in your travels.

We send lots of love and think of you often.

Much love,

Mother

Then there was a piece included from Father, which surprised me: a news summary compiled for me and my brother, since both of us were away from home.

(Prepared for you and Alastair, by Father with his love)

NEWS SUMMARY .... for the FEAR exiles .... as at 3rd MAY 1977

The official Jubilee celebrations begin in London on May 4th when the Queen and Prince Phillip will be presented with a "loyal and humble" address by both Houses of Parliament at a redecorated Westminster Hall.

Red Adair headed a team of Texan trouble-shooters to cap the blowout of a Norwegian oil rig in the North Sea. For five days three tons of oil a minute poured into the sea but there was no fire. They evacuated the 112 men on the platform. The oil slick has now almost disappeared.

Richard Nixon makes his post-resignation television debut on May 5th in a series of 1½-hour interviews with David Frost. They paid the former president £400,000 for the 29 hours of videotaping from which the series was edited. Nixon still resists the public verdict (70% said guilty) on his cover-up of the Watergate scandal, despite tough questioning by Frost.

Margaret Thatcher says a future government will outlaw the closed-shop and the Conservatives' would not hold a referendum to test public opinion on the subject.

The condition of fourteen IRA prisoners, now in the seventh week of a hunger strike, is described as "deteriorating fast". They are allowed daily visits by relatives now they have been transferred to a military hospital.

An RAF Canberra today crashed on a terrace of eight houses killing three children and two of the plane's crew. Casualties could have been higher as the plane, trying to land a mile from the runway, crashed only 200 yards from a school in Huntingdon.

The Soviet Union is thought to be negotiating with the Israeli government for the renewal of diplomatic links which were broken off by Moscow during the 1967 Arab-Israeli war.

The four main High Street banks announced a second cut in their base rates in eight days. This latest reduction – by half a point to 8½% - means they have cut base rates seven times since the turn of the year when they stood at 14%.

The exchange rate for the £ against the dollar is 1.72.

The Queen's picture will, after all, appear on a chamber-pot to be produced by a Stoke pottery. The Lord Chamberlain who said the Jubilee idea was in bad taste relented when the pottery said they would put two handles on the chamber-pot and call it a "planter" so it could be used for indoor plants.

Three young men passed around a cannabis "joint" as they drove along the M23 after a day out at Gatwick. But in the car was a hitch-hiker they had picked up near Horley, and as they drove into Reigate, the man announced he was a police officer, ordered them to drive to the police station and then arrested them. This week they were each fined £5.

After 100 days in office, President Jimmy Carter will visit London next week.

A middle-aged man who landed at Gatwick has sparked off a Lassa fever scare. He is still in strictest quarantine while they test him for the deadly and very infectious virus. They have warned commuters who used trains from Gatwick to London on April 21st to see their doctors if they develop a feverish illness before May the 13th.

Britain's reserves rose by £300m in April to its highest-ever point. The reserves have risen, by smaller amounts, every month this year. The National Enterprise Board has announced a before-tax profit of £51m. British Leyland made a profit but Rolls Royce a loss.

As always it was great to get letters from home. I felt guilty about Sarah and wondered whether she was serious about coming out to see me.

17

Leaving work

It was Friday 13th May when I told Jim about the Tootsies job as we rode to work.

'Great news, Fred. Well done. I knew you didn't fancy labouring all summer. When do you want to finish?'

'If I work for the next two weeks, is that OK with you? A family I know from home are on holiday in Majorca from May 27th. I'd like to visit them for a few days, before starting at Tootsies.'

Jim nodded in agreement. 'That works well for me. Two lads from Leicester are arriving before the end of the month. One is an experienced labourer and the other a qualified carpenter. They can start as soon as they get here. I hope this has been a learning experience for you. I appreciate the way you got stuck into the job.' He smiled and continued, 'I have good news. Today will be the last time you are on the roof. From next week you'll be inside with Chris.'

'Sounds brilliant, Jim. Thanks again for the opportunity. It's been hard work but helped me get through my first few weeks here.'

'You're welcome, I'm just glad it worked out for you.'

* * *

In the afternoon, the skies clouded over and there was a sudden shower. I sheltered until it passed. It only lasted ten minutes at most. Once it finished, I made my way across the roof with caution as I carried two buckets full of concrete.

As I neared the edge where the bricklayers worked, I slipped on the wet surface and fell backwards. My head hit the floor with a thud. The buckets of cement flew from my grasp. One landed on top of me and covered my legs with the gooey mixture. The other tipped over the side of the building. They told me later it missed the Spanish guys by inches.

There were screams from below, '¿Qué pasa?' – What's happening?

With a loud clatter on the stairs, Chris and Jim rushed up to see what was going on. They looked horrified as I lay spread-eagled on the roof.

Chris peered at me. 'Are you OK, Fred?'

I felt the back of my head as I tried to stand. 'Not sure, I must have slipped. Sorry, I've spilt everything.'

Chris had a concerned look on his face. 'Don't worry about that.'

He helped me sit upright. There was blood on the floor, and he checked the wound. 'You have a nasty gash. Let's move you downstairs and get it sorted.'

I brushed the cement from my legs with a rag Jim gave me. The bricklayers arrived on the roof and swept up the mess.

Chris sat me down and got his first-aid box. He cleaned the gash with cotton wool and surgical spirit. It stung like hell.

'I thought you might need stitches, but the wound looks clean enough, and it's stopped bleeding. Be careful when you comb your golden locks though. Try to avoid that area while it heals. I imagine it will be sore for a while.'

'Thanks, Chris. That was stupid of me. I should have taken more care.'

He smiled. 'Something similar has happened to all of us. You were lucky it wasn't more serious. I'd suggest you sit in Jim's car and recover. You've had a shock and need to take it easy. Jim can mix up more cement and I'll run it across the roof. The bricklayers only have one wall left to complete and are due to finish today.'

'OK, Chris, thanks for taking care of me.'

As I sat in the Seat, a throbbing headache developed. It stayed with me for the next two days. I had a quiet weekend. By Monday morning, the worst of the pain had subsided.

As Jim had promised, we started work inside, and I tried to help Chris with the plastering. At first, I got more plaster on me than the walls, but I got the hang of it after a while and developed a routine. It was tiring but at least I was away from the heat of the sun.

On Wednesday, I woke to torrential rain. It continued most of the day, making the drive to and from the job difficult. On the building site, water flooded through the unsealed roof, and down two of the walls we had plastered. The ground outside was sodden. Jim called a halt at lunchtime, and we headed back to Es Cana.

On Thursday, we covered the roof with lengths of tarpaulin to prevent further leaks. Then we repaired the damage from Wednesday's storms. Heavy showers continued until Friday midday when the sun and blue skies returned.

* * *

79

My final week on the building site passed with no further incidents. On Monday and Tuesday, Chris and I finished plastering the remaining walls and ceilings.

The final three days I spent helping Jim with the project he had worked on for the past two weeks. It was a large hot tub with enough room for four people. In the bathroom, on the top floor, it faced out of a wide window, with views through the trees towards the Bee Gee's villa.

It was Jim's pride and joy. He had created an intricate mosaic which covered the inside surface of the bath. He carried on with this as I spread grout between the pieces. Once it was dry, I polished the stones until they gleamed. Twice I dislodged some of the mosaic, and Jim rushed over in a temper to repair the damage. I had never seen him that way. There was an awkward silence as we got back to work, which made a change from Jim's non-stop talking. He forgave me after a while, and I tried to be more careful. His chatter resumed.

We finished on Friday and he dropped me off at Tony's, handing over my final wage packet of 2000 pesetas. We shook hands before he drove away.

I was in a mood to celebrate.

After a wash and a change of clothes, I walked to Grannies. Mick and Pat were there talking to two men, and Pat beckoned across as I entered the bar and gave me an Estrella.

'Hi, Fred. Come and meet Syd and Dave. They've driven from England and arrived this afternoon. They're starting work with Jim on Monday. Maybe you can help them get orientated.'

They both looked tired. I stepped over and shook their hands. 'Pleased to meet you both. Jim said he was expecting you, but I didn't realise you were driving. How long did it take?'

Syd, a tall lanky guy, with short dark hair, gave me a weary smile. 'We started out from Leicester on Tuesday afternoon and caught the Dover ferry at 9 pm. After taking it in turns driving overnight through France, we made it to the Spanish border at 10:30 Wednesday morning. We were hoping to catch the ferry from Barcelona in the evening.'

I looked at them startled. 'Wow, you must have been speeding to make it in that time.'

Dave, who was chubby with a flushed complexion and long fair hair, grinned. 'We weren't hanging about. Everything had gone well until then. There were complications at the border though, because of paperwork problems with the car. After a five-hour delay, we made it through, but we had to pay the customs officials for the required documentation.'

Syd grimaced. 'Cost us 2800 pesetas. We hadn't planned for that and had no cash left for the ferry when we arrived in Barcelona. I think we'd have missed it anyway. We had to stay in the outskirts overnight and slept in the car. It's an old Ford Cortina and not very comfortable. I was in the front and Dave in the back.'

Dave continued their story, 'Then about 6 am two policemen on motorbikes pulled up, tapped on the windscreen and gestured at us in a menacing way. We don't speak Spanish and unlike the customs officials, they spoke no English.' He rubbed his chin. 'We didn't know what we'd done wrong, but as they had guns, we didn't argue. After a lot of waving of hands and shouting, we had to pass over most of our remaining pesetas until they drove away.'

Syd took a deep breath. 'We arrived in the city and had to wait until the banks opened, so we could change one of the travellers' cheques we brought with us. Once we had cash again, things improved. We had breakfast as we were starving, then headed to the port and booked tickets for the evening ferry. We arrived this morning and had a look round Ibiza Town, before driving across the island. Got here an hour ago.'

'Sounds like you could do with another beer.'

They both nodded in agreement and I ordered more drinks from Mick.

We clinked glasses. 'Cheers, lads. Welcome to Es Cana. I've worked with Jim for the last six weeks. Finished today as I've got a bar waiter job lined up. From what he said, you're both much more experienced at building work than I am. I'm sure you'll fit in fine. Where are you going to be staying?'

Syd and Dave looked at each other, and then glanced at Pat.

She clarified, 'My dad has organised a room for them at Tony's on the first floor. I was trying to explain to the lads how to drive there. It might be easier if you showed them. Would you mind?'

My smile widened. 'No, of course not.'

We finished our beers, and I accompanied Syd and Dave to their battered Cortina.

I exclaimed, 'That's weird, your number plate's got my initials on it.'

They both looked at me confused.

'RJF. Oh, Fred is my nickname, my real name is Robert John Fear,' I explained.

They laughed and Syd shrugged his shoulders. 'The plates may be worth more than the car, Fred.'

We piled in and I guided them around the coast road and up the dusty track to Tony's Bar.

18

Time off

On Saturday morning, I ran into Syd and Dave as they finished their breakfast in Tony's, and grinned as I joined them. 'How's your room?'

Dave smiled back. 'We planned to go out for a few beers but were so tired we crashed early. It was so nice to have a bed after the last couple of nights discomfort.'

They were about to meet Jim to talk about the job, so they promised me a drink later and slapped me on the back before they left.

Sue brought over my breakfast and gave me a hug. 'As you've finished work with Jim, I presume you won't need your packed lunches any longer.'

I squeezed her hand. 'Thanks for doing those for me Sue. I'm not sure how I'd have survived without them.'

She brushed back her long brown hair. 'My pleasure, happy I could help.'

After breakfast, I walked over to the Red Lion. I hadn't been there for two weeks and wanted to check if any post had arrived. Tich gave me a broad smile as I entered the bar.

'Fred, great to see you again. How's it going?'

I sat on a stool as he uncapped a San Miguel. 'Cheers, Tich. I'm doing well. How're things with you?'

'Improving. We were very busy last night. I've been told you're starting at Tootsies in a few days. Is that right?'

'Yes, finished with Jim yesterday, and start a week on Monday. In the meantime, I'm taking time out to go over to Majorca, and meet up with friends from home.'

'Sounds great. Best of luck. I'll get your post. Then I need to stock up the shelves.'

Tich returned and handed over four letters. The first two were from Mother and Sarah. The others were from Janice and Tena, to whom I had written postcards in April. I read them first.

Janice was the oldest daughter of the landlord and landlady who ran the Prince Albert in Bletchingley for five years before taking on another pub, The Angel in Woodhatch. After they moved, I'd dated Janice for three months before my 1976 holiday in Ibiza. She was only fifteen and her parents kept a close eye on us.

Dear Fred,

I am so glad you've settled in. It seems like you are having a wonderful time. It was a pleasant surprise to hear from you.

I'm sorry I missed you last time you came over as I would have liked to say goodbye.

I leave school this year, so there are only a few weeks before I can get rid of this awful uniform. My original plan was to go to Reigate sixth form college to do A-Levels, but I am so fed up with school, I want to work instead. Besides, I need the money.

I've changed since we last met. My hair is longer, and I've gained much of that confidence you tried to instil in me.

Thinking about it, I learned a lot from going out with you.

I still dislike living here. The people are so horrible, it's unbelievable. Never mind, enough about me and my troubles. Ibiza is a great place, isn't it? I shall think of you out there in all that sun. You'll be so brown when you get back.

You must be careful you know. Girls go wild about blond blokes with blue eyes and a suntan.

Good luck and best wishes.

Lots of love,

Janice

Tena and Tim were regulars at another pub I frequented, The Crown in Nutfield. Sarah and I often socialised with them and I had promised to write.

Hi Fred,

Thanks for the postcard, it was great hearing from you.

Do you hope to get a job in a bar when the season starts? You'll have girls flooding around you: blond hair, blue eyes, and tanned from labouring.

I should imagine the nightlife out there is great, with so many hotels and clubs.

I've bought a new car, a Mini 1000 H reg. for £400. It goes like a bomb compared to the Vauxhall.

I saw Sarah up the pub the other night, looking fed up. She's missing you a lot.

The weather is not too good here. It's sunny in the morning, then pours with rain in the afternoon.

I can't afford to go abroad this year after buying the Mini, so I shall go somewhere here.

Well, must go now. Take care of yourself.

Love,

Tena

Next, I read Mother's latest news.

My dear Robert,

Greetings again from this green part of Surrey. It is damp underfoot in the Kip-walking fields. [Kip was our Sheltie dog.]

Father sends you a message: "Don't let yourself get into a tight-corner with finances. Just let us know if you need a loan to help get you through." So please remember that if it is ever necessary.

We had a letter from Alastair. He hopes you are getting on well. He had news from St Lawrence's Mental Hospital and can start work there on June 1st. So, I am sure that will please him.

You will miss the Jubilee high jinks. Jubilee Day is June 6th. There are many jubilee mugs, plates and various souvenirs etc, including a plant potter. It was a chamber-pot, but they could not have the queen's portrait on one of those. Television has programmes reminiscing over the last 25 years, so it is even percolating to me that a Jubilee is in the offing.

Chris enjoys work, although she feels they do not pay her as much as the other women there. But she has bought herself a nice watch by saving something each week.

This comes with love from us all and thinking of you.

Your loving,

Mother

I'd saved Sarah's for last and opened it with anticipation.

Dear Fred,

Thank you for your letter which I received today. It arrived fast considering you only posted it on Thursday. How are you keeping, have you decided about your job yet?

Saturday, I visited the fair on the common with Pat and Malcolm. It was a laugh until we rode on the switchback. I fell and hurt my leg and now have a great black bruise. It was also very muddy, and I lost one of my shoes as the mud came up to my ankles.

I had to go to the opticians to have my eyes tested, so I've got to find £5.80 for new lenses.

Please, when you write about Kevin call him Andy as my mum sometimes looks at your letters.

I am writing this letter in my lunch hour and I've just had one of my many phone calls from Kevin, but it doesn't worry me anymore. I just say I'm not in and put the phone down.

Well, I must go now.

Lots of love,

Sarah

It was fantastic to get the news from home. I read the letters several times.

My mind wandered. Was it my imagination or were Sarah's letters becoming more distant? Had my feelings towards her changed? I did not think of her as often as I did at first. How would I feel by the end of the season?

19

Trip to Majorca

I woke up on Monday morning as it got light. It took a few seconds to realise I had the week free. My plan to take a break in Majorca had only been an idea until then. I knew a boat left Ibiza Town at 10 am for Palma. I decided to catch it and threw a few belongings into my black duffel bag.

As an afterthought, I stuffed in the tent and sleeping bag. After I had fastened the money-belt around my waist, I pulled on a t-shirt, shorts and sandals. The door to my room did not have a lock, so I wedged it closed.

Upstairs, I found Sue as she prepared the restaurant for breakfast. 'Fred, what are you doing up so early? I thought you had finished work.'

I gave her a broad smile. 'A family I know from home are on holiday in Majorca, so I'm taking a break to visit them. Could you please tell Tony? I'll settle my bill for May when I get back on Thursday or Friday.'

Sue gave me a hug. 'Have a great time. Don't worry, Tony will be fine with that. I hope you find your friends. I assume you know where they are staying.'

I hitched the bag on to my shoulder, pecked Sue on the cheek, and ran off to catch the 7 am bus to Santa Eulalia.

* * *

Brian and Sheila lived near to us in South Nutfield. I knew them from the Station Hotel, the local pub I worked in during the winter and had frequented since I was 16. They were in their late twenties and had two young sons, Jamie and Charlie.

Brian had his own building business. Most of his work was in the village and surrounding area. He had gained a reputation for being reliable and a hard worker. Sheila did the accounts and administration. They were a well-liked couple and visited the pub once or twice a week in the evenings while Sheila's mum babysat the boys. I often talked to them about my plans to spend a season in Ibiza. In my last week at the pub, I got them to write details of their visit in my address book. Sheila jotted: *Brian & Sheila, Hotel Balis, Arenal, Majorca - 15 days – Arrive Friday 27th May.*

* * *

The bus arrived on time and the connection in Santa Eulalia worked well. There were frequent stops, as locals on their way to work boarded. Spanish voices rang around me. I saw the countryside in a new light and became absorbed in the scenery as we rattled along the main road to Ibiza Town.

We arrived with an hour to spare before the ferry. After buying an open return ticket to Palma for 625 pesetas, I sat at a pavement café near the harbour and ordered a coffee and a ham roll. I consumed them while enthralled by the bustle of life around me. Fishermen docked with their early morning catches and sold fish from the sides of their boats. Tourist buses arrived. Different nationalities were guided by their respective tour leaders along the promenade towards the Old Town.

Boats thronged the harbour as our ferry made its way through their midst. It was a medium-sized vessel with room for around 200 passengers. I looked back. My eyes strayed to the Old Town with the fortress and cathedral topping the hill. White buildings glistened in the bright sunlight. My thoughts drifted to my time there with Kim and her parents over three weeks earlier. I wondered where they were on their European adventures.

As we sailed along the southern coast of Ibiza, I gazed at the undulating coastline fringed with pine trees. The boat passed Santa Eulalia and Es Cana in the distance before we headed out into the choppier waters of the Mediterranean Sea between Ibiza and Majorca. I dozed in a seat on the top deck and soaked up the sun as it blazed from vivid blue skies.

Before I knew it, the four-hour journey was over. As the ferry approached the wide Bay of Palma, I caught my first glimpse of the capital, Palma de Mallorca. After Ibiza, everything was on a much grander scale. The boat navigated towards the harbour to the south-west of the city, and I pulled out my map of Palma. To the east were the sweeping sandy beaches and tall tourist hotels of Arenal, where I planned to meet up with Brian and Sheila. I saw a plane taking off from the airport nearby.

In contrast to the small white buildings of Ibiza Town, the architecture was multi-coloured and much larger. On a hilltop to the west of the harbour stood the imposing Bellver Castle, a distinctive circular-shaped fortress. The massive Santa Maria cathedral dominated the horizon as we approached the port.

I disembarked and walked eastwards along the pavement, with the sea to the right and a busy street to the left. My plan was to walk to Arenal. Palm trees provided welcome shade when the heat became too intense. I hoped to find a small café to get refreshment, but the road was endless, and I wilted.

At a junction, I crossed to the other side and saw people at a bus stop. I joined them and got on a bus to the City Centre. The driver took several coins from my hand as I offered the pesetas I had in change. A seat at the rear was free. I collapsed into it and gathered my strength.

The distance I had covered in an hour took five minutes to travel on the bus, and we soon arrived back where I had started. We turned right and weaved through the narrow streets, before arriving at a stop near the Old Town. I rang the bell. The driver drummed his fingers on the steering wheel.

'*Muchas gracias señor,*' I exclaimed, as I jumped down to the pavement.

He waved back before driving away.

There was a small café nearby, with tables outside, that looked perfect. I sat and asked for a beer and the menu. The middle-aged waiter spoke good English.

He gave a slight bow. 'Yes, sir. Do you want draught or bottled beer?'

'Is the bottled beer cold?'

'It is in a fridge. We have either Cruzcampo or San Miguel.'

'Could I try a Cruzcampo, please?'

'I'll bring your drink and the menu straight away.'

As I sipped on the chilled beer, I read through the small menu which had descriptions in both Spanish and English. I ordered the *Menu del día* (Menu of the Day) which comprised three courses, bread and wine for 175 pesetas.

The waiter served the first course of stew and rice within ten minutes.

It was delicious. I had forgotten how hungry and thirsty I was. The beer was finished, so I poured a glass of red wine from the carafe. It had an earthy taste, which became more palatable by the third glass. I washed it down with the water provided and nibbled on small slices of fresh bread.

The second course took longer to arrive, and I had finished the carafe by the time it did. I ordered a second one, before I tucked into the succulent chicken, roasted in a rich sauce. The spicy cannelloni made an excellent accompaniment. I washed this down with more water and red wine.

By the time dessert arrived, I felt heady. My tongue tingled from the sweetness of the cake and coldness of the ice cream. Any thought of going to Arenal that evening faded from my mind. It was 6 pm, and I would have to spend the night in Palma. As I paid the bill, I asked the waiter about accommodation.

He raised his eyebrows. 'A few hostels here in the Old Town are cheap, but they are often full at this time of the year. If you have no luck around here, there are more expensive hotels over by the cathedral you could try.'

I thanked him and strolled up the narrow winding street in search of a room.

* * *

The waiter was right.

The hostels in the Old Town were full. The cheapest hotel room was over 2000 pesetas per night and too much for my meagre budget.

I remembered there was a large park near the harbour and wandered in that direction. On the way, I stopped at a crowded bar. After the wine earlier, my mouth was dry. I ordered a bottle of water to quench my thirst, along with brandy and Coke for a change.

Four brandy and Cokes later, I wobbled towards the park. I found an area at the far end sheltered by hedges and trees. It was after midnight and quiet. I decided to pitch my tent and stay there for the night.

I had tested erecting the small one-man tent in our garden back in England. It took less than five minutes. This time it was much more difficult. The ground was hard, so hard I could not bang the pegs in without bending them. After ten minutes of frustrating effort, I gave up. Instead, I used the tent as a groundsheet and placed my sleeping bag on top. I clambered in and laid back.

Myriad sounds from the city merged into a lullaby that sent me to sleep.

20

Finding my friends

A rising sun and the sound of voices woke me after a disturbed night's sleep.

The quiet spot I had chosen the night before was full of people sitting on benches in the surrounding square.

As I slipped out of my sleeping bag, accusing eyes turned in my direction, but then glanced away again. I had slept in my shorts, so I pulled on a t-shirt and donned my shoes in a hurry before I packed my bag.

There was a drinking water fountain nearby. I refreshed my parched lips and dampened my tangled hair before moving to a vacant bench.

Although it was still early, streams of Spanish workers paced along the park's pathways, on their way to work in the city. Others sat on benches and read newspapers while they drank coffee and ate breakfast purchased from a nearby café.

I walked over to the café and ordered a coffee with two pre-made rolls. As I enjoyed my breakfast at a table outside, my thoughts turned to a plan of action for the morning.

I pulled out the map of Palma. On it, I found a scale in the bottom right-hand corner I had missed the day before. The distance I had walked along the seafront was only three kilometres, although it seemed more. The road that stretched around the coast to Arenal was closer to ten kilometres. To walk that far in the heat made little sense.

The Tourist Office was marked on the map. It took twenty minutes to get there. I waited until it opened at 9 am to find out which bus to catch, and where the Hotel Balis was in Arenal.

A stunning, dark-haired young lady in a smart uniform opened the door to the Tourist Office.

I explained what I needed.

She pulled out a thin booklet and thumbed through it. 'There is a departure from the harbour bus stop at 10:20 am that stops in El Arenal. It takes an hour. I'll check the closest place for you to get off for Hotel Balis.'

I beamed a smile at her. 'That's very helpful of you, thank you.'

'You're welcome. I'll write the name of the stop. Show it to the driver.'

She scribbled a street name on a scrap of paper and passed it over. 'When you leave the bus, cross the road and turn to the right. You will see the Hotel Balis in front of you. I'll mark it on this map in case you lose your way.'

'Great. I'll also need somewhere to stay. Do you know of a hostel with rooms at a reasonable price?'

The young lady tugged at her earlobe and smiled. 'My uncle owns a small hostel in Arenal. I'll telephone him to see if he has any spare rooms.'

After five minutes on the phone, she turned and smiled confirmation. 'There is a spare room at a rate of 750 pesetas per night, but it's only free tonight and tomorrow.'

'Perfect. I'll take it.'

She gave me the name and directions, marking it on the map. I shook her hand and thanked her before I headed for the door.

* * *

The bus arrived ten minutes late, but we were soon underway.

As I paid the driver, I handed him the piece of paper. He nodded and said something in Spanish.

We drove along the road I had walked the previous day. The sea sparkled in the bright sunshine. A cooling breeze blew through the open windows as the bus headed eastwards out of Palma, stopping at regular intervals. After a while, the route diverted away from the coast towards the airport where several passengers disembarked. The driver got off and helped a group of new arrivals stow their cases. Two planes landed on the nearby runway.

As we drove into Arenal, I saw the long thin strip of sandy beach along the right-hand side of the main drag, and groups of sun-worshipping tourists laid out on the sand between straw-covered shacks, which I assumed to be beach bars. Bathers dotted the sea as they refreshed themselves from the baking sunshine.

The road curved around the cove ahead and ran through an area of high-rise hotels built over recent years to cater for the booming tourist trade. They rose as tall as fifteen storeys and swamped the skyline, a huge contrast to Ibiza where local authorities did not allow buildings above five or six storeys.

A shout from the driver signalled that this was my stop. I smiled at him as I disembarked. He returned the smile, helping several other passengers unload their luggage.

There was a long queue at reception as a group of English tourists checked in to the Hotel Balis. I waited by the swimming pool while the two receptionists dealt with the incoming guests. Scores of families occupied sunbeds. A slide at the far end was in constant use, as children whooshed into the water with screams of delight. Parents sat under parasols keeping a wary eye on their youngsters.

Looking upwards I counted twelve floors, with eight rooms and balconies on each level facing the pool. The midday sun shone with intense heat. I wandered over to the bar in the corner. A straw-thatched roof shaded it and there were stools around the rectangular counter. I ordered a draught beer to quench my thirst.

Twenty minutes later, I glanced over and saw the reception desk was empty.

'Good afternoon, sir. How can I help you?'

'I'm looking for a family that's staying here, friends of mine from England. They should have arrived here last Friday, the 27th.'

'OK, I can check for you. What are their names?'

My mind went blank. 'Their first names are Brian and Sheila, but I can't remember their surname. They have two young boys with them.'

The receptionist looked confused. 'It would be easier if you knew their full names. We have over five hundred guests staying here.' He thumbed through the handwritten register with a deep frown on his face. After five minutes of searching, his face lit up. 'I have found a family of four and the parents' initials are B and S. Does the surname Cooper sound right?'

A stupid grin came over my face. 'Yes, that's them. Sorry, I should have remembered. Can you tell me what room they are staying in?'

'I'm sorry, sir. I cannot tell you that. It is company policy. I can only say they have checked out for the day. I think they are on an organised tour. Do you want to write a message? I will make sure they get it when they return. The tour is due back at 5:30 pm.'

He gave me a piece of paper and a pencil. I scribbled a quick note and suggested I meet them near the reception desk at 7:00 pm.

I smiled as I handed over the note. 'Thank you very much for your help.'

'You're welcome, sir. I don't finish until 6 pm, so I'll hand this to them when they come back.'

I waved goodbye as I strolled out of the hotel and headed to the Tierramar.

My room was small but adequate and had the luxury of an en suite shower. I washed off the grime of the past twenty-four hours and got a comb through my tangled hair. Refreshed, I lay on the bed and drifted off to sleep.

21

Meeting up at last

I arrived back at the Hotel Balis with time to spare. Brian and Sheila weren't there so I walked over to the bar and sat at a table with a good view of reception, ordering a Cruzcampo from the waiter. He brought it with a small plate of appetisers. I sipped on my drink and nibbled on the olives, cheese and nuts as half an hour passed.

There was still no sign of my friends, so I asked for one more beer and waited.

The clock above the desk ticked by. I wondered if my note had been mislaid and became impatient as it got close to 8 pm. The waiter asked if I wanted another Cruzcampo, but I was getting hungry, so I paid and walked over to the young lady at reception.

I coughed to attract her attention. 'Good evening, could you help me, please?'

She looked up from her paperwork and gave me a weary grin. 'Yes, what can I do for you?'

I explained the situation, but she knew nothing of my message. As I asked her if my friends had returned from their outing, I saw Brian and Sheila with their sons in tow, heading towards the desk.

Brian was over six feet tall, well built, with short fair hair and blue eyes. Sheila was two or three inches shorter, with long dark hair tied back in a ponytail, and hazel eyes. They both had good tans already. The boys were tall for their age and the image of their father. Jamie was eight and Charlie was seven. They didn't notice me straight away, so I called across, 'Found you at last!'

They both looked over in surprise and beamed as they saw me. Their two young sons looked up at me puzzled.

Brian shook my hand while Sheila gave me a hug and asked, 'When did you get here, Fred? We've been out on a day trip and were due back at 5:30, but the coach broke down. We waited while they tried to carry out repairs. In the end, they sent a replacement bus.'

As Brian fetched the room key, he read my note. 'Sorry to have kept you waiting, Fred. Do you want to stay here while we get changed? We won't be too long. Then we can have something to eat.'

'Sounds good. I'll just have another beer while I wait.'

* * *

The meal was buffet style, and they asked no questions when I joined the family in the restaurant.

Tired out, the two boys stayed silent as we adults chatted about the latest news from home.

I mentioned the gossip from Sarah about Bob stripping off at the pub and everyone else joining in.

Brian and Sheila stared back at me open-mouthed, before Brian answered, 'We've heard rumours there have been goings-on, but we weren't aware of that. Thank God we are never there after closing time. I wonder how they felt the next day.'

I chuckled. 'Hungover I'd imagine. It's amazing what goes on behind closed doors in such a small village, isn't it?'

Sheila cringed and changed the subject, 'I saw Sarah in there one evening with Carol and Tish. She didn't talk much but seemed down and must miss you.'

'Yes, it's difficult for her. We often exchange letters and my family keep in touch with her. But I don't know how we'll both feel if I stay in Ibiza the whole summer.'

Sheila took the boys upstairs after dinner as they were falling asleep at the table. Brian and I moved to a nearby bar for more beer. We agreed to meet in the morning after breakfast and spend the day by the pool. It was great to meet up with friends from home.

* * *

We met up on Wednesday as planned.

Brian had reserved sunbeds with a table and two parasols. The boys were wide awake again. They spent their time on the slide and splashing around the pool. Brian, Sheila, and I sunbathed, chatted and took the occasional dip.

They asked me about life in Ibiza and I told them what I had been doing since I arrived. I ended with the news of the job at Tootsies.

A smile raced across Sheila's face. 'I'm sure it will work out. You have a great way with customers.'

My face reddened. 'That's nice of you, I never looked at it that way.'

I changed the subject, 'How's business, Brian? You must be busy this time of year.'

He glanced at his hands. 'It's tough going. With inflation the way it is, people are reluctant to spend money. We are getting plenty of small jobs, but that's not where the real profit lies. I hope things will pick up again soon.'

Conversation waned, and we relaxed back into our sunbeds to soak up more sunshine. Time flew past, and I enjoyed the company. It was late afternoon when we went our different ways. Brian and Sheila had a meal organised for the evening and I planned to return to Ibiza the next day. We said our farewells, and I asked them to send my love to Sarah.

After a shower at the hostel, I set out to explore Arenal.

The streets heaved with tourists. Bars and restaurants along the main street were full to overflowing. I meandered towards the seafront and found a quieter beach bar where I sat, ate *tapas*, and drank beer. I watched the sunset behind the castle in the west. A while later, I noticed the full moon as it rose above the Bay of Palma against a darkened sky in the east.

Then I started a bar crawl around Arenal. I switched from beer to vodka and orange. My mood lightened. I forgot the time and where I was. The map was back in my room, so I became disorientated. Eventually, I found an English bar on the seafront and asked for help in locating the hostel. By then I was drunk and had forgotten its name, so I chatted to an English couple for ages though I've no idea what we talked about. From what I recalled their flight was leaving in the early hours, and they were in a similar state.

I must have found the hostel, as I woke up in my bed on Thursday morning.

Two weeks after I returned to Ibiza, I got this letter from Ealing.

Dear Fred,

I bet you didn't think I'd write, but I've just come across the name and address you wrote in my notebook in the bar in Arenal.

My name is Susan and the fella I was with was Ron. We talked to you at the bar along the seafront, remember? Hope you found your hostel OK after you left us.

97

I'm sitting in my back garden topping up my tan. It is warmer here today than it was in Majorca. Stupid isn't it?

After leaving you on Wednesday night, we made for our hotel, where we had a cup of coffee, and I fell asleep in a large armchair.

I was tired and kept dropping off wherever we had to stop and wait.

We landed in Luton at 5:15 am. It was freezing. As soon as I got home at 7:00 am, I went straight to bed and slept most of the day. Woke to find I had picked up a nasty cold but dragged myself to the pub to have a drink of whisky and lemonade.

Well, I trust you got back to Ibiza OK. Drop me a line and let me know how you are getting on. I can't believe your real name is Fred, so I only hope you get this.

Nice talking to you.

From Susan

22

Back home in Ibiza

I woke up late on Thursday morning and missed breakfast at the hostel. Faint memories of the night before drifted back, and I had a wretched hangover. I checked out of the Tierramar and paid my bill of 1500 pesetas.

On the way to the bus stop, I walked past a bar with a board advertising English Breakfast for 140 pesetas. I sat outside and ordered one, along with a Cruzcampo. The sausage, bacon, fried eggs, mushrooms, fried bread, black pudding, and baked beans went down well, as did the beer. I felt much better afterwards.

The bus I caught took a direct route to Palma and was at the harbour in thirty minutes. With time to spare before the 3 pm boat, I found a small café where I drank two coffees with brandy. The ferry arrived at 2 pm, and I joined the queue to get on board.

It felt like I was going home.

Although I had enjoyed my three days in Majorca, it was a relief to be returning to Ibiza. I relaxed on deck in the afternoon sun, soothed by a cool breeze as the ferry ploughed through a choppy sea.

After a couple of hours, I glimpsed Es Cana in the distance. My heart leapt. A further twenty minutes passed, and we drew into the harbour. The familiar sight of the cathedral and fortress of Ibiza Town brightened my spirit. The white buildings glistened as the skies reddened and the sun set.

I decided not to rush back to Es Cana but spend the night in Ibiza Town instead.

The first two hostels I checked in the Old Town were full. The third, in a narrow side street, had a room free in the basement for 450 pesetas. It was basic and reminded me of my place in Es Cana. After a wash in the shared bathroom, I headed out to explore.

The winding streets were buzzing with tourists. This time I paid more attention to the surroundings. On my earlier visit, Kim's beauty absorbed me, rather than the wonders of the Old Town.

As I walked upwards through the cobbled lanes, I heard loud music off to my left. In a small side road, an impromptu party was happening. It was an amazing sight. Scores of revellers gyrated to sounds from a set of decks outside one of the boutiques. We were treated to an eclectic mix of tracks from Bob Marley, Jimi Hendrix, The Doors, Led Zeppelin, and Pink Floyd.

I heard hints of languages from across the world. Participants wore weird and wonderful clothes. The word "freaky" sprang to mind. Oblivious to the crowd of onlookers, couples cavorted around the street and passed joints to each other.

Another small group drew on a chillum. Looks of contentment spread over their faces. Wafts of hashish smoke drifted on the warm evening air. Bottles of beer were raised to thirsty lips. The atmosphere was electrifying, and I stood gazing at the goings-on for a good half hour.

After I had dragged myself away, I followed tourists along the winding paths, past bars, restaurants, specialist shops and hippy stalls.

I found my way back to the spot on the battlements where Kim, Gary, Lorna, and I had gazed out across Ibiza Town. At night-time, it was even more enchanting. The moon was still full and reflected off the gentle swells of the sea. The lights of the buildings highlighted their white brilliance, and weaving lines of people trailed between them.

It was getting late. My stomach reminded me I needed food. As I headed downwards, I saw the sign to a courtyard restaurant. Hidden from the main street and surrounded by apartments, there were views of the castle and cathedral bathed in moonlight.

The waiter showed me to a small table in the corner. I indulged in several *tapas* dishes he recommended and washed them down with three bottles of San Miguel.

After a while soaking up the atmosphere, I wandered around the streets taking in the vibes. It was after 2 am when I returned to the room.

My decision to stay the night had been rewarded.

* * *

I woke early on Friday and grabbed a breakfast of coffee, fruit juice, bread and honey.

Passengers filled the bus to Santa Eulalia. After a struggle, I got a window seat near the front. The joy of being back was still with me as I took in the now-familiar scenery. Trees swayed on either side, small hills topped by villas stood out in the distance, and white buildings dotted the road at regular intervals.

Excited voices, some from locals and others from tourists, filled the air as the bus stopped at various points along the route. Dusty earth wafted over the tarmac in places, a gentle breeze blew through the open window, and the warmth of the sun glowed on my face. We soon arrived in the main square of Santa Eulalia.

I needed cash to pay my tabs, so I walked to the branch of Banco De Credito Balear I had used before. A group of customers formed outside as it was not yet 10:30 am. When a cashier pushed the doors open, everyone rushed past him. I joined the back of the first queue to have my documents checked.

This time I knew what to expect. I waited with patience as my position in the line advanced at a slow pace. I handed over my passport and five £20 travellers' cheques to the same elderly cashier.

After a long wait, I received my documents and the slip of paper. It showed 11,730 pesetas at a rate of 118, less the bank's commission. An hour later, I wandered out into the blazing early afternoon sun with the wad of notes safe in my money-belt.

With 5000 still left over from the building work, I hoped this would last until mid-July. I planned to pay my tabs for June with wages and tips from Tootsies.

Thirsty by then, I walked across the square to Fred's Bar. It was as gloomy as I remembered but provided a respite from the heat outside. Heads turned as I entered, but the rustling of newspapers resumed almost straight away. Mad Mike was not there. I assumed it was too early for him.

I ordered an Estrella and stood at the bar. In England, I would have got talking to someone else within minutes. Here it was different. Regulars kept to their own cliques. Outsiders were viewed with suspicion. After another beer, I made for the entrance and escaped the oppressive atmosphere.

Moments later, I was on the short bus ride back to Es Cana.

* * *

The wedge under the door was still in place.

Removing it, I entered the room and a wave of heat hit me. I reached up and opened the two windows. A faint breeze stirred the air. I checked around and everything was in order. After unpacking my duffel bag, I stripped off and laid on the bed for a short siesta.

When I woke, sweat covered my body. I walked along the corridor to the bathroom and ran a cold bath, in which I soaked for five minutes. Refreshed, I dressed in clean clothes then strolled upstairs for something to eat and to pay my tab.

Tony had just started his shift and gave me a broad grin. He shook my hand. '*Hola,* Fred, welcome back. Did you have a good visit to Majorca?'

I sat at the bar and sipped the bottle of San Miguel he passed me. 'It was great, although hectic compared with Ibiza. How have things been here?'

He gave me a thumbs-up as he served other customers. 'Now it's June the season has changed gear. All the rooms are booked out, and the restaurant is getting much busier.'

I smiled back. 'Great news. You must be happy with that. When you have time, could I have my tab for May?'

Tony reached behind the bar and handed me a piece of paper. Scrawled on it were: Rent – 31x90 = 2790, meals & drinks – 1710, work supplies – 20x120 = 2400, laundry – 400, Total – 7300.

I cringed, as it was more than I had calculated, but it seemed in order.

Tony grinned as he folded the wad and stuffed the notes into his wallet. 'Cheers, Fred. Nice doing business with you.'

23

Catching up

After a meal at Tony's, I strolled along the dusty road to Tootsies.

I wanted to make sure my start on Monday was still going ahead.

By the time I arrived, it was late afternoon. The outside area was full. Gordon looked agitated as he took orders for food and drink. I waved across at him. He acknowledged me with a brief nod.

Inside, Ray was behind the counter with a young barmaid, both rushed off their feet as they served drinks and carried out meals to waiting customers. I joined the queue at the bar.

Ray grimaced. 'Fred, good to see you. We tried to get hold of you on Tuesday. It got busy sooner than we expected, so we wanted you to start this week. I asked at Grannies, but Mick told me you'd gone away.'

My brow furrowed. 'Sorry, I was in Majorca to meet friends from home. Can I give you a hand now?'

'Yes, please. Could you collect empties from outside and wash them for us?'

For the next hour, I carried in trays of glasses, washed them in the large sink, and dried them. After I had moved them to the shelves around the bar, I repeated the exercise.

In the meantime, a huge pile of plates had accumulated. The chef, a stocky Welsh guy called Duncan, was red-faced, and at the end of his tether. I proceeded to the kitchen sink to wash and dry the dishes. After another hour, the backlog was under control.

The rush subsided. Ray passed me a beer. 'Thanks for helping. It was manic there for a while. Could you come in tomorrow and Sunday to help as well? Then we'll apply for your work permit on Monday.'

The extra money would be a great help, so I nodded in agreement. 'What time did you want me to start?'

'Midday should be fine.'

Gordon and Duncan sat slumped at the bar. The barmaid, Sylvia, served them both a beer. That revived their spirits.

I chatted to Sylvia for a while. She was a pretty redhead from Manchester. Like me, she had been in Es Cana on holiday in 1976 and came back to look for work. She found a room at the Las Arenas apartments on her first day. Ray and Gordon took her on straight away. She was thrilled with how things had worked out.

It was 11 pm when I arrived at the Red Lion. Customers lined the bar waiting for drinks. Roger, Margaret and Tich served them as fast as they could. I caught Tich's eye, and he handed me a San Miguel and then my post. There were two letters. I recognised Sarah's handwriting on the first. The second had a Bletchingley postmark, so I assumed it was from the lads. I sat outside and sipped my beer as I opened them.

Dearest Fred,

I received your letter this morning. The postal system doesn't seem too bad my end.

I hope you are not working too hard on the building site.

The weather here has been awful, frost in the morning and rain all day, although today it has been hot. It looks like my suntan this year won't exist.

On Monday, Pat and I are going to a slimming place in Earlswood. It costs £2.10 per hour but will be worth it if I lose a lot of weight. (Don't worry it'll be off the hips).

I plan to cut your sister's hair and see your parents on Sunday. We arranged to meet last week, but they had to go out and I was ill with a terrible cold.

The photos I got weren't very nice, so I shall send you this one. It's of me and my nan at our Christmas Party.

I seem to be getting on all right at work. Today I permed Pat's hair so now she is curly. I do quite a lot of Shampoo and Sets. Monday night I set my nan's and I also do my mum's.

I must finish. Really miss you and can't wait for the time when I see you again.

All my love,

Sarah

FRED,

WE HAD TO CANCEL HOLIDAY AND BOOK UP AGAIN FOR 8 PEOPLE. WE'RE GETTING A CHEAP RETURN FLIGHT FOR £52 EACH, BUT THE CATCH IS YOU'RE MEANT TO BE A HOMEOWNER ABROAD OR HAVE AN ADDRESS, LIKE A VILLA OR APARTMENT. SO, WHAT WE HAVE DONE IS PUT DOWN THE RED LION. I DON'T THINK THEY'LL CHECK UP. IF THEY DO, CAN YOU ASK TICH TO TELL THEM WE'RE STAYING IN THE DIGS ABOVE THE LION AND THAT SHOULD DO THEM.

WE'LL BE ARRIVING ON 3RD JULY AT ABOUT 12:50. AS THAT'S A SUNDAY AND YOU AIN'T WORKING, MEET YOU IN THE RED LION. CAN YOU HAVE A LOOK AROUND IN ES CANA FOR A ROOM WHERE WE CAN LEAVE BAGS AND WASH, YOU KNOW NOTHING TOO EXPENSIVE? HOPE YOU'RE OK OUT THERE. THIS IS WHO'S COMING: MUTTS, SIV, SAM, PERV, GILES, TUZZ, KOOK, NICKI.

SO, TELL TICH TO BE OPEN AND WE'LL HAVE A GOOD PISS UP.

DROP US A POSTCARD TO LET US KNOW YOU GOT THE LETTER.

ANYWAY, SEE YOU LATER.

LOVE AND KISSES,

MUTTS & SIV

The photo of Sarah touched me. Her image had faded from my mind after almost two months away. A pang of guilt hit me when I thought of how I had been unfaithful to her.

I was shocked to find out about the change of plans from the Bletchingley gang. I thought only Mutts, Sam and Siv had booked to come in July. Now there would be eight of them. I was unsure how I could get them cheap accommodation at the height of the season.

It was past midnight when I went back inside for another drink. The earlier crowds had subsided. I sat on a stool at the bar and ordered a vodka and orange from Tich, who asked about my trip.

'It was good to catch up with friends and hear all the news from home. Looks like you're getting busy here.'

A smile brightened his face. 'It's been crazy since the weekend, which is great. The season has picked up sooner than normal. We've doubled our takings compared to the same week last year.'

I told him I'd be starting the next day at Tootsies.

Tich leant across and patted my shoulder. 'That's great, hope it works out for you. They can be tough taskmasters, so take care.'

'Yes, Sue warned me too. I'm sure it will be fine. By the way, one of the letters you gave me was from Mutts and Siv. You know I was expecting them next month. Well, eight of them are now booked for Sunday, July 3rd, early afternoon. Do you want to have a look?'

He took the piece of paper and read it. 'Interesting, Fred. I don't think the charter companies ever follow these things up, but if they do, we can cover for them. We'll make sure we're open Sunday lunchtime. That could turn into quite a session, I imagine. You'll have problems finding accommodation for them though. Do you want me to ask around?'

'If you could, that would be great. I'll check with Tony, although he told me earlier he was booked out. I'd better get off soon as I'm working tomorrow. Could I settle my tab?'

Tich leafed through the small notebook until he found my page. 'It comes to 1655, not too bad.'

I reached into my money-belt and counted out the notes. Then I dug into my pocket to find coins for the rest. 'There you go. I won't be around so much this month. If you hear about a place for the lads, can you leave a message for me?'

'Will do, take care.'

'Cheers, mate. You too.'

24

Bletchingley lads

I could not sleep.

My mind churned as I worried about money, work, and finding a room for the lads.

Thoughts turned to how I first got to know people in Bletchingley. The village was two miles walk from where I lived. After a mile up the hill from South Nutfield to top Nutfield, you headed east along the A25 for another mile to get there.

In the autumn of 1971, I went out with a girl called Ali, whose parents owned a local shop on the corner of the Bletchingley housing estate. Two years younger than me, she attended Reigate County School for Girls.

I attended Reigate Grammar School for Boys. Situated at the top of a hill, it was on the bus route that ran along the A25 out of Reigate towards Redhill. I took the bus and changed at Redhill to pick up the train to Nutfield station (which to confuse things is in South Nutfield), before walking the five minutes home.

Ali caught the bus with a group of other girls from Reigate County. They were often at the back of the top deck when I boarded. My memory of how we got together was vague. Once we did, I stayed on the bus as we headed out of Redhill along the A25, through top Nutfield, and alighted at her stop in Bletchingley. We then spent time together at her place.

Besides our afternoon liaisons, we met at weekends and walked in the fields. There was a youth club where they held discotheques which we visited sometimes on a Saturday evening. I saw a few lads from the village whilst there. On the lookout for girls, they were interested in stronger drinks than those offered at the youth club.

In 1972, my O-Level exams took priority. I had to study hard to get the grades to qualify for Sixth Form. Ali and I drifted apart.

* * *

In the summer of 1974, I had finished school after taking my A-Levels.

At 18, I could drink in pubs, although they often questioned my age. My drinking had started at 15, when I joined the school rugby players after matches for two or three pints at a local pub in Reigate. Because of the company I kept they always served me. This caused problems with my father as it became obvious, on occasions, that I was drunk when I got home. He made me walk a straight line and sent me to my room without food if I wobbled away from it.

One Friday evening that summer, a group of lads from Bletchingley came into the Public Bar of The Crown in Nutfield on a pub crawl. I recognised three of them from the youth club two years before. The gang wore denim or leather jackets with jeans and boots. Each of them had their nicknames in brass studs on the back of their jackets. Most of them had long hair. I learned later they referred to themselves as Greasers.

They were rowdy but caused no trouble. I chatted to a guy called Biff, and we got on well. He was a stocky fellow, with black curly hair, and a menacing grin. I remembered Mutts, Sam and Tuzza from the youth club. They persuaded me to join them as they continued their pub crawl.

We crossed the half-finished bridge over the new motorway (M23), which was due to open in 1975. Several of the lads played dare by hanging each other over the railings. This scared me, as the drop to the tarmac surface of the road below would have killed anyone who slipped. They trusted each other and there were no accidents.

Once in Bletchingley, we had a pint each in three pubs: William IV, Red Lion and Plough. Then we headed back to the Prince Albert, the lads' local. It dated from the 19th Century and had low wooden beams. The Saloon Bar took up most of the front of the pub but we made for the Public Bar. This comprised a small area, with limited access to the bar through a hatch. Down a step at the back, you came to a cramped smoke-filled room with a dartboard. We ordered drinks and crowded into the back room to play a game of Killer.

Names were listed on the chalkboard to the right of the darts board. There were nine of us and we put 20p each into a bowl. 20p bought a pint of beer. The winner took the £1.80 in the pot.

The scorer chalked three marks against each name to represent the number of lives. Each player threw a dart to select a number. Then we aimed for the bullseye with a single dart. The closest started the game.

We threw three darts each and tried to hit a double of our number. Once this happened you became a killer. After that, the aim was to get doubles of the opponents' numbers and take away their lives. The last one left with any lives won the game.

It was a fast and furious game. Most of my new mates played as members of the Monday night darts team. My inexperience showed as I didn't even manage a double before I was "killed". After ten minutes, there were three players left: Biff, Mutts and Tuzza.

Biff still had one life left on a 20. Mutts had two on a 17. Tuzza had one on a 5.

Tuzza hit a double 20. Biff was out. Mutts missed the double 5. Tuzza scored a double 17. Mutts hit double 5 and raised his arms in victory. The winnings disappeared into his pocket.

He was keen for another game, but I dropped out and took over the chalking, as the other eight threw in their coins. Biff won the second round and another guy, Siv, won the third.

A loud bell rang, meaning they had called last orders. Everyone crowded around the hatch to get a final pint before the pub closed at 11:00 pm.

Light seeped into my room as these memories flooded back. I leaned over and set my alarm clock for 10 am. My mind returned to Bletchingley.

Over the following months, I spent a lot of time with the Bletchingley lads. I became part of the Monday night darts team and one of the crowd. My darts ability was not good enough to play in the matches, but my talent for numbers meant I became a scorer for the team.

Even when I started work in London, I made sure I got to the Monday evening matches. They played these at the Prince Albert and other pubs that took part in the local league. I also joined the lads at weekends and enjoyed their company. They were a rough-and-ready bunch, but genuine in their nature.

I passed my driving test and bought a clapped-out grey Ford Anglia for £50. This started a new era in my relationship with the lads, as I drove them to darts matches or on outings to other pubs and parties. Even though I was driving, I often drank three or four pints during the evening. One time, this almost lost me my licence.

Six of us had been to a party in nearby Oxted. It was past midnight as I dropped my passengers off at their homes around the Bletchingley estate. As I pulled up outside the final drop-off point, there were flashing lights in my rear-view mirror. A police car drew up in front of us and two coppers got out. I wound down my window, and they told me to get out of the car.

They smelt the beer on my breath and asked if I had been drinking. I said I had only drunk two pints, but they did not believe it and wanted to breathalyse me. Before they could fetch their equipment, an urgent message came through on the radio. They returned to their car and drove away. I had a lucky escape and was more careful after that incident.

Mutts and Sam were often amongst my passengers. Siv had a car too, and we drove in convoy. This was how I got close to the three lads that joined me on the holiday to Ibiza in July 1976.

We hatched the plan on a snowy evening in early January 1976, huddled around our beers in the Prince Albert. Siv suggested the holiday idea, as he had heard of a cheap deal. Within minutes the four of us agreed, and he booked it the next day.

That was the day that changed the direction of my life.

25

Starting at Tootsies

Even when I slept, vivid dreams ebbed and flowed.

The alarm clock disturbed my slumbers, and I sprang out of bed. After a quick wash, I got dressed and headed upstairs.

Sue greeted me with a grin as I ambled into the restaurant, 'Hiya, Fred. Nice to see you again. Tony said you met up with your friends in Majorca. Did you have a good time?'

'Yes, thanks. I enjoyed it but it felt like I was coming home when I left.'

Her green eyes sparkled. 'It happens to all of us. This island has a magical effect and draws you back. I wouldn't live anywhere else now.'

I sat at a vacant table on the veranda. Sue followed me. 'Did you want any breakfast?'

'Could I get a full English and a mug of tea, please? I'm working at Tootsies from midday and need to build up energy.'

She raised her eyebrows. 'Oh, I thought you weren't starting until next week.'

'That was the original plan, but they got busy earlier than expected. I was there yesterday afternoon to make sure the job was going ahead, and they roped me into work. I ended up washing glasses and plates. They've asked me to do the same today and tomorrow. On Monday, Ray will help me apply for my work permit. Then I'll start as a bar waiter.'

A slight frown crossed her face. 'Well, I suppose that's good news. Be careful they don't take advantage.'

I scratched my head. 'Thanks for the warning, Sue. Tich said something similar.'

* * *

The sun blazed from a cloudless sky as I walked to Tootsies.

It was 11:45 am when I arrived, and most of the outside tables were full.

Gordon beckoned me over. 'Great to see you, Fred. Thanks for yesterday. Could you do the same today? There's already a backlog of glasses. If it gets quieter later, I'll give you instructions on the work we

111

need you to do from Monday. For now, it's a case of firefighting to keep things under control.'

'No problem. I'll get stuck in straight away.'

At the bar, I waved to Ray and Sylvia, who were serving a queue of thirsty punters. I popped my head into the kitchen and said hello to Duncan. He nodded a sweaty face in my direction.

After grabbing a tray, I worked around the tables collecting empty glasses and finished plates. Gordon collected orders. Then he served drinks and meals. He became more frustrated as the afternoon progressed. Waiting customers often asked me to take an order or settle their bill, but I had to decline and concentrate on what I was doing.

I moved between the bar, kitchen and outside, trying to balance priorities of getting empties, plates and cutlery cleaned, dried, and re-stocked. At one point I stumbled over a step and almost sent a tray of glasses flying. I recovered just in time and steadied myself before disaster struck.

The madness subsided around 4 pm. We had worked without a break. I sat at an empty table with Gordon and he offered me a Ducados. He leaned across and lit it. The smoke hit my throat, and I reached for my glass of iced water.

He shot me a grin. 'They are harsh, aren't they? Sorry to throw you into the deep end with work, but you seem to be coping. We'll pay you cash in hand for the weekend and then you'll be on the books.'

'Will I be taking over what you've been doing?'

'That's the idea. We have two Spanish lads starting on Monday. They'll serve meals and clear up the glasses and dishes. You'll take orders from customers. Ray and Sylvia will get the drinks ready at the bar and you'll serve them. When you're asked for the bill, add it up and collect the cash.'

'I saw you had a notebook. How does that work?'

'When you take an order, place the piece of card under the second sheet, and carbon paper between the two pages.'

He pulled out the book from his waistband to show me. 'Write the table number in the top right-hand corner. There's a table plan at the back of the book. Write out the orders with prices next to each item. The menus show the cost of meals and drinks. Keep the orders for food and drink separate. Once you've done that, tear out the top sheets and hand them to the bar staff. They will deal with the drinks orders and pass food orders to the kitchen.'

I tried to take it in as he continued, 'When customers ask to pay, add up the bill. Make a note of the total on the final order in your book for that table. If you get tips, you can pocket those. The rest of the money goes into your wallet. Watch out for anyone who tries to sneak off without paying. It happens sometimes. If it does, shout for me or Ray.'

A worried look came over my face. 'It sounds complicated.'

Gordon gave me a reassuring smile. 'Don't worry. We're here to help if you have any problems. We'd better get back to work. The late afternoon crowd are arriving after their day on the beach.'

* * *

The sun was setting when I finished.

Duncan served me a plate of fish, chips and mushy peas. The glass of draught Estrella went down well.

The walk to Tony's seemed longer than normal. After a quick bath and a change of clothes, I headed for Grannies. There were several spare seats at the bar.

Mick spotted me as I sat down. 'Welcome back stranger. How's it going?'

I gave him a tired grin. 'Good, thanks. I started work at Tootsies sooner than expected and just finished for the day. I came in to sort out my tab. Hope you didn't think I'd forgotten.'

A mischievous smile crossed his face. 'Ray was looking for you on Tuesday. I told him you were away. Everywhere has got busy earlier than normal this year. Let me get you a drink and I'll see what you owe.'

Moments later, Mick passed over my vodka and orange. 'Looks like you need this. Your tab came to 2950.'

I reached into my money-belt and fished out three 1000 peseta notes. My eyes were beginning to droop. I retired to my room and slept like a log.

* * *

Sunday at Tootsies was less busy.

After clearing the empties, I had time to help Gordon as he took orders and served customers. He showed me the table layout, and we ran through the prices of meals and drinks. The system made better sense as I watched it in action.

In a quiet moment, he advised me, 'One important thing you must learn is to socialise with the punters. They might annoy you sometimes but be pleasant with them and take time to chat. This is something I still find

113

difficult. You'll get better tips and they'll come back more often if you remember their names and make them feel comfortable.'

I nodded with enthusiasm. 'Thanks, Gordon. That's great advice. I'll do my best.'

Before I left that evening, Ray gave me 2000 pesetas for the work I had done at the weekend.

* * *

Ray arrived at 8 am on Monday.

I had eaten a good breakfast and was waiting for him outside Tony's.

He shouted across, 'Morning, Fred. Climb in.'

I clambered into the front passenger seat of his beaten-up jeep. We bounced along the dusty track until we reached the main road and headed out of Es Cana towards Santa Eulalia. There was silence as Ray drove and concentrated on the traffic ahead, a real contrast to the rides with Jim and his chatter. I sat back and appreciated the beauty of the surrounding countryside. Farmers were already hard at work tending their animals and crops.

Arriving in town, we pulled into a small side street and Ray towered above me as we walked to the office that issued work permits.

He turned, grinned, and spoke for the first time since we had left Tony's, 'We have to wait fifteen minutes until the office opens at 9 am. It's best to get here early, to be near the front of the queue. You have got your passport, haven't you?'

'Yes, don't worry, I have it here.'

'I know their procedures. Let me fill out the forms and I'll do the talking. The whole conversation will be in the local dialect. Just smile if the officer asks you anything and look at me for guidance.'

At 9:15 am they showed us into a small room. We sat at a table where Ray completed the paperwork. After a long wait, a woman guided us to another room where a uniformed man sat behind the typewriter on his desk. He took the file of papers, my passport and a wad of pesetas from Ray.

There was a conversation between the two of them as the official filled out a form on his typewriter. He glanced in my direction once and asked me something I didn't understand. I deferred to Ray. He answered on my behalf.

The officer soon completed the form, signed it, and showed me where to put my signature. He then used an official stamp to validate my passport. After scooping the money into a drawer, he handed the passport back to me.

I turned to the relevant page and inspected the stamp. It excited me that I was now officially registered in Ibiza.

Two hours after our arrival we were outside again in the hot June sunshine.

Ray explained, 'They'll send your application off for approval. As with most things in Spain, this takes a long time. They're more interested in getting the pesetas than anything else. You now have permission to work. The only problem might come in a few weeks if they turn you down. I've never known it happen though.'

'Thanks, Ray. I hope it goes through.'

The flicker of a smile passed his lips. 'Right, let's drive back to Tootsies and you can start work. Gordon said he's told you most things. If you have any questions, just shout.'

I grinned back at him. 'I'm looking forward to getting started.'

26

Struggling at work

Gordon was showing the Spanish lads around when we got back to Tootsies.

Sylvia was behind the bar. Duncan prepared meals in the kitchen. Ray left to get supplies from the supermarket. There were a few customers outside.

Gordon strolled toward me. 'So, are you ready for action?'

I snickered. 'Yes, raring to go. Where do you want me to start?'

'Let me introduce you to Manuel and Carlos first. They speak limited English, but for what they do that shouldn't be a problem. Although most of our customers are tourists, locals come here sometimes, and they can talk to them. Also, by law, we have to take on Spanish people.'

He took me across and made the introductions. They both looked nervous. I smiled and shook their hands.

I tried my limited Spanish, '*Buenos dias, ¿Cómo estas*?' – Good morning, how are you?

Manuel replied, '*Muy bien gracias, ¿y usted*?' – Very well thanks, and you?

At that point, my Spanish faltered. Those months of learning deserted me. I grinned in response.

Gordon intervened. He spoke the language well and explained to them what I would be doing. They nodded that they understood.

Gordon gave me a brand-new order book and a wallet with a float of 1000 pesetas in a mixture of notes and change. I positioned the card and carbon paper in the book and stood by the entrance to the bar.

My first customers were an English family with two children.

I approached their table. 'Good afternoon, what can I get you?'

The father looked up at me. 'Two beers, a lemonade and a Coke. Can we have the soft drinks in bottles with straws?'

I scribbled the order and added the prices. 'Yes, that's no problem. Did you want any food?'

His eyebrows furrowed. 'We might have something later.'

I nodded and ripped the first sheet from the book. The carbon paper fell to the floor. I picked it up and dusted it off. That was not a good start.

At the bar, I handed the order to Sylvia. 'Can they have the soft drinks in bottles with straws, please?'

She smiled and prepared the drinks. I took the tray out to the table and passed the glasses and bottles around.

As Gordon had suggested, I tried to strike up a conversation. 'So, where are you from? How long are you here for?'

The mother gave me a smile. 'We're from Guildford in Surrey and are staying at the Hotel Cala Nova for two weeks. We arrived on Saturday.'

I gushed, 'That's interesting. I attended school near there, in Reigate, and my family lives in a village called South Nutfield.'

The father looked uninterested, but his wife was friendly. 'Yes, I know Reigate and I've heard of the village. Have you worked here long?'

My grip on the empty tray tightened as I noticed people had arrived on nearby tables. 'I came to Es Cana two months ago but have only just started here. Sorry, I must go now as there are other customers to serve. Let me know if you need anything else. My name's Fred.'

I pulled out my book, shuffled the card and carbon paper, and headed for the next table.

* * *

An hour later, I was struggling to cope with the stream of orders, serving the drinks, and settling bills.

There was no time to chat, and I became frustrated as customers clicked their fingers or shouted to attract my attention.

Despite that, I remained in control. Gordon gave me words of encouragement. The two Spanish lads were a great help as they cleared tables and brought meals out from the kitchen. Sylvia helped me when I got confused with which drinks belonged where.

I made it through to 5 pm. Gordon took over for half an hour while I had a break. Duncan served me a snack of a toasted ham sandwich, and I relaxed in the late afternoon sun, smoking a cigarette.

After that, I stayed on top of things until I finished for the day at 8:30 pm, as the sun was low in the sky. I even got my first tip of 100 pesetas, which cheered me up no end.

Gordon sat with me as I drank a beer and had a meal of cottage pie with gravy. 'I know how you feel, Fred. It's difficult, isn't it?'

'Tougher than I thought. Do you think I coped OK?'

'Not bad for your first day. Just try to relax. It's difficult talking to customers when you're rushing around, but I'm sure you'll get used to it after a while. Wednesday will be your real test as it's Hippy Market day. As we're nearby, many tourists drop in after their visit.'

I gave him a weak smile. 'The last thing I want to do is let you down.'

Gordon patted me on the shoulder. 'Don't worry. We're in this together.'

* * *

I started again at 10 am on Tuesday.

Ray congratulated me because everything had agreed when they tallied my takings against the paper slips from the previous day. That encouraged me, and my mood improved as I eased myself into the day's work.

Before I knew it, the garden was full again. I coped better and had brief conversations with the customers. This reflected in the number of tips I took. When I emptied my pocket, I had accumulated 350.

On the Wednesday, as Gordon had warned, Hippy Market day became manic with floods of tourists during the afternoon. I panicked at one point and was close to tears.

Gordon recognised I was in trouble and stepped in to assist. 'Take it easy, Fred. It's not the end of the world. We all struggle to cope sometimes. I'll help you until things get quieter.'

A grateful smile crossed my face.

It calmed down early in the evening, but I had lost confidence in myself. I questioned whether I was right for the job, even though I had taken over 500 in tips.

Thursday started with disappointing news.

My takings had not tallied, and they were 400 pesetas under. I apologised but didn't know where I had gone wrong. Ray accepted my apology but warned me if it happened again, I would have to pay any difference from my wages.

I felt depressed, and my mind was pre-occupied. Although I tried to pick myself up and get stuck into work, the day dragged. I coped with the orders but was not in the mood for friendly banter with customers. This showed in my tips as I only got 250.

As I sat and ate my meal, there was a strained atmosphere between myself and the others.

* * *

It occurred to me that I had done nothing about finding accommodation for the lads.

Tich had said he would ask around, so I popped into the Red Lion to see if he had found anything.

I took a stool at the bar.

Tich spied me and came over to shake my hand. 'Are you OK, mate? You look sorry for yourself.'

'I'm fine but work at Tootsies is tougher than I imagined.'

He gave a concerned glance as he passed me a San Miguel. 'Robbie found it tough as well and he was more experienced than you. He often came in here to vent his frustration and vowed never to come back. If it gets too much, I'm sure you'd find something else.'

I clasped his hand. 'Thanks, Tich. I appreciate your support. Sorry to bother you again, but did you ask about accommodation for the lads?'

'Yes, I did. There is a local guy, Pablo, who comes in here. He owns four blocks of holiday flats nearby. I saw him on Tuesday evening and asked him. There is one family room that might be available as he's just received a cancellation for early July. It'll be a tight squeeze for your eight mates, but there's nothing else. He'll get back to me by the weekend and I'll let you know.'

'That's fantastic, mate. Thank you. They only need somewhere to crash and have a wash, so I hope it works out.'

A group of girls arrived at the far end of the bar. Before he turned to serve them, Tich reached behind the counter and handed me a letter, grinning.

'Here you go, mate. Maybe that will cheer you up.'

It was from Sarah. As I sipped on my beer, I read her latest news.

Dear Fred,

Thank you for your letter of the 24th May which I received today. I am glad you are getting on well out there.

Over the last week, our weather here was great, and I got a good tan (in my lunch hour).

My weight-watching is going well, and I lost 12 lbs in a week. I'm on a diet of meat, fish, eggs and three pints of water a day, but no alcohol.

A diet like that always has side-effects, which I found out. I blacked out at work on Wednesday, but I am fine now.

It sounds as though you won't want to come home when your six months is up. But it's not all bad news here.

I'll pop in to see your parents and sister tonight as I am going to a football match in South Nutfield.

The Top 10 has some nice records in it now. 10cc's record is all right. I like the Eagles, and Rod Stewart, which is number 1. The ELO has got a great single out too.

What is your hair like, are you still washing it every few days? Mine is growing.

The photo I sent was not a good one. I'll send you another when I get a chance. When I went to Brighton with Christine, we took photos of each other, so I'll see what they are like.

My mum sends her love. I am missing you more than ever.

All my love,

Sarah

It was great to hear from Sarah again, but her blackout concerned me. I never thought of her as overweight and was worried she had lost so much. My feelings for her swept over me and at that moment, I wanted to be with her more than anything else.

27

Election day

After a good night's sleep, I arrived at Tootsies on Friday in a better frame of mind.

Determined to stay on top of the work, I wanted to prove I could cope. The perceived strains from the evening before had evaporated and I was more at ease.

Sylvia grinned as I walked into the bar. 'Morning, Fred. You look happier today.'

I gave her a hug. 'Thanks, Sylvia. Sorry, I worry too much and just need to be more positive. I don't hide my feelings well, do I? How are things with you?'

She returned the hug and looked me in the eyes. 'I'm finding it difficult too. Let's stick together and we'll get through this. After all, it's what we both dreamed of doing.'

Ray glanced over and smiled in our direction.

Something had puzzled me, so I turned and asked him for an explanation, 'I've noticed loads of posters on buildings, telegraph poles and lampposts. There are also vans driving around the streets with people shouting through megaphones. What's going on?'

He threw his head back and laughed. 'Oh, didn't you know? There is an election happening. It takes place next Wednesday, June 15th, and has been planned since Franco's death eighteen months ago. This is the first time the Spanish have had the chance to vote for a government since 1936, before the outbreak of the Civil War.'

'I hadn't realised. No wonder they're getting excited.'

Gordon overheard us and joined in, 'It's quiet here compared to the mainland, from what I've heard. There have been demonstrations in Barcelona and Madrid ahead of the elections, as none of the parties from the Second Republic can take part, except for the Communist Party.'

My eyes widened. 'What's the Second Republic?'

Gordon sipped on his coffee. 'It was in existence from 1931 to 1939 and ended when the military dictatorship was established under Franco. If you're interested, I've got a book at home you could borrow.'

'Yes, that would be great. I studied History at A-Level, but never learned about Spain.'

'I'll bring it in tomorrow. Anyway, enough history lessons for now, I can see punters arriving. Let's get going.'

* * *

I settled into a routine at Tootsies and made it through the weekend with no real problems. It was busy, but we worked better as a team. Gordon and Ray helped when I became stressed and made sure I didn't get behind with serving customers. My tips improved as I found time to chat and smile more.

They gave me the Monday off, after seven straight days of working as a bar waiter. I slept until early afternoon.

After a meal at Tony's, I walked to the Red Lion. Roger and Margaret were there. Tich had the evening off but left a message. Pablo had confirmed the family room was available and I should contact him to find out more. There were directions to where he lived.

After a quick drink, I strolled over to his apartment and knocked on the door. A frail old woman answered, and I asked to see Pablo. She shouted for him and within a minute he appeared. He was short and stocky, with a thick moustache, olive skin and a permanent frown on his face.

We shook hands, and I enquired about the place. He said I should follow him and led the way to the first floor of a nearby block of apartments.

He opened the door and explained in a gruff voice, 'Here is the main room with two double beds and a sofa. There are a pair of sunbeds on the balcony. The bathroom is through there at the back. How many of your friends did you say are staying?'

An involuntary twitch cracked the edges of my mouth. 'There will be eight of them. It looks a tight squeeze but is better than nothing.'

Pablo nodded. 'It is the height of the season. They are lucky this is available. As you are a friend of Tich, I'll offer an excellent rate of 2000 per night. You must pay a deposit of 4000 which you get back if they leave the apartment in good condition. Your friends must pay 28,000 when they arrive.'

I stood stunned for a moment. It was a lot of cash, but I had little choice. 'When do you need the deposit?'

He scowled. 'Today.'

I unzipped my money-belt, pulled out four 1000 peseta notes and handed them to him.

We shook hands. The deal was done.

On my way back to the room, I picked up a postcard and scribbled a message to the lads. In it, I explained what I had organised. The cost to each of them, including the deposit, was £35.

* * *

The sound of megaphones on the streets subsided on Tuesday.

Electioneering was not allowed on the day before the vote. There was an air of excitement and anticipation among the local people, although most tourists were unaware of the coming election.

Most of the shops closed for the election. The Hippy Market took place though, and Tootsies was packed. We struggled to cope with the streams of customers.

Crowds of locals turned out for the vote at the central polling station in Es Cana. According to opinion polls, the result in the Balearic Islands was a forgone conclusion for the UCD (*Unión de Centro Democrático* - Union of the Democratic Centre). This did not lessen the enthusiasm of voters, keen to fulfil their democratic rights after over forty years of dictatorship.

It was at the weekend, when I saw a copy of *The Guardian* newspaper from Thursday 16th, that I found out about the disturbances which had accompanied the election on the mainland.

The article headlined "Left ahead in cities in Spain's election" mentioned that in the first democratic vote since 1936, turnout had exceeded 80 per cent. This was despite the demonstrations and bombings that continued in many parts of Spain. Three people, including two policemen, had been hurt by a bomb explosion in Seville. Another two policemen were injured in Barcelona when a Molotov cocktail was thrown at their vehicle. There were also four explosions in Pamplona and two in Cordoba.

Full article: https://www.theguardian.com/world/2009/jun/16/democratic-spanish-elections-1977

28

Meeting Helen

Two weeks had passed since I started work at Tootsies.

During that time, I was too tired to go out most evenings. This Friday was different. I fancied a night out at Grannies.

I arrived at 9:30 pm. Liz was sitting at the bar, while her 18-30 crowd were engaged in drinking games.

The stool next to her was free, so I joined her. 'Hi, Liz, nice to see you. How are you?'

She turned and gave me a tired smile. 'Not too bad, Fred. This latest group is hard going though. Would you like a drink?'

Graham served us. 'They must be keeping you busy at Tootsies, Fred. We've not seen you for ages. What do you want?'

'Vodka and orange, please. It's been manic. I'm so tired after work, I go straight to bed most nights.'

He threw ice into a glass, poured an over-generous measure of vodka and topped it up with a small amount of orange juice. 'That should wake you up, mate. Enjoy.'

I winced as I sipped it. '¡Salud! Liz. Thanks. Good health.'

We clinked glasses, and she knocked back a third of her whisky and lemonade.

She grasped my hand and whispered in my ear, 'Fred, I've got to get back to my crew in a minute. Could I ask you a big favour?'

I gave her a wary nod. 'Depends what it is, Liz.'

Her grip tightened. 'Don't look now, but there's a girl sitting on her own at the end table on the terrace. Her name's Helen. She's part of the group that arrived three days ago. I'm having real problems getting her to join in with anything. She's shy and doesn't drink much. Could you keep her company for a while? Don't let on I asked you.'

My face brightened. 'That would be a pleasure, Liz.'

I left it for five minutes. After ordering another drink, I headed out to the terrace and wandered to the end table. There were two couples engaged in conversation. Helen was trapped in the corner.

I asked the foursome, 'Is that space free?'

They looked up at me. One couple stood to let me in, and I sat opposite Helen. She glanced at me for a moment, before turning away. A slender girl, she had short brown hair, green eyes and a pale complexion.

Every time I tried to catch her attention, she glanced down at the table, embarrassed.

My opening line was not a classic one. 'Are you here on holiday?'

She gave a slight nod but said nothing.

I tried again. 'Are you waiting for your boyfriend?'

This time she giggled. I had to strain to hear her whispered reply, 'No, he's in England. I'm on holiday with a girlfriend from home.'

'Is she around? I haven't pinched her seat, have I?'

She gave me a sweet smile. It transformed her face. 'No, that's OK. She's with the group over there. I fancied being on my own for a while.'

I sat back and sipped on my drink. 'Sorry, I didn't mean to disturb you. I've been working all day and just want some peace too.'

Her face brightened. 'No, that's fine. It's nice to have company. I can't stand the antics of the group I'm on holiday with. They're too boisterous for me. My friend, Sandra, seems to enjoy their company though.'

'You don't seem like an 18-30 type of girl. What possessed you to come on holiday with them?'

'Sandra persuaded me. She thought I needed a break from work and my boyfriend. I wasn't aware of the 18-30 Club's reputation before I came here.'

My glass was empty. 'Did you want another drink? Sorry, I didn't catch your name.'

'I'm Helen. I'd love a Coke, please?'

Graham was collecting glasses, so I called him across, 'If you've got a moment, mate, could I have one more of these and a Coke for my friend here.'

He gave me a knowing grin. 'No problem. I'll bring them over.'

* * *

As the night progressed, Helen became more talkative, and I enjoyed her company.

I broached the subject of the boyfriend and was surprised by her reply. 'I don't get on with him anymore. We've been together since school days, but he's become too obsessive. I jumped at the chance when Sandra asked me to come on holiday.'

'How old were you when you first met him?'

'We were both fifteen. My father's a minister, and his family attend the church. I had to go to every service and Simon was a welcome distraction. We got on well and had deep discussions about our religious beliefs.'

'So, how did the relationship develop?'

Helen tugged at her hair. 'Simon was my first boyfriend. I thought he was my destiny. Five years on, I'm not so sure. He has very strong Christian beliefs, while I'm disillusioned with religion. The latest thing is, he wants to get married and have children. I feel trapped by the whole situation. This time away might well be the breaking point.'

'But you're not enjoying the holiday either, are you?' She was close to tears, and I reached across to hold her hand. 'What I've learned, Helen, is you need to stand up for yourself and grab every opportunity you can. It shocked everyone at home when I came out here to work. Nobody understood why I wanted to throw away a promising career and risk everything. But it felt right, and I knew I had to do it.'

Helen pulled out a tissue and dried her eyes. 'You're right, Fred. It is Fred, isn't it? I heard the barman call you that.'

'Yes, sorry, I forgot to introduce myself. Fred's my nickname.'

'So, what's your real name then?'

'Robert. Fred was a name given to me by a teacher at school, and it's stuck ever since. My surname is Fear, and he used to call me Freddy Fear. In the last couple of years, mates have called me Fearless Fred. I sort of like that.'

Helen's smile returned. She glanced across at the 18-30 crowd. They were falling about all over the place. Liz was trying to herd them towards the disco. Sandra came across, and Helen introduced me to her friend.

Sandra gave me a drunken grin and slurred, 'Nice to meet you, Fred. Take care of Helen, won't you?'

She swayed towards the entrance.

* * *

126

We left not long afterwards and made our way to the seafront.

Restaurante Es Cana was closed, so we sat at a table and listened to the gentle waves lapping against the shore. I put my arm around Helen's shoulders, and she didn't resist. We felt comfortable in each other's company. Other sounds faded into the background as we cuddled.

She broke the silence. 'Do you have a girlfriend, Fred?'

'There is a girl in England I was going out with, and we keep in touch. I met her last autumn. We grew close and I miss her, but I'm not sure how it will work out.'

'Sorry, I know I'm being nosey, but have you met anyone else since you've been here?'

I frowned. 'I've had two one-night stands, but they were nothing serious. Have you ever been with anyone except Simon?'

'There was only one other boy. It was a brief fling. I lost my virginity to him last year. Simon was away on a religious retreat and I got drunk at a party. One thing led to another, and this lad took me back to his flat. We had a wild night, but I regretted it afterwards.'

'Did Simon ever find out?'

'No, although he had suspicions something had happened. He still thinks I'm a virgin though and doesn't believe in sex before marriage. The crazy thing is I enjoyed that night, but I still feel guilty about it.'

I didn't know what to say after hearing Helen's confession. We sat in silence for a while, before I remembered about work. 'Look, Helen, I need to get to bed. I've got to start work at 10 am, and that's only eight hours away. Maybe we could meet again tomorrow evening when I finish my shift at Tootsies. Can I walk you to your hotel?'

'Sorry, Fred. I've been so wrapped up in myself, I forgot about your work. Would you mind walking me back? I'm staying at the Hotel Caribe.'

Holding hands, we made our way across the wasteland. Outside the hotel, we had a passionate embrace. Helen agreed to come and meet me after work later that day. Back in my room, I fell asleep thinking about her.

29

Trouble at Tootsies

I woke with a start from a vivid dream, as my alarm clock kicked me into action.

Memories flooded back from the previous night. I had the tinge of a hangover, but my first thoughts were of Helen. She was a sweet girl, and I looked forward to seeing her again.

I had a quick wash and got dressed. On the way out, I grabbed a sandwich and a mug of tea at Tony's.

My mind was in turmoil as I walked towards Tootsies. Dread overcame me as I thought about being there until September. It was too much like hard work. The initial enjoyment of having the job had vanished.

There was a tense atmosphere when I arrived. Duncan, Ray and Gordon were in the middle of a heated discussion. Sylvia stared in astonishment from behind the bar.

I edged towards her and whispered, 'What's happening?'

She put a finger to her lips. 'Sit down. It's all going to blow up in a minute.'

Sylvia was right.

Duncan confronted Gordon and shouted, 'I've done my best, and you replace me with a Spaniard who isn't even a qualified chef. I want my money now, you wanker.'

Gordon pushed him back.

Ray towered over him. 'Keep it down, we'll pay you what you're owed. I'm sorry it hasn't worked out.'

Duncan scowled up at him. 'I want my cash now.'

You could have cut the silence with a scalpel.

Ray put an arm around Duncan's shoulder and steered him towards the rear of the bar.

* * *

The uneasy atmosphere continued through the busy afternoon.

Gordon and Ray introduced us to Mateo, the new chef. He had worked in a restaurant in Liverpool and spoke excellent English, with a scouse accent. The food he produced looked good, and he got on well with Manuel and Carlos.

I struggled to cope with the flood of customers, and Gordon had to step in to help again. Sylvia looked glum behind the bar. We exchanged anxious glances throughout the afternoon.

It was a relief when Helen arrived as I finished work for the day. Her smile cheered me up. We sat at a table and shared my meal of fish and chips.

Helen explained that the rest of the 18-30 group had gone for an evening barbecue on a beach in San Carlos. Sandra was with them, so the room they shared was free. She suggested we go back there to have some time to ourselves.

I used the bathroom and had a welcome shower. The bath at Tony's was a pain to use and took ages to fill. I enjoyed the steady stream of water as it washed away the day's stress.

Refreshed, I sat on the balcony with Helen. In a sleek white dress, she looked radiant. While I was in the shower, she had been downstairs to the bar and bought me a vodka and orange. This time she sipped a gin and tonic rather than Coke. We sat for a while in silence. The sky darkened and the first stars appeared.

Helen turned and smiled. 'So, tell me about yourself, Fred. Our conversations yesterday were more about me.'

A grin crossed my face. 'And very interesting they were too.'

I reached across to hold her hand. 'I was born in Leicester. My family were in a religious sect called the Exclusive Brethren. Have you ever heard of them?'

'No. Are they like the Plymouth Brethren? I've heard of them.'

'They come from the same origins, but Exclusives are much stricter. You can't mix with anyone outside the sect. They ban radios or televisions and forbid you to read newspapers. Assembly meetings on Sunday are compulsory. They made me read bible passages out loud at the services from as young as seven. At junior school, I couldn't attend morning assembly or religious classes of any kind.'

Helen gazed at me wide-eyed. 'That sounds awful.'

I squeezed her hand. 'Yes, it was. I don't talk about it much. When you're involved, it seems normal. You become indoctrinated, even brainwashed by their teachings and way of life. You are born into the sect and know nothing else. They forbid marriage to outsiders and expect you to marry young and have children. If you leave the sect, they allow no contact with any of your former friends or family.'

She leaned over and stroked my leg. 'You must have left the Exclusives. Otherwise, you wouldn't be here. Are the rest of your family still members?'

'No, our whole family left. My father took the brave step of leaving when I was nine years old. At the time it was traumatic, and I can remember my grandparents trying to persuade me to come and live with them. We saw none of our relatives again after they excommunicated us. Although it was disruptive, I always respected my father for getting us out when he did.'

Helen sipped her drink. 'I've concluded religion does more harm than good, don't you think?'

My arm slipped around her shoulder and we snuggled close together. 'I do these days. My parents have strong Christian beliefs, but I'm what they refer to as a backslider. From the age of fourteen or fifteen, I rebelled against what they had taught me to believe. This caused real friction with my father and we still don't see eye to eye. My mother is more understanding of the reasons for my rebellious ways.'

She gave me a kiss on the cheek and lay her head on my chest. 'Well, you seem to have come through it OK. It's great you've made the break and travelled here on your own. I wish I could do that.'

I stroked her forehead. 'Maybe you will one day.'

She raised her head, and we kissed.

We became lost in each other. Hands roamed as our lips and tongues explored. We moved to Helen's bed and continued our embraces. We touched each other with heightened passion and removed our clothes. The lovemaking was tender and prolonged.

Exhausted, we lay back on the bed and glowed with satisfaction.

Helen whispered in my ear, 'That was incredible. I didn't know it could be so enjoyable. My first time was much rougher, and I never came like I did with you.'

I stroked her hair and pulled her close. We once again explored each other's bodies. After a while, we drifted off into a light sleep, wrapped in one another's arms.

Sandra returned at 2 am in a drunken state. I made my excuses and left.

Helen had booked a trip for Sunday evening to see a show of *Ibithencan* dancing in a nearby village. We agreed to meet on Monday and spend my day off together.

* * *

On Sunday morning, I awoke in my bed and could still smell Helen's perfume on my skin.

Work was tougher than normal. There was a strained atmosphere after Duncan's departure. Sylvia looked unhappy while Ray and Gordon avoided our glances. Early in the afternoon, they both disappeared in Ray's jeep and we had to cope on our own. The outside tables filled with people and I struggled to keep up with the orders.

My concentration drifted several times as I thought about Helen. Manuel and Carlos did their best to help but only made matters worse. Orders got misplaced, and I had to placate annoyed customers as they waited for their food and drinks. I found it hard to believe Gordon was not around to step in and help.

An hour after they left, Ray and Gordon returned. They had someone else with them. He looked familiar, but I didn't have time to stop and think. Instead of coming to our aid, they walked into the back room and closed the door.

I became more frustrated and was close to tears. I struggled to handle the increased levels of customer complaints and pleaded with Sylvia to ask Gordon to come out and help.

She looked nervous and shook her head. 'Sorry, Fred. They said we shouldn't disturb them.'

Moments later, the three of them came out. Ray called over and asked me to join him in the back room. Gordon took my notepad and wallet before he and the other guy headed outside to take over the serving of customers.

It clicked. The mystery man was Robbie, the bar waiter who had left the previous year, vowing never to come back. He must have changed his mind.

I sat at the table opposite Ray. He seemed upset and couldn't look me in the eyes.

His voice croaked, 'Fred, I'm sorry, but we will have to let you go. Robbie has come back, and we've agreed to take him on again. I know you've tried your best, but we can't afford two bar waiters. We need someone we can rely on and you've struggled since you started, haven't you?'

I nodded in agreement. 'Yes, it's not turned out the way I thought it would.'

He gave me a nervous smile. 'We'll pay you for your time here. I don't have the cash now, but you can come back tomorrow afternoon to collect it. You've worked 12 days and we'll pay you a full day for today. Gordon and I agreed we'll stump up the tax and pay you as though it was cash in hand. Does that sound OK?'

'Sounds fair enough. I'm just sorry I didn't live up to your expectations.'

We shook hands. Ray took me to the bar and asked Sylvia to pour me a beer. Once he had gone outside, I brought her up to date on what had happened.

Her eyes glistened. 'I'm so sorry, Fred. You don't deserve this.'

I beamed a smile at her. 'Don't worry, Sylvia. It's a blessing in disguise. I'm sure you'll be OK, and Robbie is a much better bar waiter than I could ever be. You'll get on with him fine.'

She came from behind the bar and gave me a soothing hug.

30

Change of plan

My mood as I walked along the dusty road to Es Cana surprised me.

I felt elated in the warmth of the late afternoon sun.

Margaret was in the Red Lion with Roger. She smiled as I approached the bar. 'Great to see you again, Fred. What can I get you?'

'A cold San Miguel would go down a treat. Thanks.'

She reached to the back of the fridge to find the coldest beer. After uncapping it she passed it over. 'That should be nice and chilled. Enjoy. So, how's everything with you?'

I took a deep slug. 'Well, I should say I've got bad news, but in fact, I'm relieved. They sacked me from my job at Tootsies. I'd only been there for two weeks, but Robbie came back, and they've taken him on again.'

Margaret's eyes widened. 'I'm sorry to hear that. Ray and Gordon are ruthless with their employees. They fired Duncan too, didn't they? He was in here yesterday drowning his sorrows. You sound like you've taken the news better.'

I couldn't help smiling. 'It was hard work, and I wasn't enjoying it. I'm not sure how much longer I could have stayed. They've forced me to change my plans, but I hope to find something else soon. Any ideas?'

'Ask John at El Cortijo. He needs help handing out leaflets on the beach. It's not well paid but would make you some pocket money. I'll mention it to Roger to see if he knows of any other opportunities. Oh, I almost forgot, there's a letter here for you.'

She reached under the counter and handed it to me. It was from Sarah. I opened it straight away.

Dear Fred,

Thank you for your letter which I received this morning. I am glad you had a great time over in Majorca.

I am pleased you liked the photo. It was not that good, but it was the only one I had that was clear.

I hope you get on well in your new job. You still seem to be enjoying yourself.

We went to the Post Office Club on Tuesday the 7th. It was great. Everyone was plastered and very friendly. A pint was only 15p. There were loads of raffle prizes, but I didn't win anything.

On Monday, I streaked your sister's hair. She now looks like a blonde instead of the red streak down the back of her hair.

I will close now, take care.

Lots of love,

Sarah

It seemed to me that Sarah and I were growing further apart, but I was in no position to criticise.

Roger came over and passed me another San Miguel. 'Sorry about Tootsies, Fred. I'll keep my ears open and let you know if I hear of anything.'

I leaned over the bar and shook his hand. 'Cheers, mate. Much appreciated.'

He gave me a broad grin. 'No problem, I'm sure you'll find something else soon enough.'

Sunday evening became a blur. After two more bottles of beer in the Red Lion, I moved on to Tony's, and then Grannies where I shared my news. Although everyone sympathised, nobody was surprised. I drank more than I should have done and staggered back to my room in the early hours.

* * *

A severe hangover greeted me the next morning as I struggled out of bed.

Late for my meeting with Helen, I stumbled through the Hotel Caribe reception. She sat there with a slight frown on her face.

I slumped beside her. 'Sorry I'm late. How was your evening?'

She took my hand. 'It was interesting. What about you though? You look upset.'

I tried to concentrate but felt sick. 'I had a bad afternoon at Tootsies. They sacked me.'

Helen stared at me. 'That was sudden. What did you do wrong?'

I shrugged. 'Nothing I know of, although I had struggled with the job. Robbie, the bloke who worked there for the last two seasons came back. They hired him again and fired me. I have to go there later this afternoon to pick up my wages.'

She tightened her grip on my hand. 'Oh, Fred. I'm sorry to hear that. What do you want to do until then?'

'Not a lot, if you don't mind. I've got a serious hangover from last night. Would it be OK if we lay by the pool?'

She jumped to her feet. 'I'll just run upstairs and change into my swimming costume. Do you need to collect your stuff?'

'Yes, I wasn't thinking. I'll go back to my room and get changed. Shall we meet in half an hour?'

She gave me a kiss on the cheek. 'Sounds good, see you then.'

* * *

We spent the afternoon on sunbeds, shaded by a parasol.

A few beers and sandwiches helped the hangover. In Helen's company, my mood brightened. The conversation was light-hearted, and we often held hands, kissed, and looked deep into each other's eyes. Later, I left Helen and made my way to Tootsies. We planned to meet again at 7 pm and go out for a meal.

It was strange arriving as an ex-employee. The place was buzzing. Robbie had slotted back into his role with ease. I recognised how much better he coped with the job, as he laughed and joked with customers. Sylvia was also more relaxed behind the bar and waved across as I entered.

I flashed her a grin. 'Hi, how's it going?'

She glanced in Robbie's direction as he headed out of the door with a tray of drinks. 'All right. He's a friendly enough guy and I seem to get on OK with him. It's just a shame it didn't work out for you, as we got on so well together.'

'Oh, don't worry. I'm sure I'll find something else soon. To be honest, it's worked out for the best. Is Ray around? I need to collect my wages.'

'He's in the back with Gordon. They've been to the bank today, so should have everything ready for you.'

I gave her a thumbs-up, walked to the office and knocked on the door.

They gave me a shifty look as I entered. Gordon came across and slapped me across the shoulders, before going outside.

I sat at the wooden table opposite Ray as he inspected the piece of paper in front of him. He turned it round in my direction, so I could read it. 'This is what Gordon and I reckon we owe you. We've done our best to be fair. We will pay you for 13 days, no deductions. By our reckoning that works out to 10,400 pesetas at a rate of 800 per day.'

I took the calculations and studied them. They had paid me eight hours a day at 100 per hour, although I often worked longer. I knew it was futile to discuss this and make the situation worse.

'So, what do you think, Fred?'

My eyebrows shot up, but then I smiled. 'That's fair enough. Thanks for sorting it out so fast.'

He opened the tin cash box in front of him and counted out the money. I checked it, folded the wad and put it in my pocket. I'd transfer it to my money-belt later. All I wanted to do was get out of there.

As I turned to leave, Ray said, 'There is one other thing. Every Wednesday, on Hippy Market day, we have a table out front selling our t-shirts, sweatshirts and caps. We run the stall between us but wondered if it might interest you while you search for other work. You would earn a fixed commission on each sale. What do you think?'

I had not expected that. It was better than nothing I supposed. After a moment's thought, I nodded. 'Yes, I could do that. What percentage?'

'Discuss it with Gordon on Wednesday. I'm sure you'll do well. Everybody on the way to and from the market walks past the front of the pub. Arrive here for 9 am and you can help set up.'

We shook hands in agreement.

Ray guided me to the bar and poured me a beer.

I sat outside in the late afternoon sun and watched Robbie, the smooth operator, in action. He was fantastic at the job and looked like he had never been away.

31

Spending time with Helen

For the next week, Helen and I spent as much time as possible in each other's company.

Her hotel room became our escape, and we enjoyed many loving hours there. Our time together was precious as she had to leave the following Monday morning. Sandra appeared now and then but was often away on 18-30 activities, or with the lad she had hooked up with. She spent most nights in his bed.

* * *

On Wednesday, Helen came with me and helped set up the stall at Tootsies.

Gordon explained how it worked, 'T-shirts are priced at 250 pesetas, sweatshirts are 450 and caps 200. You'll get 5% commission on everything you sell. The t-shirts and sweatshirts come in small, medium and large, with a variety of colours. The caps are one size, with elastic headbands, and are blue or white. I'll leave you a small money float to start with. If you need any change during the day, just give me a shout.'

We nodded in agreement and took up our positions behind the table.

The number of tourists flooding the road to the Hippy Market took me by surprise. When I worked as a bar waiter, I was only aware of those who came into the pub. They were a fraction of the crowds I saw now. It was a popular event and renowned across the island. Coaches brought visitors from other resorts and we were in the perfect position to attract them.

Helen and I made a good team. We soon had flocks of people around the table. Helen came out of her shell. She was excellent at attracting the tourists and persuading them to buy. At first, I was more reserved and only handled the money side. After a while, I got into the flow and enjoyed the buzz of selling.

At lunchtime, Gordon gave us a short break, so we walked around the market, which was in a large wooded area with stalls along the dusty tracks in the gentle shade of the trees. We saw tables stretching off into the distance. Groups of hippies chilled out nearby. Families with children performed yoga. Long-haired, bearded, and bare-chested men played guitars and flutes. Women strummed on tambourines. The distinctive smell of hashish smoke swirled around the place. Without exception, the hippies seemed laid back and satisfied with their lifestyle.

The stalls sold a variety of tourist paraphernalia, all handmade: jewellery, bangles, necklaces, purses, rag dolls, paintings, embroidered dream catchers, dresses, shirts, and much more, displayed on small wooden tables or hung from lines of rope tied between the branches of trees.

I kept an eye out for Alex and Sharon from the Barcelona ferry but could not see them anywhere.

After a quick snack, we returned to Tootsies and took over from Gordon. It got even busier as tourists came back from the market. Our best success was with families who wanted matching gear. The afternoon flew by and the crowds did not quieten until after 6 pm when with Gordon's help, we packed away the unsold items. He counted them, took the money and disappeared to the office where he calculated our sales for the day.

Helen and I retired to the garden.

Robbie served us. 'Hi, it's Fred, isn't it? What can I get you?'

I gave him a nervous smile. 'Could I have a beer and a Spanish omelette?'

Turning to Helen, he asked her what she wanted.

She looked at him with apprehension. 'I'll have the same as Fred.'

He showed no sign of embarrassment at what had happened and wrote out the order. He returned with the beers and placed them in front of us without a word.

We relaxed in the late afternoon sun and sipped our drinks.

Gordon came out ten minutes later and smiled. 'Well done both of you. It's been a successful day. In fact, it's the best we've had all season.'

We both grinned at him as he continued, 'You sold 87 t-shirts, 34 sweatshirts and 55 caps. The cash agreed to the peseta, so I am impressed. Your share is 2400.'

With that, he counted out the money and handed it over, before going back into the bar.

I gave half to Helen. She protested, 'No, that's fine. I only came along for the laugh.'

'You've earned it, so please take it.'

With a reluctant shrug, she put it in her purse.

Carlos brought out the meals. Famished after a hard day's work, we wiped the plates clean within minutes. Helen paid the bill. We walked back to her room at the Caribe for a shower and an evening of passion.

* * *

On other days, we went for long walks or bike rides. Afterwards, we relaxed by the pool soaking up the sun. In the evenings, we discovered local restaurants and enjoyed the Spanish cuisine. We also visited Grannies and sat out on the terrace, happy in each other's company. Helen became more self-confident. She felt comfortable enough to drink more and her inhibitions lessened.

Cortijo's was our spot to end the night. Helen proved to be a great dancer. We bopped around to Status Quo, Abba, Baccara, 10cc, Showaddywaddy, Wings, Queen and many others. Then came the slower numbers, and we lost ourselves in each other for song after song.

Our special favourite was *Don't Go Breaking My Heart* by Elton John & Kiki Dee.

As each day passed, we got closer and closer to one another. We dreaded the Monday morning when Helen would have to go home.

* * *

On Saturday night, there was an 18-30 fancy dress event at the Caribe called Guys 'n' Dolls. It involved the lads dressing up as women and the lasses as men. Liz persuaded us to take part.

Helen dressed up as Laurel, and Sandra as Hardy, while they suggested I go as Marilyn Monroe. They borrowed clothes from Liz, who had a large stock of fancy dress for such occasions. Both were ready within half an hour. They then turned their attention to getting me prepared.

I had a shower and came out with a towel wrapped around my waist. The girls then set about styling my hair. It was long, blond, and wavy anyway, but they used a hairdryer and tongs to create a Marilyn-like style. I had a fringe swept over to the right on top and ringlets at the side and back.

Helen removed my towel while Sandra disappeared to buy us drinks from the bar. She helped me dress in satin knickers, suspenders and stockings of hers. That was a turn-on and Helen's eyes widened as she saw me get aroused. She could not resist and pushed me on to the bed, pulled the panties to one side, and went down on me. After that diversion, she dressed me again. Then she strapped a bra padded out with cotton wool around my chest.

Sandra returned with the drinks. Helen produced the white dress she had worn on our first night of passion together. With her help, I climbed into it, pulled the straps up over my shoulders and smoothed it over my hips. It was a perfect fit.

We sipped on our drinks: vodka and orange for me, gin and tonic for Helen, and rum and Coke for Sandra. Then they started on the next stage, the make-up.

Sandra applied the foundation first. Helen added light blue eyeshadow, pencilled my eyebrows, and brushed black mascara along my eyelashes. Then came the bright red lipstick. As a finishing touch, she added a beauty spot at the bottom of my left cheek.

The girls stood back and smiled with satisfaction at their handiwork. I glanced across at the mirror and could not believe the transformation.

There was one thing missing, shoes. I tried some of Helen's, but they were too tight. A pair of Sandra's fitted better. They had three-inch stiletto heels. I toppled on them when I first stood up. Although I had worn four-inch platform shoes in the sixth form at school, the heels had been much wider and easier to wear.

After a few minutes of practice, I got used to them. The girls gave me instructions on how to hold myself and swing my hips as I walked. Although I hated to admit it, I was enjoying myself. The final touch was a small silver clutch bag in which I put cash, cigarettes and a lighter. We were ready to go.

We must have made a sight walking into the large room where the party took place. Laurel on one side, Hardy on the other, and an unrecognisable Fred in the middle bearing a striking resemblance to Marilyn Monroe. There were a few stares as we entered.

Waiters circled with trays of drinks. I drank three glasses of champagne in quick succession and became giddy. There were sausage rolls and vol-au-vents to soak up the alcohol.

Liz came over. She complimented the girls on their outfits and stared at me in disbelief. 'Fred, is that you? You look amazing. You'll have the lads chatting you up before you know it.'

The evening passed in a haze of drink. Other great characters included lads dressed as Abba dancing queens, Suzi Quatro and flower power hippy girls. The lasses' outfits varied from Charlie Chaplin, Elvis Presley and Tom Jones to hairy-chested disco dancers and pimps. Everyone had a hilarious time and booze flowed.

Towards the end of the night, the music changed to slower romantic tunes. There were odd couples engaged in close moves on the dance floor. Sandra, dressed as Hardy, was with her lad who was dressed in a blouse and a mini skirt that showed off his hairy legs. Suzi Quatro clung to Tom Jones, and a dancing queen snogged Charlie Chaplin.

The sight of Helen and me as Laurel and Marilyn must have been even stranger, as we held each other tight and kissed. At 3 am, we staggered back to Helen's room and collapsed on her bed where we fell asleep. As light seeped through the curtains, we undressed and cuddled under the sheets.

32

Sad farewell

I turned over in my sleep and fell on to the tiled floor with a bang.

The bed was narrow. Helen shifted over to the far side as I clambered back in beside her. In our half-awake and still drunken state, we made frenzied love as the realisation dawned on us that this was our last day together.

We awoke again after midday, both with terrible hangovers. I glanced in the mirror and realised I had make-up smudged across my face. Helen fetched aspirin from her handbag and then set about wiping me clean.

In the shower, we soothed our aching bodies and held each other close under the stream of hot water. Neither of us wanted to let go but soon relented when the water ran cold.

As we dried ourselves off, the door opened, and Sandra appeared.

She looked in a worse state than we were and gave a weak smile. 'Hi guys, sorry but I've got to crash. We ended up in a room on the third floor last night. The eight of us kept drinking and playing party games. It turned into an orgy and I haven't slept yet.'

Helen and I got dressed and left Sandra to recover.

* * *

On the seafront, the sun blazed out of the clear blue sky. We found shade under a parasol at Restaurante Es Cana and sat at the same table we had occupied on our first night together when the place was closed.

After a bottle of San Miguel each, we felt more human. The afternoon drifted by as we nibbled on *tapas* and drank more beer. Talking was difficult as neither of us wanted to face up to Helen's imminent departure. We watched the world go by and soaked up the warmth of the sunshine.

At 4 pm, we returned to the hotel for a late siesta. Sandra was still flat out, so we drew the curtains, lay on the bed and snoozed.

In the evening there was a farewell party in Grannies, but we weren't in the mood for more partying. Instead, we took a gentle stroll to a nearby garden bar and had a jug of sangria between us as the daylight faded. We cuddled together on the hard, wooden bench and clinked glasses.

Helen's green eyes sparkled as she held me close. 'I'm not sure where this week has gone. I've had a fantastic time and don't want to leave.'

Squeezing her hand, I gave her a gentle kiss. 'I feel the same. I'm so glad I came over to talk to you when I did. You've been fantastic company and I've grown very fond of you. I wish you didn't have to go home. What will you do when you get back?'

She squinted as the last rays of sunlight shone over my shoulder. 'I've thought a lot about that. You've given me so much confidence. I'd forgotten what it's like to believe in myself. I want to come back here later in the season. First, I need to get the money together, so I'll try to find extra work.'

'If you came back, you could always stay in my room. It isn't much but better than nothing.'

'Oh, I'm sure that won't be necessary, and I couldn't impose on you. With luck, Liz can find me a place.'

I changed the subject, 'What do you think will happen with you and Simon?'

She put her head in her hands for a moment and then peeked through her fingers. 'This will finish us. He'll know something has happened, even if Sandra says nothing. Besides, you've taught me what it's like to love someone. Simon and I never had that. It won't be easy breaking up with him but for my sanity and self-confidence, I've got to go through with it.'

'There's no point staying in a relationship when you're not happy. How will he react?'

Helen buried her head in my shoulder. I stroked her hair as tears flowed. After a few minutes, she pulled herself together and sat up straight. 'I don't think he'll take it very well. He's set on getting married and having children. I must be strong and stay as far away from him as possible. It won't be easy as our parents are close. I hope my mum and dad will understand.'

There was nothing else to say. We held each other tight and embraced, oblivious to the tourists sat at the nearby tables.

* * *

Later in the night, after a few dances at Cortijo's, we made our way back to the Caribe.

The coach for the airport was leaving at 6 am.

We climbed the circular staircase, intending to spend our last hours in Helen's bed. There was a sudden shout from behind us and a clatter of feet on the stairs. '*Señor, señor*, stop there.'

I turned to see the figure of a tall Spanish guy pointing at me. '*Señor*, you cannot go to this lady's room. You do not stay at this hotel. Please leave.'

Thoughts raced through my head. There was no arguing with him. Why did it have to happen now though?

I nodded and headed back down the stairs. Helen grabbed my hand and joined me. We made our way through the car park and found a low narrow wall to sit on.

There was a chill in the air and the moon was high in the sky. We smooched, hands caressing through our clothes. Eventually I jumped up and pulled Helen to her feet. 'Come on, let's go to my room. It's a real mess, but at least we'll be alone.'

We hurried across the wasteland, down the stairs and along the corridor. By the time we landed on my bed, we had strewn our clothes across the concrete floor. Our passion exploded as we made love for the last time.

Exhausted, we lay content in each other's arms, but dreading the hours to come.

Helen still had to pack her cases, so at 4:30 am we got dressed. I planned to go with her to the airport, so we could spend every minute together.

The single light in my room went out. It plunged us into darkness. I figured the bulb had gone, but when I peeked out into the corridor, the lights were out. There had been a power cut.

We edged our way along the corridor and up the stairs. Stars sparkled in the sky and the moon glowed, but there was no light coming from any of the buildings.

At the hotel, there was the twinkle of candles and Helen made her way to her room to get packed. I waited outside and smoked cigarette after cigarette. Daylight edged over the horizon.

* * *

The coach journey was raucous.

There had been chaos as Liz rounded up her Club 18-30 crowd and got the cases loaded. Most of them were still drunk from the party and belted out loud songs on the way to the airport.

Helen and I held each other tight in the back seat, trying to ignore what was going on around us.

Our farewell at the airport was difficult, and we both ached with sadness. Helen was the last of the group to go through customs. As she turned to wave goodbye, I saw tears streaming down her face. I blew her a final kiss and headed out of the terminal.

Liz had organised the new crowd that had arrived on the plane Helen caught home. She came over before we got on the coach and gave me a hug.

'Thanks for looking after Helen, Fred. You made a real difference to her holiday, and it looked as though you enjoyed her company.'

'She's a lovely girl. I'll miss her.'

The return trip to Es Cana was not as rowdy, but even at that time in the morning, Liz got them in the mood. Before we reached Santa Eulalia, everyone was singing along to the Club 18-30 anthems.

It was 8:30 am when we arrived at the Caribe and by then they had restored the power.

Tired out, I headed to my room.

As I drifted off, my thoughts turned to the girls I'd spent time with over the past few months. I realised my attitudes were changing. Sarah had been the love of my life over the winter, but now I thought of her less and less. The phrase "out of sight, out of mind" popped into my head. I'd enjoyed my times with Micky, Cathy, Kim, and now Helen. But what would happen when I met someone else? I argued with myself that I didn't want to commit to one girlfriend anymore. I was still young and there'd be time for commitment as I grew older. For the moment, I just wanted to enjoy myself and have fun.

These thoughts morphed into dreams as I slipped into a deep sleep.

33

Meeting Alice

It was late afternoon by the time I woke, after a day full of vivid dreams.

The sun streamed through the windows and sweat covered my body. Helen's aroma still pervaded the sheets and a wave of sadness swept over me.

The bathroom was free, so I ran a bath. As I soaked in the tepid water, my eyes drooped, and I dozed. A loud knock brought me to my senses.

'*Hola,* will you be long?' A male voice on the other side pleaded, 'I need to work soon.'

As I sprang up and wrapped the towel around my waist, I shouted, 'Just finished. I'm emptying the bath now.'

I pulled the plug and opened the door. It was Roberto, who worked upstairs at Tony's. 'Sorry, mate. I forgot the time. I didn't realise you stayed here.'

A smile brightened his face. 'That's OK, *amigo. Si*, Pedro and I both have rooms here.'

I gave the bath a quick clean as he entered the room. 'Sorry again, Roberto, I'll catch you later.'

His reply followed me along the corridor, '*Hasta luego*, see you later.'

* * *

Tich greeted me with a huge smile as I walked into the Red Lion. 'Fred, how's it going? Haven't seen you for ages.'

I shook his hand with enthusiasm. 'Good, thanks. Yes, it's been a while. Did you hear what happened at Tootsies?'

'Roger and Margaret told me. It didn't surprise me, as I knew Robbie was back. What surprised me was that you ran the t-shirt stall for them last Wednesday. I thought you would have learned your lesson.'

My face dropped. 'I get you, but we made good money. Helen helped me and we earned 2400 between us.'

Tich opened two San Miguels, and we clinked bottles as he leaned across the bar towards me. 'Are you meant to be working this Wednesday?'

'Oh shit, I'd forgotten. I've been so wrapped up with Helen for the past few days, it slipped my mind.'

'Just be careful. The sooner you get out of their clutches the better.'

'Cheers, mate. I appreciate you've got my best interests at heart. I have to find something else though. Any ideas?'

Tich scratched his head. 'There's always handing out leaflets for John at Cortijo's, but that's only pocket money. The only other place might be Grannies. I overheard Mick and Pat moaning the other evening about their new Spanish barman. Why don't you ask them?'

'Great idea, thanks. Is there any post?'

'Only one letter. I'll get it for you. Your mates are arriving this Sunday, aren't they? Pablo said you'd paid a deposit on the room for them.'

I nodded in agreement as he passed the letter. It was postmarked Bletchingley and looked like a reply to my postcard. I ripped it open and read it.

To Fred,

Well, it's nice to hear from you again mate. Thanks for the postcard. If you could book the apartment, we would be most grateful. We will square up when we arrive, and you have my promise on that. After arguing over the price, we agreed in the end.

I don't know if they told you that Nicky from Redhill was coming. Well, she has changed her mind. Sam does not need a place as he wants to doss on the beach. So, what we want is a room for six and as cheap as possible because money will be bloody tight for some of us.

Siv will be there until the football season starts. Mutts and Sam are staying on and then going up to Germany. Me, Ian, Giles and Kooky are leaving after a fortnight.

Anyway, I hope you are well and taking care of yourself. Looking forward to seeing you soon.

All the best,

Steve Alias TUZZA

P.S. We finished 4th in the Darts League and won the Sportsmanship Shield again.

Tich gave me a worried glance as I stopped reading. 'Anything wrong?'

I uttered a nervous laugh. 'No, it's fine. There's just been a change of plan. One person has dropped out and Sam plans to doss on the beach, so there will only be six of them staying at the apartment. I hope it doesn't cause complications with money.'

Tich gave a look of disapproval. 'Not sure that's such a good idea of Sam's sleeping on the beach. The police clamp down during the tourist season. I'll have a word with him when they arrive.'

'Great. I wouldn't want him to get arrested.'

After one more beer, I said goodbye and took a slow wander around the seafront. The sun was setting behind me, so I sat on the beach and soaked up the atmosphere until it got dark.

* * *

Graham was behind the bar in Grannies.

'How's it going Fred? I see you're on your own tonight. Has your latest conquest gone home?'

'Yes, Helen left this morning. I'm missing her, but I'll get over it. Could I have a vodka and orange?'

'Don't worry, you'll soon find someone else.'

As Graham placed the drink in front of me, he pointed towards his fellow barman who was staring into space at the far end of the bar. 'Have you met Eduardo yet? He's our new Spanish employee.'

I shook my head. 'No. I haven't had the pleasure.'

Graham shouted his name. He scuttled towards us. 'Eduardo, this is Fred, a friend of ours and a regular customer.'

He reached across and gave me a limp handshake. '*Buenas tardes, Federico*, good evening, pleased to greet you.'

It amused me how he had given me a Spanish name. He was my height with short black hair, a tanned face and deep brown eyes. 'Great to meet you, Eduardo. Are you enjoying the work?'

He glanced over his shoulder at Graham, who had gone to serve another customer. 'Eez OK but Gra-ham is a funny man. We do not see, how you say, eye by eye?'

I snickered. 'You mean eye to eye; you don't get on with him?'

He gave me a trusting look. '*Si*, eez very difficult. He does not like me I think.'

148

I sipped on my drink. 'These things take time, I'm sure you'll be fine.'

An awkward smile crossed his face. 'I hope so, *Federico*. *Hasta luego*, see you later.'

With that, he shuffled back to the other end of the bar and resumed his stare into space.

I sat at the only empty table on the terrace and people watched.

A small group of English tourists joined me, two girls and three lads. I stood to let them in and perched myself at the end of the bench where the girls sat. The guys opposite them were deep in conversation and took no notice of me.

I overheard them mention the 18-30s and assumed they were from the group who arrived that morning. After a while, my curiosity got the better of me and I asked, 'Sorry, I couldn't help overhearing you talk about the 18-30s. Are you on holiday with them?'

Annoyed at the interruption, the lads frowned at me.

The closest girl brushed her shoulder-length blonde hair aside and gave me a slight grin. 'Yes, we arrived last weekend. We go back next Sunday morning.'

'Oh, I didn't recognise you and thought you'd arrived with the main group today.'

A sign of recognition came over the girls' faces, although the lads feigned disinterest. A smile lit up the blonde girl's face. 'You dressed up as Marilyn Monroe at the party on Saturday, didn't you?'

I felt myself blush. 'Yes, that was me. My name's Fred. I don't remember seeing you there, but I was drunk. What are your names?'

Her blue eyes widened as she introduced her friends, 'I'm Alice. This is Jane. We know each other from home in Berkshire. The boys are Alfie, Reg and Dennis.'

I gave Alice and Jane a peck on the cheek, before shaking hands with the lads. 'Pleased to meet you. So, how are you finding the 18-30 experience?'

Alfie repositioned his spectacles. 'The five of us have stayed away from most of the partying. None of us drinks much and we don't enjoy the wild ways of the main group. That's why we hang around together. Liz, the courier, has given up on us, although we get on with her well enough.'

'Yes, I've seen a lot of the wild behaviour. Most of them lose control after a few drinks. Liz encourages it.' I looked at my glass, which was empty. 'Can I get refills for any of you?'

They glanced at each other before shaking their heads.

Alice gave me a sweet smile. 'No. don't worry, Fred. We're heading off for a walk along the beach, before going back to the hotel for a good night's rest. We're hiring bikes for the day tomorrow and want to make an early start.'

'OK, nice to meet you all. Hope to see you again soon.'

Alice winked at me. 'Oh, I'm sure we will. I look forward to that. Enjoy your evening.'

My heart was beating fast as I walked to the bar for another drink.

34

More trouble at Tootsies

It was two days later, on Wednesday, when I met Alice again.

Tuesday had been a quiet day. I spent a relaxing time at the Panorama pool sunbathing, swimming and reading. After an evening meal at Tony's, I walked to Grannies, hoping to catch up with Alice and her friends. There was no sign of them. After several beers, I retired at 10 pm as I had an early start at Tootsies.

Running the stall alone was a sharp contrast to the previous week. I soon realised Helen had been the main attraction for customers. I struggled during the morning as potential punters drifted past and I could not grab their attention. My enthusiasm waned, and I only sold a handful of items.

I sensed Gordon's disappointment as he relieved me for a short lunch break.

After a quick snack and a drink, I returned, determined to improve my performance as tourists meandered back from the Hippy Market. Trade picked up for a while. I found once there was a small crowd around me, others came over to join them. It then became difficult to keep track as people fired questions and tried on the merchandise.

My mood improved as I sold more of the stock, but it was hard work. At one point I ran out of change. I looked around for Gordon but could not see him anywhere. Instead, I had to dip into my money-belt. Later in the afternoon, when other customers had replenished my supply, I stuffed the equivalent amount back.

It was 4:30 pm when I spotted Alice and Jane. They both looked fantastic in revealing tops and hot pants. I waved at them as they walked past on the opposite side of the road.

They didn't see me, so I shouted across, 'Alice, Jane!'

They turned with surprised looks before they recognised me and came over.

Alice gave me a broad grin. 'Fred, what on earth are you doing here?'

'Long story. Can I tell you later?'

She drew closer and held my arm. 'Yes, I'd like that. Jane has got a date with Paco, a waiter from the Caribe, and the three lads are going to Ibiza Town for the night. So, I'll be on my own. Where do you want to meet?'

I beamed back. 'Shall I pick you up from the hotel reception, say 8:30 pm?'

Alice gave me a gentle peck on the lips. 'I'll see you then.'

The girls turned and walked away. Alice glanced over her shoulder and blew a kiss. She had a skip in her step, and I heard the excitement in her voice as she chatted to Jane.

I was in a daze.

The rest of the afternoon dragged. I lost concentration. Selling t-shirts was the last thing on my mind. Six pm arrived and the flow of tourists became a trickle. Gordon came out and helped me pack away the stock, counting it as he did. He took the float and takings to the office and told me to meet him in the garden. I ordered a beer and had a chat with Sylvia at the bar. Five minutes later Gordon stormed out and beckoned me to follow him.

As we sat at a table, he muttered, 'I'll keep this brief, Fred. After the success last week with your young lady, this week has been a disaster. You only sold 22 t-shirts, 8 sweatshirts and 15 caps. I could have done better myself.'

I fidgeted in my seat as his face reddened. 'And the takings didn't agree. You were 450 pesetas short. I saw you put cash in your money-belt this afternoon. Did you think I wouldn't notice?'

I became flustered and defended myself, 'But that was to replace change I had taken out earlier. Are you calling me a thief?'

Gordon fumed, 'How else do you explain the shortfall?'

'I don't know. Maybe someone stole a sweatshirt while I wasn't looking.'

'Well, it's not good enough and you must cover the loss yourself. You earned 605 pesetas, so I'll deduct it from that.'

He slammed a 100 peseta note and 55 in change on the table.

As he stood up, Gordon glowered at me. 'Don't worry about coming back next week. I'll find someone else.'

I stared at his back in disbelief as he stormed off.

With a gulp, I downed the remains of my beer and got away as fast as I could. Tears welled up. As I hit the dusty track sobbing wracked my body. I could not believe what had just happened.

By the time I arrived at the Red Lion the tears had dried, but Tich noticed how upset I was.

He took me to one side, and I told him everything.

He gave me a sympathetic grin. 'Didn't I warn you, Fred? You're better off out of there. Don't worry, you'll find something else soon enough.'

I tried to smile, but it was more like a grimace.

Tich guided me to a table in the corner. 'Sit here for a while. I'll get you a brandy to settle your nerves.'

He came back with a San Miguel, a large measure of brandy, and a letter. 'There you go, mate. They should cheer you up. Give me a shout if you need anything else.'

I stood, grasped his shoulder, and shook his hand. 'Cheers, mate, I don't know what I'd do without you.'

He returned the handshake and sat me down again. 'You're welcome. We've got to stick together. It can be tough sometimes.'

Half the bottle of beer disappeared in seconds. The bite of the brandy hit the back of my throat. I calmed down as I opened the letter, which was from home. There was a note from my brother Alastair and another from Mother.

Dear Rob,

I cycled home from university two weeks ago and started work last week. The cycling took four days from Stirling. I joined up with a friend at Huddersfield to cycle to Newark.

We've just seen England draw with Argentina 1-1. On Wednesday evening, England drew with Brazil 0-0. They are on a summer tour of South America.

I hope you are feeling well and enjoying your job.

It has rained over here for the last two days.

It is 9:25 pm.

Love From,

Ali

My dear Rob,

A hasty note to put in with Alastair's.

Thanks for your letter and all the news. You will be back from Majorca and into your new job by now.

People are always asking after you at the Free Church. Yesterday Janet and Ted were there with their children and wanted all the up-to-date news. Ted was most interested that you had gone alone.

Elections are upon you I hear, and 129 parties to choose from. The mind boggles.

The Jubilee was fantastic when it arrived. Two of my friends were in London on Jubilee Day. They saw the Queen. Everyone's kindness and friendliness in the crowds impressed them.

The weather has been wet and unlike June. Last night we had great thunderstorms and dazzling lightning, but today has gone muggy, after a November-like fog early morning.

Chris and Sarah have seen a lot of each other over the past few weeks.

Father is recording today. It is my full day at the surgery. We have two folks on holiday: Sheila in Spain and Mrs Peters in France.

Postage has gone up so I must check the rate for Europe.

We all send our love.

Much Love,

Mother

I read them over a couple of times as I sipped on the brandy, which was strong but soothing.

What struck me most was how things had changed since I wrote to Mother at the start of the month. I had not envisaged the end of June would find me unemployed again. I had enough cash left to cover rent and bills but would soon need to change more of my remaining £240 in travellers' cheques. Without work, I could not see me surviving beyond the middle of August.

On a more positive note, I had a date lined up with the beautiful Alice. I needed to go back to the room and get changed.

With a cheery wave to Tich, I headed out of the door.

35

Getting to know Alice

Alice looked radiant, with her glowing face framed by wavy blonde hair.

Her blue eyes sparkled as I approached, and she rushed over to give me a hug. I held her close and felt the warmth of her breasts through a thin blouse.

She wore a tight mini skirt that emphasised her curvy hips and slender legs. Even with platform shoes, she was shorter than me.

I looked her up and down. 'You look fabulous, Alice. I feel like a tramp dressed in jeans and a t-shirt.'

She gave me a sweet smile and held my hands. 'You're fine. Have you been drinking though? You reek of alcohol and your eyes are bloodshot.'

'Yes, sorry. The afternoon went downhill after you left. I'll tell you about it in a while. Have you eaten?'

She shook her head. 'No. I was waiting to see what you wanted to do. Did you have somewhere in mind?'

I guided her out of the hotel reception. 'Let's go to the Restaurante Es Cana. They do great local food there and we can get a table overlooking the sea. I'll tell you then what happened this afternoon. What do you think?'

She held my hand tight and pulled herself into my side. 'Sounds great. I've not been there. Most of the meals I've eaten have been in the hotel.'

I placed my arm across her shoulders. Alice cuddled up and wrapped her arms around my waist. We walked over the wasteland towards the seafront, then followed the road around the bay. A cool breeze blew off the sea, which was refreshing after the heat of the day. The sun sank behind the hills in the west and the almost full moon peeped over the horizon in front of us.

The waiter recognised me and showed us to a secluded table on the veranda. We ordered drinks. I had a San Miguel and Alice a Coke.

We were hungry, so I asked the waiter what he would recommend. His suggestion was the speciality of the day, *Paella de Marisco* (seafood paella), with ingredients that 'come fresh from the bounty of the sea surrounding the island'.

Alice and I smiled at each other. We nodded in agreement. It sounded delicious.

While we waited for the food, I told Alice what had happened at Tootsies over the previous couple of weeks. She looked horrified as I ended my story with the happenings from the afternoon.

She reached for my hand across the table. 'Now I understand why you needed a drink. That's a terrible way to treat someone. You're better off out of there.'

The paella arrived soon after. The portions were generous and there was an amazing selection of seafood mixed in with the rice. After admiring it for a minute, we dived in. Silence reigned as we savoured the delicious flavours. Both of us finished our plates.

Alice sat back and rubbed her stomach. 'That's the best seafood dish I've ever tasted. Everything was so fresh. Thanks for bringing me here. It's lovely. I wouldn't have known about it otherwise.'

We resumed our handholding across the table. I grinned at her. 'It was the first place I came to when I arrived in April. The food is always good, and the atmosphere is just right. I love being able to sit outside in these beautiful surroundings. It's such a contrast to England.'

Alice gave me a quizzical look. 'What made you decide to move out here?'

I told her about coming on holiday the previous year with three mates. 'The others are coming back on Sunday with four others. Mutts and Sam will try to find work. Siv wants to stay on until the start of the football season.'

I pulled out my pack of Ducados and offered Alice a cigarette.

She looked at it with disdain and shook her head. 'No, thanks. I've never smoked. It's a disgusting habit. How long have you been hooked?'

'Since I was fourteen. I'll try not to smoke when I'm with you, I promise.'

I put the unlit cigarette back into the pack.

Alice glanced away. 'Oh, don't worry, have one. Both my parents indulge, so I'm used to it. I know it's meant to be enjoyable after a meal. It's just not for me.'

I retrieved the cigarette and lit it, blowing the smoke to one side.

My bottle of beer was empty. 'Did you want another drink, Alice?'

'Something different would be nice. Could I have an orange, please?'

The waiter came to clear our plates. I asked him for a San Miguel and a fresh orange juice.

I gazed into Alice's eyes. 'Do you ever drink alcohol?'

She giggled. 'Sometimes, on special occasions. I enjoy a glass of champagne if it's available and Babycham is OK. I don't like the sensation apart from that. Do you drink every day?'

I swallowed hard. 'Yes, I suppose I do.'

A gentle sigh escaped her lips. 'It sounds like you need looking after. Someone needs to take you in hand and mother you.'

My eyebrows shot up. 'Do you think so? Maybe I'm too used to my little habits. I started drinking when I was fifteen.'

Alice chuckled. 'I'm surprised they served you in pubs. Even now you've got a young-looking face. You can't be older than nineteen.'

It was my turn to laugh. 'I turned twenty-one in October last year. How old are you?'

'Have a guess? Most people think I'm older than I am.'

'I don't know. Twenty?'

Her face lit up. 'I'm only eighteen. My birthday was in April. Thanks for the compliment though.'

'You're mature for eighteen. You remind me of my first real girlfriend. Wendy was fourteen when I met her, and I was seventeen. We were together for nine months and she devastated me by going off with someone else.'

I glanced at her for a reaction, but she remained straight-faced.

'Have you had any serious relationships?' I asked.

Alice paused for a moment and sipped on her drink before she answered. 'I've led a sheltered life and only been out with two boys. Neither lasted more than a few weeks. They were after more than I'd give them. Both wanted to sleep with me, but I'm determined to keep my virginity for the right person. I expect you've been with a few girls, haven't you?'

I blushed at her directness and stuttered, 'There have been several. Wendy was the first. Although three years younger, she was more experienced than me, and I learned lots during our time together.'

She gave a slow nod of understanding. 'I'm sure you'll find the right person one day. It's possible you already have and just don't know it yet.'

Her eyes sparkled, and she gave me a seductive wink.

With our drinks finished, I paid the bill and suggested we take a walk along the beach.

* * *

We had an enjoyable stroll which involved much kissing and cuddling.

Alice proposed we go to El Cortijo and dance the night away. It was past midnight by the time we arrived.

John was on the door and shook hands. I introduced him to Alice, and he welcomed her with a peck on the cheek. He waived her entrance fee of 100 pesetas. Locals got in for free anyway.

As Alice walked to the toilet, John pulled me to one side. 'Tich told me about the way Tootsies messed you around. If you need work, you could always help me by handing out leaflets on the beach. I'd give you some pocket money and free drinks in return. Why don't you come here at 10 am and we can get you started? Maybe your young lady could come along too.'

I smiled and shook his hand. 'That would be great, John. Thanks a lot. I'll make sure I'm here for ten.'

Alice returned, and we headed through the crowds to an alcove on the far side of the dance floor. I spotted Alan in his distinctive kilt and waved across.

After serving drinks to a nearby group he joined us and shouted above the noise, 'Fred, how are you doing? Sorry to hear about Tootsies.'

I struggled to make myself heard, 'I'm fine, thanks. Looks like business is going well here.'

A wide smile spread across his face. 'It's been our best summer yet. Would you both like a drink on the house?'

I turned to Alice. 'This is Alan, a friend of mine. Do you fancy a Babycham, or something else?'

After a moment's thought, she mouthed, 'A Babycham would be nice.'

Alan leant over the table and shook Alice's hand. 'Great to meet you. Are you having a vodka and orange, Fred?'

I nodded in confirmation.

Alice and I relaxed in each other's company. The dance floor heaved, and the disco ball sprayed colours across the chaotic scenes. Everyone danced with gusto as the D.J. played hits by Status Quo, Rod Stewart, Abba, Queen, Thin Lizzy, Brian Ferry and ELO. It was hot in the disco and perspiration covered the dancers' ecstatic faces as the tempo increased.

Absorbed in each other's presence, the atmosphere was hypnotic. Our first round of drinks soon disappeared, and we ordered a second, and then a third. The crowds thinned out, and the music became slower until only couples remained. We joined them and pressed up against each other as we moved around the dance floor, lost in a long embrace.

* * *

After a fantastic night, I walked Alice back to the Caribe and kissed her goodnight.

My hands strayed under her blouse.

She gave out a satisfied moan, before pulling away. 'One step at time darling, one step at a time.'

I stroked her hair. 'I won't do anything unless you want me to.'

We talked and Alice agreed it would be fun to help hand out leaflets, so we planned to meet the next morning outside Cortijo's.

After another prolonged kiss, we said goodnight. Alice headed upstairs.

I walked on air as I made my way back to my room.

It was 4 am.

36

Handing out flyers

My alarm clock woke me at 9 am and I sprang out of bed.

After a quick wash, I walked upstairs for breakfast. Sue was working.

She smiled as I strolled into the restaurant. 'Morning, Fred. How's it going? We saw Tich yesterday evening and he told us what happened at Tootsies. I'm sorry they treated you that way, but you're not the first and won't be the last I'm afraid.'

I gave her a hug. 'Thanks. It's a relief to be out of there. John offered me some work handing out leaflets, so I'm meeting him at ten. If you hear of something else, please let me know.'

As I sat at the table, she massaged my shoulders. 'I will. What about Grannies? Mick and Pat are unhappy with Eduardo, their Spanish barman. Talk to them.'

I looked up at her. 'Tich mentioned that too. I've met Eduardo. He doesn't get on with Graham, does he? I'll have a word with Mick or Pat when I see them. It's the type of work I enjoy.'

'I'm sure you'd fit in well. You're a hard worker. There's no harm in asking. Sorry, I need to serve customers, did you want something to eat?'

'Could I have an English Breakfast and a mug of tea, please?'

She took the order to the kitchen and within minutes I was digging in.

* * *

Alice was waiting outside El Cortijo, looking stunning in hot pants, frilled top and laced sandals.

John, Alan, and two Spanish guys were busy cleaning the place. John waved across and joined us at the front desk.

He shook our hands. 'Thanks for coming.' A bundle of leaflets lay on the counter. 'These flyers allow free entry to the disco before 10 pm and are valid until Sunday night. The aim is to generate more trade when we first open. Most customers don't arrive until 11 pm or later. There are two hundred flyers here. Start by handing them out on the beach. Target groups of lads or lasses and give them one each. Tell them about the disco and how fantastic it is. Maybe you can talk to the girls, Fred, and you the boys, Alice. You should be able to hand out most on the beach, but if you have any left, try one or two of the hotel pools.'

Alice gave an enthusiastic nod. 'Sounds great, John. Should be fun. We could try the 18-30s at the Caribe later.'

John ran a hand through his short silver hair. 'Great idea. If you enjoy it, you could do it again tomorrow. I hope by then you'll have generated enough interest for the weekend. I'll pay you 200 pesetas upfront for today's flyers and another 5 for each customer that produces one at the door. You can have a free drink each night you come in until Sunday. What do you think?'

I gave him a broad smile. 'Sounds brilliant, John. Thanks for the opportunity.'

After another shake of hands, we set off on our mission.

We split the leaflets between us and headed to the main strip. The sun beat down as we wove our way along the beach amongst the parasols and sunbeds. Alice soon found a crowd of lads and aroused their interest. She had no problem convincing them. My first group of lasses were keen, and I enjoyed talking to them.

By the time we reached the far end of the beach, we had handed out half the leaflets. We talked through the reactions to our spiel. Most of the recipients knew of Cortijo's and had been there at least once. There was enthusiasm for the free entry idea, and a few promised to get there early on at least one night.

Encouraged, we walked back along the beach and identified tourists we had missed or those who had arrived within the last hour. At the start of the beach again, we still had a quarter of the flyers left. These soon disappeared as we made our way around the captive audience at the Panorama and the 18-30 crowd at the Caribe.

It was 2 pm when we finished. I suggested we spend the afternoon at the Panorama pool. Alice popped upstairs to change into her bikini and then accompanied me to my room while I changed and threw a towel, book and suntan lotion into my straw bag. Alice laughed when she saw me with what she described as my "straw house".

We found a quiet corner that was perfect. We messed around in the water, sunbathed and talked about everything and nothing, enjoying each other's company. Enthusiastic kisses and cuddles interspersed our idyllic time together.

* * *

Three days flew by. On the Thursday evening, we had a meal at the Panorama, before walking to Grannies where we sat on the terrace, oblivious to everything going on around us.

Mick and Pat worked behind the bar but were very busy, so I didn't get a chance to talk to them about the job. Alice drank Coke and I had several beers.

After midnight we moved on to El Cortijo where we saw John and updated him. He told us forty customers had redeemed their flyers at the door, and we agreed to repeat the exercise in the morning. We slow danced our time away. When the disco closed, I walked Alice to the hotel. After a passionate kiss, we said our goodnights and I got back to my room after 4 am.

Friday's distribution of leaflets was not as successful because we hit some of the same people as the day before. There were eighty left and we handed these out wherever we went during the day. We enjoyed the rest of the afternoon at the Caribe pool and Alice passed a batch of flyers to Paco, Jane's boyfriend, so he could give them to hotel guests.

It was July 1st, and I had tabs to settle. Alice joined me in the evening as we visited the Red Lion first, where the bill came to 2250. Next, we stopped at Tony's Bar for a meal of omelette and chips. Tony handed me the standard scrawled piece of paper and I gave him 5225. Our final stop was Grannies where I paid Mick 3200.

Alice looked shocked as I passed over the wads of cash. It also concerned me as I counted what I had left in my money-belt, 5200 pesetas. Another visit to the bank would be required soon.

We were both tired and skipped Cortijo's. After a romantic walk along the seafront beneath a brilliant full moon, I escorted Alice back to the Caribe. I knew sleeping with her was not on the agenda but was more relaxed and accepting of that. I was in bed by 2 am and lay awake for a long time thinking about her. When I fell asleep, she was ever-present in my dreams.

On Saturday, we hired bikes and cycled westwards along the coast. It was a glorious day and we were both in high spirits, despite knowing she was leaving soon. We lived for the moment and revelled in each other's company. Early afternoon we stopped off at a deserted cove. We embraced to the sound of lapping waves as we lay back on a towel.

* * *

At 5 am on Sunday I sat outside the Caribe as Alice hurried upstairs to pack. She didn't want me to come to the airport, so we embraced while Liz rounded up the 18-30 crowd. Jane was in tears as she held on to Paco until the last moment. Alice didn't cry, but I missed her the moment the coach left.

After they had driven off, Paco joined me for a coffee before he started work. He confided how much he felt for Jane and that he planned to join her in England when the season was over.

It was 7 am when I got back to my room and I knew sleep would be sparse. The lads were arriving early in the afternoon. I set my alarm for midday.

37

Bletchingley lads arrive

Five hours later, the alarm clock jolted me into action.

I splashed water on my face, brushed my teeth, and headed upstairs for breakfast. Pedro and Roberto were working as Tony and Sue had the day off.

Syd and Dave, the guys working for Jim at the building site, sat at a corner table so I joined them. I hadn't seen them since their arrival, although I often saw their battered Ford Cortina with its memorable number plate parked at the back of the restaurant.

I smiled at them. 'How's it going? Is Jim keeping you busy?'

They both grinned. Dave had his hair tied in a ponytail and appeared to have lost weight.

Syd looked exhausted. He rubbed his eyes before answering, 'It's tough. We weren't expecting it to be so hot and both of us are struggling. Jim's a hard taskmaster and we've been working long hours, including Saturdays.'

'Still at the Bee Gees villa?'

They shook their heads. Dave gave me a weary look. 'No, we were only there for the first few days. We're now at a new block of apartments on the outskirts of Santa Eulalia. There are only the two of us, Chris, and two Spanish guys. Jim is worried because the contract is due for completion by early September, and we're running behind.'

Roberto interrupted and took my order for breakfast. The others ordered a bottle of beer each.

I glanced at them. 'Do you think Jim needs any more help?'

Syd looked startled. 'You're not thinking of coming back are you, Fred? Tich explained what happened to you at Tootsies.'

I laughed. 'No, that was the last thing on my mind. A few of my mates are arriving from England this afternoon. Mutts and Sam want to stay on longer and are keen to work.'

Syd looked at me with interest. 'Well, I could always ask Jim. I told him on Friday we needed extra help. He said he'd think about it. We could have a chat with them today to see if they'd be interested, then I could talk to Jim tomorrow. Where are you meeting them?'

I rubbed my stubbled chin. 'The Red Lion. I'd expect them to be there by three.'

Dave grinned. 'We're going there after here, so I'm sure we'll run into them.'

I reached over and shook their hands. 'That's great, thanks. If you see them first, just say we've spoken. You can't miss them. They're a rowdy bunch.'

* * *

I heard them halfway down the alley to the Red Lion.

When I walked in, the lads were playing a game of Killer darts and didn't notice me. Syd and Dave had introduced themselves and joined in. There were bottles scattered everywhere, many of them empty.

At the bar, I caught Tich's eye. 'Hiya, how long have they been here?'

He gave me a nervous smile. 'They got here just before 2 pm. A minibus dropped them off, and they poured in here well-oiled already. I don't think they've stopped drinking since leaving home this morning. At this pace, they'll drink us out of beer.'

I shuddered. 'Oh dear, I hope they behave themselves. I still need to get their money, fetch the key from Pablo, and show them the apartment. Have you talked to Sam about his idea of sleeping on the beach?'

Tich shook his head as he passed me a San Miguel. 'No, sorry. It's been chaotic ever since they arrived. Maybe you can mention it when you speak to him.'

I sat at the bar and watched in amazement at the antics going on around the dartboard.

Siv spotted me first and screamed across, 'Fred, what are you doing over there? Come and join us.'

With reluctance, I walked over, and my drunken mates surrounded me, eager to shake my hand or slap my back.

Siv could always hold his drink. Mutts and Sam were also under control. Tuzza, Ian, Giles, and Kooky not so much. Their excitement at being on holiday was clear.

Once they had finished their latest game of Killer, I pulled Siv to one side. 'Can you help me collect the cash? I need to pay off the landlord and pick up the key.'

He shuffled with embarrassment. 'They've been squabbling over money. Sam wants to sleep on the beach, but the others argue he should still put in his share. They don't want to stump up the deposit either as they say they'll make sure the place is clean when they leave.'

'That's awkward. I lost my job at Tootsies and cash is tight for me too. If we don't get the deposit back, then I lose the 4000 I've paid.'

'Don't worry, mate. If that happens, we'll make sure we cover it.'

I gave him a nervous grin. 'OK, but I'm not happy. Can you ask Sam to talk to Tich about sleeping on the beach? He doesn't think it's a good idea as the police crack down on it this time of year. I'll get 4000 from each of the others in the meantime.'

Siv handed over his share and walked over to have a word with Sam. Moments later, I saw Sam head to the bar where he became engrossed talking to Tich.

It took a while to collect the money, but I had 24,000 pesetas in my pocket.

Sam came towards me with a sheepish grin on his face. 'Sorry, Fred. Tich explained about the beach and I've decided it's best if I stay in the apartment. The problem is I've only got 2000 I can give you right now. The rest of my cash is in pound notes. Tich says Roger will change it for me, but he's not around until tomorrow.'

I agreed to wait until the next day, explaining my reserves were running low. I knocked back the rest of my beer, before heading off to pick up the key from Pablo.

Pablo wasn't there but the frail woman I had seen before, who I presumed was his mother, gesticulated and showed me on her watch he would return in two hours.

I took a stroll along the seafront and the warmth of the late afternoon sun helped calm my nerves. I stopped at the Restaurante Es Cana for a beer and a snack. Tourists packed the beach, and it reminded me of the time I had spent there the previous year. I reflected on how things had changed in the intervening twelve months.

When I returned, Pablo answered the door and beckoned me inside. I counted out the 28,000 pesetas. He nodded with approval and handed me two keys to the apartment. Pablo stressed once again I would only get my deposit back if they left the place in good condition. I hoped the lads would remember their promise.

* * *

It was after 8 pm when I got back to the Red Lion.

The atmosphere was even more frantic and getting out of control. The lads were jumping around to tunes on the jukebox and singing along at the top of their voices. There was one song they kept putting on – *Sailing* by Rod Stewart. There seemed to be little sign of the drinking slowing down. There was no beer left, so they had moved on to spirits.

Tich glanced at me in exasperation. I tried to take command of the situation and walked towards the dartboard where another game of Killer was underway.

I shouted above the noise, 'Lads, could I have your attention. The apartment is ready for you. When you've finished can we head over there?'

They nodded in my direction and then returned to the darts, which was reaching a climax.

Half an hour later, after a lot of persuasion, the seven of them picked up their bags and were ready to go. I led them out of the Red Lion. It must have been a spectacle as they staggered and swayed after me towards the apartment block.

I tried to quieten them as we entered the building, but they clattered up the stairs dragging their luggage. Their drunken voices echoed along the corridors.

As I opened the door they pushed through together. Once inside, it was obvious how cramped conditions would be for them. There was little space for the bags and the lads argued over who would sleep where.

Siv turned and slurred, 'Fred, this is tiny. Are you sure there was nothing else? We were expecting much more for 2000 pesetas a night.'

'Sorry, mate, you were lucky to get this. It's the height of the season and everywhere's full. You only got this place because of a cancellation. Pablo offered you a special rate because of my connection to Tich.'

He gave me a bemused grin.

I handed him the keys. 'There are only two of these, so you need to work out amongst yourselves who takes charge. Please make sure you don't lose them.'

As I left, I heard drunken moans and groans as the lads argued over the sleeping arrangements. Who would share the double beds? Who would sleep on the sunbeds? Who would get the sofa?

By then I was beyond caring. I was annoyed they had not even thanked me for organising things.

I wandered back to the Red Lion and helped Tich tidy up the mess they had left behind. Visions of the state of the apartment in two weeks' time flashed through my mind.

After clearing up, we sat at the bar, dazed. There were no bottles of San Miguel left, so Tich poured himself a whisky and Coke while I had a vodka and orange. We had several more as we tried to recover our senses.

It was after midnight when I headed home. My mind churned for a long time before I fell into a restless sleep.

38

Feeling homesick

Bizarre dreams kept waking me. As the first filters of daylight streamed through the windows, I gave up trying to rest and got dressed.

I was in a sombre mood as I walked along the beach and then the coast path to the east of Es Cana.

The sun was still low in the sky. Faint wisps of cloud danced on the horizon. A gentle swell moved across the water and sunlight glistened off the peaks of the waves. Fishing boats weaved their way from the small harbour. As always, the aroma of pine pervaded the air and birds twittered to greet the new morning.

Under normal circumstances, that wonderful atmosphere would have cheered me up but the way the lads had treated me weighed on my mind and I could not shake the gloom that overwhelmed me. I missed Sarah and beat myself up about how I had betrayed her.

I ambled onwards to try and clear my frustrations, but negativity took control. I felt homesick and regretted my decision to come to Ibiza. Had I made a huge mistake leaving Sarah and my career behind?

After a while, I turned around and headed back. The sun burned my back and sweat poured down my face. I was thirsty. My thoughts shifted to the refreshing taste of a beer. I knew I should eat but the idea of beer became an obsession.

The first place I spotted as I approached Es Cana beach was the Hotel Miami. I headed two hundred yards inland and found the entrance. The reception was quiet. No-one questioned me as I strolled across to the bar and ordered a draught beer. I glanced at the clock and saw it was only 10:30 am.

My first drink did not touch the sides and a second soon followed. By the fifth, my stomach grumbled, and I asked for a bowl of peanuts. I knew I had to slow down, so I found a shaded spot by the pool where I sat and pondered my situation. The alcohol only made my melancholy worse.

I lay on a sunbed and fell asleep.

When I awoke two hours later, the veil of gloom had lifted somewhat. I had a splitting headache from the beer but otherwise, my feelings were more positive.

I thought I'd better catch up with my mates, so I headed for the Red Lion.

Roger greeted me. 'Fred, how's it going? You've just missed the lads. They've gone to Tootsies as we've got no beer left until this afternoon's delivery.'

'Hi, Roger. How were they today? I assume Tich told you the state they were in yesterday.'

He flashed me a smile. 'Subdued and hungover. Mutts, Sam and Siv were apologetic and said none of them remembered much about leaving here. It shocked them when they asked to pay. It was over 5000 pesetas.' That was £43 – more than double my tab for the month.

I glanced at the floor. 'I'm so sorry, Roger. I came back to help Tich tidy up the mess, but I've never seen them that way before. Did they settle up?'

He leant across and grasped my shoulder. 'Don't worry. We've experienced much worse. I changed a few five and ten-pound notes for them. It got sorted in the end. Sam left this for you.'

He passed over an envelope which I opened. It contained the 2000 pesetas he had promised.

I smiled back at Roger. 'Thanks for sorting them out. I hope they calm down. As there's no beer, could I have a vodka and orange? I need to settle my nerves.'

He turned, poured the drink and handed me three letters. 'The post has just arrived. Trust it's good news.'

'Cheers, Roger. Let's hope so.'

I opened the letters. There was one from Sarah. The second included notes from Mother and my younger sister, Christine. The third was from Helen. They had arrived within a week of being written. I assumed my post in the other direction was just as quick.

With my drink and letters in hand, I sat at a table in the alley. I needed cheering up and hoped the news from home would help.

Dear Fred,

Thanks for your letter which I received at the weekend. I am glad you are OK but sorry to hear about your job at Tootsies Bar.

The weather here has been dismal, although I went to Lancing yesterday, and it was hot. It must have been hot as I only wore a cotton shirt and skirt.

On Saturday, I cut and blow-dried Christine's hair and cut Alan's short again. He looked a lot different when he left than when he came in.

There have been no more blackouts. In fact, I'm fine.

I bought the Muppets L.P. last week. It is great.

My hair is now down to my collar, so I have it parted in the middle and flicked back both sides. Since I lost weight, I cannot wear a fringe as it makes me look long in the face.

I will close now but write again soon. Please take care of yourself and I look forward to seeing you again.

All my love,

Sarah

My dear Robert,

Thanks again for your news plus a little Chris gleaned from Sarah last weekend. It sounds as if we might see you soon and I look forward to that.

I took Chris to St. Olave's hospital this morning. It is near London's dockland and part of the Guy's Hospital group. All being well she should be minus her tonsils by this time tomorrow. She was cheerful about it and I'm confident she'll make friends there. I've enclosed a letter from her she wrote before we left.

Alastair is now getting as much driving practice as possible. His test is on August 22nd.

The garage says my car engine needs an overhaul, but I'm not sure if it's affordable.

Any thoughts on going to university in the autumn? It might be a worthwhile thing to consider.

Lots of love and see you soon.

Mother

Dear Robert,

Sorry I haven't written before.

I am still working at Spectrum but I'm trying to find a job elsewhere. I can't manage on the money and have run out of things to learn there, so it's getting monotonous.

Alan and I have been going to the Station Hotel. Now we're known there, people ask after you. One girl behind the bar said you'd written to them.

Sarah has taken charge of my hair. She cut it last week and put streaks in yesterday.

Ali's back now. I had to store my clothes in your room, so I have a problem when you are both here at the same time.

I don't want to sound selfish but... if you want to buy me a birthday present then get something silver, if it's true how cheap it is out there.

You asked me before you left if I thought I'd miss you, well I do very much.

Write again soon.

All my love,

Chris

Dear Fred,

I hope you didn't miss the coach back. We were lucky because we boarded the plane as soon as you left, although it didn't take off for twenty minutes. Thanks for coming to the airport with me. Was the power still off when you got back?

I'm keeping my fingers crossed you get a job because the weather here is enough to depress anyone. Not only is it cold and cloudy, but I got soaked when I popped out at lunchtime as I forgot to take a coat. I should have brought nice weather back with me.

It was 11 am yesterday when I got home. I was so shattered I slept most of the day. I don't expect you got up very early either. Everyone is so white over here that my tan looks great.

Thank you again for a fantastic 11 days. I didn't realise two people could grow so fond of each other in such a short time. You helped me sort myself out and although I'm depressed at being in England and not in Ibiza, I feel great in myself. I seem to have regained my self-confidence and am like a new person (I hope that doesn't sound too silly and you can understand what I mean).

172

It's difficult going to bed early and waking up early in the morning. It's 1 am now and I'm not tired.

Tomorrow I will try to get an evening job to earn extra cash.

Are you dressing up again on Saturday? If you are and somebody takes photos, you must send me one.

Could you do me a favour, please? I left my nightdress in our hotel room under the pillow. Ask Liz for me if she's seen it and maybe she can bring it back with her in the winter? It's lilac chiffon if she wants a description.

Anyway, I'm getting writer's cramp. Good luck with finding a job. I know you will. Take care and write soon.

Love,

Helen

I read through them several times, as usual. It was great hearing from everyone, but the letters only helped resurrect the homesickness I had earlier in the day. That feeling and the vodka gnawed at my stomach and I had to eat. I peered back through the door and waved goodbye to Roger, before heading to Tony's for a meal.

39

Finding another job

The omelette and chips I ordered from Roberto settled my stomach.

After eating, I sat outside on the veranda with a beer. The sun was setting, and shadows lengthened through the trees. It was still hot. I was drowsy but in a better frame of mind.

I strolled inside after watching the sunset. There were familiar faces at the small bar in the restaurant's far corner: Sue, Pat from Grannies, and Liz the 18-30 rep.

Tony was serving drinks as I joined them. '*Hola, Fred. ¿Cómo estás?* Would you like a drink?'

I gave him a weak smile and ordered a vodka and orange.

Sue squeezed my hand. 'Are you all right, Fred? You look down.'

'I'm better than I was. My mates arrived yesterday. It upset me the way they treated me. They got drunk and didn't like the room I'd sorted out for them. For the first time since I got here, I've been homesick all day.'

'Don't let it get to you. We all go through it at some stage.'

Pat and Liz overheard. They nodded in agreement.

Liz hugged me. 'I feel like that when work gets too much, but I always remind myself how lucky I am being here and that helps.'

'You're right, Liz. I'll get over it. By the way, I got a letter today from Helen that she wrote on her first day back in England. She asked whether anyone had found her lilac nightdress. She left it under the pillow.'

Liz gave me a concerned look. 'Actually, she phoned yesterday and mentioned that. She's split up with her boyfriend and was talking about coming here in August for a few weeks. She wants to stay with you. Did you say she could?'

My eyebrows shot up. I took a slug on my drink. 'Oh dear. I may have said something, but never dreamed she'd come back. It would be difficult in that small room of mine.'

'I thought as much. You've already been out with Alice since she left. I've seen it all before. Do you want me to say anything when she phones again?'

My face reddened. 'If that's OK, Liz. Should I write and let her know?'

'No, leave it with me. If you write to her don't mention we've talked. Helen stressed I shouldn't tell you until she books her ticket later in the month.'

A difficult silence descended for a few moments. Then Pat called me over. 'Fred, can I have a word with you? Liz, Sue, and I are having a girls' night out, but I wanted to ask you something before we left.'

I walked over to the corner of the bar where she sat propped against the wall.

Her amber eyes twinkled as she whispered, 'Mick and I have discussed taking someone else on behind the bar in Grannies. It's getting busy now and Eduardo isn't up to the job. We want to reduce his hours and give him the afternoon shift when it's quieter. Would you be interested in working lunchtimes and evenings?'

A smile crossed my face. 'That's fantastic, Pat. I'd love to.'

She gave me a peck on the cheek. 'Brilliant, why don't you pop in tomorrow lunchtime to talk about it in more detail? It's Eduardo's day off, but Mick is working with Graham.'

'I need to go into Santa Eulalia to change money, but I'll come in after that.'

The unexpected good news cheered me up. I bought the girls a round of drinks before they headed off on their night out.

* * *

I had a more restful night's sleep and woke refreshed at 7:00 am.

After tea and toast in Tony's, I walked to the bus stop. Within minutes the bus arrived. I joined the jostling crowd as we clambered aboard and handed over our fares.

The excited Spanish conversation around me faded to a drone. I gazed out of the window and took in the scenery as we made regular stops to pick up more passengers. I felt a surge of excitement at the thought of getting a job at Grannies as we bounced along the dusty road. There was a haze in the air and the July sun beat down from clear blue skies.

When I disembarked in the main square of Santa Eulalia, there was still over an hour to go until the bank opened. I explored the streets of the town and made my way to the seafront. I relaxed in the shade of a palm tree and sipped on a bottle of water I had bought at a nearby kiosk.

There were the normal chaotic scenes as the bank's doors opened, but I was early enough to get to the head of the first queue within minutes. The exchange rate had improved to just under 120 pesetas to the pound, 7120 after commission for my £60. I checked the money-belt and confirmed I still had £180 left. I reckoned that should last me until October if I got the job.

It was hot in the bank and sweat drenched me. I winced at the strength of the midday sun as I stepped outside. I was soon on the bus back to Es Cana and appreciated the warm breeze through the open windows as we drove along behind a horse and cart.

* * *

Grannies was busy, and Pat sat at a table sipping a gin and tonic. Mick and Graham served a crowd of customers. They both looked hot and bothered.

I joined Pat. 'Hiya, did you have a good night?'

She chuckled. 'Yes, from what I remember. We got sloshed, and I didn't get home until 4 am. It was good to let our hair down and share our frustrations. It's that time of year when everyone gets stressed because of the heat and the amount of work we're doing. Liz is finding it more and more difficult coping with the 18-30 crowd. She was even talking about throwing it in.'

'It must be tough for all of you. I hope I can take the pressure off you, Mick, and Graham if I get the job here.'

'Mick will come and have a chat with you when it gets quieter. Do you want a drink in the meantime?'

'An Estrella would be great, Pat.'

On her way to the bar, she collected a few empties and left them by the sink. After pouring my drink, she brought it across. 'Here you go, Fred. I'd better help behind the bar and get those glasses washed.'

'Cheers, Pat.'

I sat back and observed the hectic scene around me. It was an hour later when Mick came over.

I stood and shook his hand. 'How's it going?'

'We're busy and the money is rolling in. It's just a difficult time of the year and we're struggling. Pat said you want to help. Is that right?'

'Yes, I'd love to.'

Mick studied me for a few seconds. No doubt he could see my eyes sparkling with enthusiasm. 'Well, it will be long hours, although you get one day off a week, and I can't offer you much money. Are you still interested?'

I nodded, so he carried on, 'You'll start here at 9 am to tidy up from the night before and restock the shelves. We open at 11 am and you'll work the lunchtime shift until 3 pm with either Pat, Graham or me. That person will then do the afternoon shift with Eduardo until 8 pm when you need to begin again. Two of us will work with you most nights, but on Fridays and Saturdays, there will be the three of us as it gets very busy. We close at 2 am, but sometimes later at weekends.'

'Sounds like hard work, but I'm sure I'll manage it. When can I start?'

Mick's mischievous grin lit up his face. 'I need tomorrow to let Eduardo know the change of rotas. I'm sure he won't mind as it means less work for the same money. We have to keep him on because of the rule about employing at least one Spaniard. It's too difficult to find someone else this late in the season.'

He took a swig of beer before continuing, 'I'll pay you 600 pesetas a day. Not a lot, I know, but I can't afford any more. We'll cover your tax and insurance. You'll get your wages on the last day of the month. Pat brings in snacks her mum makes, so you won't need to worry about food too much. Your drinks are free while you are working. Are you still up for it?'

'Yes, that's brilliant. I'm sure it will be a great experience. I'm looking forward to it.'

Mick shook my hand. 'Meet me by the back entrance at 9 am on Thursday and I'll show you what you need to do to get the place ready.'

I gripped his arm. 'Thanks for the opportunity, Mick.'

40

Fresh start

During breakfast the next morning, I told Sue the news and she gave me a warm hug.

'That's fantastic. I'm so glad, Fred. You deserve another break. Hope it works out for you.'

I visited El Cortijo to let John know I couldn't help with the flyers anymore. He understood and wished me the best at Grannies, paying me 575 pesetas for the leaflets handed in over the weekend.

My next port of call was the Red Lion to see if there were any letters and to catch up with my mates, as I thought they might be there.

Tich waved as I walked through the door. Once he had finished serving, he came towards me with an outstretched hand. 'I hear congratulations are in order. Well done. I knew you'd find something else. Grannies will be hard graft, but I'm sure you'll fit in.'

'Cheers, Tich. I start tomorrow, so won't be around much for the next few weeks. Are there any letters?'

He shook his head. 'No, sorry, nothing today. Several of your mates are here though. They're playing darts and have calmed down after their first day of excitement.'

He uncapped a San Miguel and passed it across the bar. I took a slurp and headed over to the dartboard.

There were only four of them: Tuzza, Ian, Giles, and Kooky. They slapped me on the back.

Tuzza rubbed his stubble and grinned. 'Do you want to put your name up, Fred? We're playing 501, double in, double out – best of three games. Loser buys the winner a beer.'

He was at the board chalking a game between Ian and Kooky. I nodded, and he added my name.

Giles sat at a nearby table, so I joined him. He was the quietest of the bunch, although you would not have guessed that on Sunday.

I grinned at him. 'Have you settled into the apartment OK?'

'Well it's not ideal, but we're coping. Ian is sharing a bed with Kooky while I'm in with Tuzza. It's embarrassing being in double beds together, so we've put extra pillows in the middle to keep us apart. Mutts and Sam have taken the sunbeds on the balcony, and Siv is on the sofa.'

'Sorry I couldn't find anything else, but it's the height of the season. You were lucky to get anywhere.'

He beamed a smile. 'That's OK. We only use it for sleeping and having a wash. There are bags and clothes strewn all over the place, so it looks a real mess, but we'll make sure everything is tidy before we leave.'

'Please do, Giles, I don't want to lose the deposit. Where are Mutts, Sam and Siv today?'

'We haven't seen you since Sunday, have we? Lots has happened since then. We went to Cortijo's on Monday evening and Siv met a girl. He's spending all his time with her and stayed in her hotel room last night.' After a sip of beer, he continued, 'Mutts and Sam started work with Jim today. Syd and Dave picked them up and took them in their car to the site. It looks as though they've got a job until the end of August at least. What about you, Fred? Have you found something else yet?'

'Yes, I start at Grannies tomorrow morning, six days a week. Come in and see me if you can.'

'I'll try to persuade the others to drag themselves away from this place. It feels like our second home already.'

Tuzza's booming voice interrupted us as he called Giles to take over the chalking. Kooky had beaten Ian 2-1. The next game was between him and Tuzza.

The afternoon slipped by and we had a great laugh. I played three games, two against Kooky and one against Tuzza. I lost them all and had to buy the beers. Apart from those fluke games earlier in the season, my talent for darts had not improved.

Mutts and Sam came in at 6:30 pm looking knackered. After a brief chat, I said my goodbyes. I wanted to get a meal and an early night. It would be my last for a while.

* * *

Mick was waiting at the rear of Grannies when I arrived at 9 am the next day.

He rubbed his eyes as he spoke, 'Morning, Fred. Good to see you are punctual. Here are your keys. There is one for the padlocked cage outside, another for the back door, and the third is for the front gate. Please make sure you keep them safe.'

After opening the rear door, he ushered me along the passageway to the storeroom and the bar area. He pointed towards the sliding doors that separated the bar from the terrace. 'Open these at both ends. The locks take the same key as the back door.'

Mick inserted the key and unhooked the latches on the first door, before sliding it open. He repeated the same at the entrance end.

He paused and checked I was following, before resuming, 'Then you need to collect any glasses from the previous night. We try to tidy up as much as we can, but there are always some left when we close. Take them over to the sink, wash them up, and leave them to dry.'

I nodded to confirm I understood.

Mick continued, 'Once that's done, take the empty bottles outside. There are a few that are returns, and they go in the crates. The others get thrown in the dustbin.'

We spent fifteen minutes collecting glasses from the terrace, bar and entertainments room. I washed them then carried the empty bottles out the back and sorted them.

Mick took me to the storeroom and explained, 'Next thing is to sweep the floors. Then fill this bucket with a splash of detergent and water. The most important place to clean is the raised decking behind the bar as it gets very sticky. Don't spend too much time with the rest. Eduardo can do a more thorough job late in the afternoon when it's quiet.'

I gave him a nervous smile. 'I'll do my best to get everything done in time.'

'You'll be fine. While you're cleaning, I'll check what we need to restock. Oh, one other thing. When you're in the toilets, give them a quick scrub to make sure they're clean. There are utensils and disinfectant in a small cupboard in the Gents. Eduardo can do them again before he leaves this evening.'

I grabbed the brush and swept the floors. After that, I filled the mop bucket and cleaned as much as I could without leaving the floor too wet. It took longer than I expected, By the time I had finished the toilets, it was 10:30 am.

Mick glanced around at what I had done. He then gave me his prepared list and explained how to stock up for the day. He unlocked the cage containing the barrels and crates of drink. We loaded the trolley with refills and wheeled it inside.

I kneeled on the decking. For each section of bottled drinks on the shelves and in the fridges, I pulled the older bottles forward and inserted the new ones behind. The spirits were on the shelf above.

Time raced by and at 11 am, I heard a key click in the gate. Graham sprang down the steps.

Mick gave me some final words of advice, 'Graham will take over now and tell you the best way to serve drinks and work out the money. The ice delivery arrives early afternoon. We keep the ice in the storeroom fridge and fill the buckets for the bar from there. If the beer runs out, he'll show you how to change a barrel. It's easy enough, so you shouldn't have any problems. Good luck.'

'Thanks, Mick, I'm looking forward to the challenge.'

We shook hands, and he headed out the back to collect his car.

Graham gave me a reassuring grin. 'Right, Fred. Let's get going.'

41

Enjoying work

My first few days at Grannies sped by and I enjoyed the work.

I got on well with Mick, Pat and Graham. We developed a good understanding and had a real laugh together. I soon learned the best ways to serve drinks, add up the rounds in my head, and ring pesetas into the till as fast as possible.

It was hot behind the bar and my long hair was a problem. As I sweated it got tangled, so I tied it back in a ponytail. That helped but was not the solution. I knew it needed a drastic cut. I found this difficult to contemplate but realised it was necessary.

During quieter times we chatted to customers. Many became regulars during their two-week holidays. We welcomed others who had visited in previous years with open arms. They were treated like long lost friends.

On Sunday lunchtime, I talked to two young ladies from Bristol, Laura and Sally. I discovered Sally was a qualified hairdresser and mentioned the problems I had with my hair. She offered to cut it for me. When my shift finished, I went with them to their room at the Miami Hotel.

Laura washed my hair over the bathtub and gave me a relaxing head massage.

Sally sat me in a chair at the dressing table in their bedroom. Laura lay back on her bed and watched as Sally trimmed my golden locks. I looked on in horror as long strands of hair fell to the floor. Ten minutes later, I had short hair for the first time in years.

I'd grown my hair long while in the sixth form at school. It was my pride and joy. As I looked at myself in the mirror, a transformed person stared back.

I offered to pay Sally for the haircut, but she refused. Instead, we agreed I'd buy them both a drink next time they were in Grannies.

Everyone I saw over the following days had to take a second look before they realised it was me.

* * *

Whilst working with Graham on the Monday lunchtime, he commented on how tired I looked. Even though I tried to get a siesta in the afternoons, I was only sleeping four or five hours a night. It caught up with me.

Graham passed me a strip of pills he said were slimming tablets and explained he used them to combat tiredness. He told me I could buy them over the counter at the local chemists. I took two and within an hour I felt more energetic and in a great mood. After that, I relied on them whenever I got tired, which was most days.

My first day off was on Wednesday, after working six straight days in Grannies. Graham was free as well but had to work the evening shift. He invited me to go with him and his Spanish girlfriend, Margarita and her friend, Pilar, for a day out. The plan was to go to Agua Blanca, a nudist beach a few kilometres along the coast. Apprehensive, I agreed to join them.

They met me for breakfast at Tony's, then we piled into Margarita's car, a bright red Seat 600 with only two doors. Pilar and I clambered into the back. After a bumpy half-hour ride along the winding coast road to the north-east, we arrived at Agua Blanca.

Before us lay a long stretch of golden sand which backed on to striking rocky cliffs. We made our way to the southern end, the permitted nudist area. Despite it being the height of the season, the beach was quiet.

We settled on the soft sand and Graham and Margarita stripped off. He was muscular and well-endowed, which made me nervous because I paled by comparison. Margarita was tall and had a beautiful body. Her long brown hair reached down to her slender waist. I found it difficult to keep my eyes off her as she walked towards the water and swam for a while with Graham.

I had brought two beach towels with me in my straw bag. Pilar lay beside me on one of them and I relaxed on the other. After some taunting from Graham, Pilar and I took off our swimming costumes. Pilar was thin and almost boy-like, with short black hair. Her breasts were small but pert. Like me, she was reluctant to stand up and parade around.

The sun beat down, and we smothered ourselves with sun cream. My private parts reddened. After a while, I used this as an excuse to pull a towel over me to hide my embarrassment. Graham had no such qualms and walked over to a nearby shack to get us drinks, bottles of San Miguel for us and *jugo de naranja,* orange juice, for the girls.

Early in the afternoon, Graham and Margarita disappeared for a long time. The last we saw of them was as they climbed over the rocks around the headland. It did not take too much imagination to realise what they had planned.

In the meantime, I tried talking to Pilar. It was difficult. The Spanish I had spent hours learning evaporated. I could not string more than a few words together. She also struggled with her English. We cuddled and had a brief kiss. I was aroused but we were in open view. We lay in each other's arms and soaked up the sun.

Graham and Margarita returned a while later, flushed, and with broad grins across their faces. The girls had a whispered conversation and glanced over at me. Pilar stood up, wrapped her towel around her waist and held out her hand.

She led me in the direction the other two had come from. Soon we found a secluded spot among the rocks and laid on our towels. Pilar was keen to take things further. She leant in and kissed me. I responded with enthusiasm, but our efforts soon fizzled out. Pilar gave me an apologetic look and tears clouded her deep brown eyes. I held her close to console her.

Before returning, we frolicked in the warm waters nearby. It was a wonderful experience and made up for our earlier frustration.

We clambered back over the rocks. Graham and Margarita snoozed in each other's arms. I fetched us more drinks to quench our thirst.

We got dressed as the shadows from the cliffs crossed the beach. As we drove back to Es Cana Graham and Margarita laughed and joked. Pilar and I held hands, but there was an awkward silence between us.

* * *

In the evening I walked to the Red Lion. I hadn't seen the lads since the previous Wednesday.

The seven of them sat around a table deep in discussion. I discovered it was about money. I bought a round of drinks and took them over. That cheered them up for a while, but the gloom soon descended again.

Mutts drew me to one side and explained the situation. 'Cash is tight. Tuzza, Ian, Giles, and Kooky have blown theirs, and want to borrow from Sam and me until we get back to England. They reckon because we've got jobs, we can afford it. But we need our money because we plan to go to Germany after finishing here.'

184

'I know what you mean. Grannies aren't paying me much, so I can't lend them any either. What about Siv?'

He fidgeted in his seat. 'He doesn't want to, as he planned to stay on until the start of the football season in August. I think he may change his mind though. Annette, the girl he met here, is flying back on Friday morning and Siv is thinking of returning early to be with her. She only lives six miles away from Bletchingley, in Hurst Green.'

'Where will you two stay when they leave?'

His face brightened. 'We've sorted that out. Jim's worried about security on the building site and asked us to live in one of the part-finished apartments. It means we won't be in Es Cana, but there's plenty to do in Santa Eulalia. We'll never be late for work either.'

I laughed. 'That's true. You must come and visit me in Grannies when you can though.'

'Yes, we'll make sure we do, mate.'

We re-joined the lads. Siv had decided to go back on Saturday and lend the others enough money to see them through until then. The partying resumed. There were smiles and laughter once again as they bought round after round of beer.

I had two drinks with them before moving on. The five who were leaving promised to come and visit me in Grannies on their last night. I stressed again they should tidy up the place before leaving. It was agreed with Tich that they would leave the keys to the apartment with him on Saturday, and he would give them to Pablo.

As I departed, Tich handed me two letters, both in the same handwriting.

42

Letters from Alice

I sat on the bed in my room and opened the letters. They were both from Alice.

Dear Fred,

Today is Sunday, and I have been home for five hours. I am sitting in the garden listening to the charts and the weather is glorious.

On the coach to the airport, Jane was sobbing the whole way. She broke my heart. I've never seen her so upset. Paco said he'll ring her up in a week. You should know whether he will as I saw you both walk into the Caribe bar and he must have spoken to you about Jane. It was a good idea you didn't come to the airport as it was awful. I don't believe I've ever been so unhappy all my life. On the bus, everyone was miserable and tired. We did not sing one song, not even any clean ones.

Liz didn't say a word on the way back either and she looked as sad as everyone else. Talking of Liz, can you give her my fondest regards and tell her Jane and I will send her a postcard from Jesolo, Italy in August.

Anyway, with the trivialities aside, how are you? Still smoking and drinking too much I suppose. If you come home and your eyes are bloodshot, I will be cross. If I told you I have just cried yet again, you'll think I'm stupid, but it's true. It must be the thought of your bloodshot eyes. Sitting here in my garden in England it doesn't register you are so many hundreds of miles away.

How is the job hunting going? I suppose you'll go to El Cortijo tonight. Have a nice time. I almost forgot, did your friends arrive OK and meet you in the Red Lion? Did you have your straw house, sorry, bag with you? I bet you had a few comments made about that.

Could I ask you for a favour? Would you send me a photograph of yourself? I'd prefer if it was one of you looking sober and not in drag. I don't mind if it's of you dressed as a girl. It's just that if I show it to anyone, they'll either think I am a lesbian or you are a transvestite.

I had better go now as I must have my tea.

One other thing. Please for my sake will you eat more and drink less.

See you soon.

Love and Best Wishes,

Alice

The next one was dated two days later.

Dear Fred,

Today is Tuesday, and I have been at home most of the day. No, I'm not fed up with work, it's my day off as I work on Saturdays. It's just one drawback of working in a shop.

This afternoon I had a driving lesson and practised the dreaded 3-point turn. I hit the kerb this time instead of going up on it, so I must be getting better.

I am sitting in the garden again. The weather here is still beautiful. What is it like in Ibiza or need I ask?

I hope your gang of friends are enjoying themselves. I can't expect you to cut back on the drinking while they are with you, can I? Just you wait until you return to England, I will sort you out. As I said before, you need someone to mother you and I'll have a good try. If you don't mind that is.

Jane rang yesterday. She is still very low and waiting for Paco to telephone.

Friends have invited me to three parties since I've been back, but I'm not in the mood. I realise that's silly because I only sit around at home moping and feeling sorry for myself. So, I might go to one, I don't know yet.

Any luck with the job hunting? Or maybe you are not bothering much, with your mates there.

Don't forget to send that photograph, will you? I've told my friends about you and they are dying to see what you look like. I hope you don't mind. If you do just tell me. I know you would anyway. Because as I discovered you are not as quiet and innocent as first impressions lead one to believe.

I'd better go now.

See you soon.

Love and Best Wishes,

Alice

After reading the letters three times I lay back and fantasised over Alice. Of the girls I had been with in Ibiza, I missed her the most. With thoughts of her racing through my mind, I fell into a restless sleep. My dreams were full of her and me together.

* * *

I woke bright and early on Thursday morning and looked forward to another week of work at Grannies.

The mornings when I worked alone getting the bar ready were the most challenging, but I soon settled into a routine and got everything finished by opening time.

Mick arrived just after 11 am and was with me for the lunchtime session.

He had some news. 'Did you hear they've devalued the peseta?'

I shook my head.

The flicker of a smile passed his lips. 'It's been all over the Spanish papers and on the radio. The government announced on Monday they were devaluing to curb inflation and boost exports. The rate for the pound has gone up from 120 to 150, an increase of 25%.'

'Fantastic news, Mick. My money should stretch further now.'

'Yes, I'm not sure how it will affect inflation though. It's running at 30% and we'll have to raise our prices again soon because of increased costs. Wages will also go up, although I don't think there'll be much impact until later in the year.'

The first customers of the day came through the door and we cut our conversation short.

* * *

A week later, an American tourist, Kevin from Rochester NY, showed me two articles in *The New York Times* from Tuesday 12th and Sunday 17th July.

The first was headlined "Spain Devalues Peseta by 24.9% To Curb Inflation" and gave the reasons behind the government's reasons for the devaluation.

Full Article: https://www.nytimes.com/1977/07/13/archives/spain-devalues-peseta-by-249-to-curb-inflation-selling-hits-dollar.html

The second had the headline "The Peseta Is Devalued" and concentrated on the benefits to American tourists and further analysis of the reasoning behind the move.

Full Article: https://www.nytimes.com/1977/07/17/archives/the-peseta-is-devalued.html

43

Friday night in Grannies

Friday nights were always manic.

Eager drinkers packed the outside terrace after a day in the sun. A queue of customers had already formed as I dived behind the bar to start my shift.

Mick, Pat, Graham and I worked together. Pat was half-cut and spent most of the time with her friends, as Mick's mood darkened. Despite that, the three of us got stuck in and served the thirsty punters.

We could drink behind the bar, provided we were sober enough to serve. Pat loved her gin and tonics and sometimes wasn't. Mick, Graham and I had regular supplies of vodka and orange but remained level-headed as we rushed around.

I expected to see the lads, as it was the last night for most of them. They didn't disappoint me. The five who were leaving: Siv, Tuzza, Ian, Giles, and Kooky, rolled in an hour after I started. They had spent the day in the Red Lion.

Mick gave them a wary glance as they staggered through the door. He pulled me to one side. 'I realise they're your mates, but they've gained quite a reputation over the past two weeks. Can you make sure they behave themselves? I'll throw them out if they become disruptive.'

'OK, I understand, Mick. I'll have a word with them.'

I ushered them into the far corner. Siv was the most receptive, so I told him what Mick had said. He assured me there would be no trouble. I poured a round of beers and put them on my tab, then handed the drinks to the lads, smiling. 'Here you go, guys. It's been great seeing you again. Trust you've had a good time. Say hi to everyone in Bletchingley for me when you get back.'

They clinked glasses.

Tuzza slurred, 'Cheers, Fred. Thanks for looking after us. Hope the rest of your season goes well. Send a postcard won't you.'

'Yes, have a safe journey home. Give me a shout before you leave tonight.'

The five of them stared at me with glazed eyes and raised their drinks in acknowledgement.

Back behind the bar, I spotted Mutts and Sam as they came down the steps. They looked shattered after a hard week's work. I beckoned them over and tipped them off about Mick's warning. They told me they would keep an eye on the others. I bought them a beer, and they headed over to join the rest.

To add to the chaos, Liz and twenty of her 18-30 crowd arrived several minutes later. Once we finished serving them, Liz slumped on a stool at the bar.

I walked over for a chat. 'Hi, Liz. Are you OK? You look wiped out.'

She gave me a weak grin. 'Hi, Fred. Good to see you've found another job. You're right, I'm exhausted. This season has been my toughest yet. I just want to pack it in and go back to England for a rest.'

'They expect too much of you. I'm not sure how you manage it. You need to take care of yourself and do what's best for you.'

'I know. The money makes it worthwhile, but it's no fun anymore. Still, things will get quieter soon.'

After a pause, I asked, 'Did you find time to phone Helen?'

'No, sorry, I've been so busy I'd forgotten. I'll give her a ring this weekend.'

'Don't worry, there's still time. I wrote to her but didn't mention our conversation. If you could talk to her that would be fantastic. I'm worried if she came back, I'd disappoint her.'

'OK, Fred. I'll sort it out. After all, it was me who asked you the original favour.'

With a deep sigh, she got up from her stool. 'I'd better make sure my crowd are behaving themselves. We were on a boat trip this afternoon and there was a lot of drinking.'

Although the place appeared busy, there wasn't much action behind the bar. Mick poured vodka and oranges for the three of us. We had a short break and a laugh at the expense of several customers.

We were low on glasses, so I collected empties, weaving through the crowds on the tables along the terrace and in the entertainments room.

The lads mingled with the 18-30s and played table football. There was a lot of noise, but everyone behaved themselves.

191

After several collection runs, I returned to the sink and washed the glasses, then left them on the drainer before rushing to take an order from the nearest group at the bar. It stayed that way for the next two hours and the three of us didn't stop. Even Pat joined in to help for a while after her friends departed.

Familiar faces came and went: Alan and John for a quick drink before opening El Cortijo, Tony and Sue on an evening out, Ray and Gordon after closing Tootsies for the day. They gave each other a quizzical glance when they saw me working. I ignored them and let Mick serve their drinks.

After midnight, customers drifted off, either to return to their hotels or dance the night away. The lads and most of the 18-30 crowd had left. A hard core of drinkers remained. Most of them were on the terrace as it was cooler there. Others sat on the stools along the bar.

Graham collected more glasses, stacking them inside each other until they formed a long column which arched over his right shoulder. Once he could no longer add any more by stretching up with his left hand, he returned to the sink and unloaded. Mick had asked him several times not to do this as it could be dangerous, but Graham insisted it was OK. Besides, he claimed, it was entertaining for people to watch.

I was washing glasses when I heard a loud crack and the sound of breaking glass. Graham had stacked the column so high it caught the top of the door frame as he ducked under it. A glass in the middle broke from the force. The rest shattered as they fell to the floor and across a table that a group of tourists had vacated five minutes earlier. It could have been disastrous.

Mick rushed out and shouted obscenities at Graham. I followed him with a dustpan and brush. The three of us cleared up the piles of disintegrated glass and placated customers nearby. Silence had descended over the bar as everyone turned around to find the cause of the commotion.

Conversation resumed to its normal level as punters returned to their drinks.

Graham never collected glasses that way again.

By 1:30 am things had quietened, and Mick suggested we close at 2 am. He spoke too soon. An influx of newbies came in with Bill, the Cosmos rep. They were a group of thirty lads and lasses from Manchester. Bad weather in England delayed their plane, and they had only just arrived.

Their thirst seemed unquenchable, and they bought round after round to make up for lost time. It always took a while for new arrivals from Britain to get used to the pace of drinking abroad. It was normal for them to rush their drinks for closing time at 10:30 pm (weekdays) or 11 pm (Friday and Saturday). The strength of the spirits also caught people by surprise as they were unused to the larger measures served in Spain.

By 3 am everybody had their fill. Bill led his group away to take them for the last hour at El Cortijo. We ushered the few remaining diehards out of the door and cleared up most of the glasses.

As Mick locked up, Graham suggested we go for a drink at Cortijo's. I agreed although Mick and Pat were ready for bed.

A bright half-moon lit our way as we walked across the wasteland. A tangible warmth hung in the air and a familiar, unpleasant smell hit my nostrils. It was a pong I recognised from the year before but had only noticed again in the last couple of weeks.

Graham saw my nose twitch. 'It stinks, doesn't it? Do you know why?'

I shook my head.

He gave me a grin. 'It's only in recent years Es Cana has become commercialised. Older properties still have cesspits in their back gardens. They get more pungent as the weather gets hotter and reach their peak of smelliness in July and August.'

'Makes sense. I wondered what it was. I suppose they'll have to upgrade the sewerage as this place develops. It's not very pleasant for tourists is it?'

'It's a big problem and will cost loads of money to fix. They often discuss it, but like many things in Spain, it always gets put off. It's the *mañana* attitude.'

We stayed at Cortijo's for an hour and drank three beers each before they closed. It was after 4 am when I collapsed on my bed. I'd be up again in less than four hours.

Days and nights flashed past this way, but I enjoyed every moment working in Grannies.

The slimming tablets helped combat my tiredness, and I survived on minimal sleep.

44

Welcome day off

I woke at the normal time of 8 am the next Wednesday and was about to get out of bed.

It had been a late night. I was on the beach talking to a girl called Lesley from Liverpool until it started getting light. We met at the weekend and got on well. She was with Bill's Cosmos crowd and was leaving at 7 am. We had enjoyed each other's company and our relationship was platonic. That made a refreshing change.

Upon realising it was my day off, I turned over and fell asleep.

When I woke up again, the early afternoon sun streamed through the windows and I was covered in sweat.

The long snooze should have refreshed me, but I was knackered. A cooling bath made me feel better. The two pills I had taken when I got up kicked in and my energy returned. I walked upstairs to Tony's and had a mug of tea and an omelette.

After a stroll along the seafront, I sat for a while soaking up the hot sun. My mood was buoyant. I thought about how lucky I was being there rather than behind a desk in London.

I assumed the lads had left on Saturday as planned. Mutts and Sam had moved to the building site, so I couldn't check with them. The only person who knew was Tich, as they had given him the apartment keys.

The Red Lion was busy as tourists dropped in for a drink after a day on the beach. Tich was on his own behind the bar. He waved across as I walked in and handed me a San Miguel before serving other customers. I sat on a stool and read a copy of the *News of the World* from the previous Sunday. When it quietened down, he came over with two San Miguels, one for him and one for me.

We clicked bottles, and he grimaced. 'Sorry to be the bearer of bad news, Fred. When the lads left on Saturday, Siv only gave me one key to the apartment. They lost the other. Pablo was fuming when I handed it to him later in the day.'

He paused and looked me in the eyes. 'It got even worse. He returned that evening in a foul mood.'

My eyebrows shot up as Tich continued, 'Pablo told me he found the room in a disgusting mess. One sunbed was in pieces, there were cigarette burns on the bedding and furniture, and rubbish everywhere. A tap in the bathroom was broken, and he's had to have the lock changed. It took four hours to clean the place and repair the damage.'

'Oh shit, I'm so sorry Tich. They promised me everything would be tidy by the time they left.'

He placed a hand on my shoulder. 'It's not your fault, but Pablo was after your blood, although he had calmed down when I saw him yesterday. You won't get your deposit back and he wants you to pay another 4000 pesetas to cover the damage and replacement lock.'

I gave him a rueful grin. 'Thanks, Tich. I'll try to get the deposit money off the lads when I return to England. Looks like I'd better avoid Pablo if I can though. Did Mutts and Sam say anything?'

'No, I haven't seen either of them. How's your job at Grannies going?'

'It's long hours and hard graft, but I'm enjoying it. We make a good team.'

'Great news. I thought you'd fit in well there. It's not perfect, but the working atmosphere is much more relaxed than at Tootsies. Robbie often comes here after work and says he regrets going back.'

My brow creased. 'I'm sorry to hear that. It was awkward when he returned, but I don't hold it against him.'

'I know he felt guilty. He wants to have a chat with you and should be in this evening.'

'Cheers, mate. I'll stay for a while. Is there any post?'

'No, sorry, but it can be erratic at this time of year. Anyway, I must get on and stock up before Roger and Margaret arrive. Do you want another San Miguel?'

I glanced at the empty bottle in front of me. 'Yes, please.'

I sipped on the beer and went back to reading the newspaper.

* * *

Robbie came in half an hour later and I beckoned him to join me. He ran a hand through his short black curly hair. His dark brown eyes gleamed as he approached.

I grinned as he perched on the barstool next to me. 'Do you want a drink? You look like you need it.'

He gave an enthusiastic nod and replied in his lilting Scottish accent, 'Please, Fred. Whisky and Coke?'

Roger came over and I ordered Robbie's drink plus vodka and orange for myself. There was an awkward silence as we waited for the drinks to arrive. Then we clinked glasses.

Robbie gave me an uncertain glance. 'I'm sorry you had to leave Tootsies the way you did.'

'Don't worry, it worked out for the best. I wasn't coping and didn't enjoy the job. Grannies is the complete opposite and I love working there.'

'That's good to know. I left at the end of last season determined not to return. But life at home was boring. I had a job in a factory, the weather was crap, and I remembered the good times I'd had here. So, I came back on the off chance I'd find work. I didn't expect it to be at Tootsies again.'

I tilted my head. 'How's it going?'

'I'd forgotten why I left. Ray and Gordon haven't changed. They're still the bullies they always were. They make me want to walk out again sometimes, but I'll try to stay until the end of the season. The money's good.'

'Yes, I'd agree with you. I get half that at Grannies, but then again money's not everything.'

Robbie chuckled. 'True, although it helps. Do you want another?'

I nodded.

He downed his whisky and ordered a round.

We talked for a long time about our upbringings. He had a tough life growing up in Glasgow and told some fascinating stories. I explained to him my Exclusive Brethren background and how I had left the bank to come to Ibiza. As the alcohol flowed, any inhibitions between us disappeared.

By our fifth drink, we had moved on to the future and what we planned to do after the season ended.

Robbie said, 'I hope to go to Hamburg in Germany. I met four English lads last week. They were here on a break from a building contract there. There's plenty of construction work in the city and not enough German workers. British people are in demand and the pay is cash in hand. They need bricklayers, carpenters, plasterers and labourers.'

'Sounds good. It'll be freezing after here though, won't it?'

He threw his head back and laughed. 'I'm from Scotland don't forget. I'm hardened to the cold. I did an apprenticeship as a bricklayer, so I'm used to being outside. What do you think you'll do?'

My eyebrows furrowed as I deliberated. 'I'm not sure yet. One thing is for certain. Although I may go home, I won't return to working in the bank. If I can get shift work in a factory, I'll do that for a few months and save enough cash before I set off.'

Robbie flashed me a grin. 'Will you come here again?'

'I could do, but it's been much tougher than I thought. Otherwise, I might hitch-hike around Europe for two or three months and end up here for the last part of the season. It depends on me earning enough money during the winter though.'

'Sounds like an excellent plan, Fred. I've always wanted to hitch around Europe. Maybe we could team up in April or May.'

I looked into his glazed eyes. 'Yes, great idea. We must keep in touch.'

It was after midnight. I finished my drink and stood up. 'Robbie, I'll make a move. I need to sleep.'

'Me too. I didn't realise the time.'

After an enthusiastic shake of hands, we shouted our goodbyes to Roger and Margaret and staggered out.

45

More letters from Alice

By my third week in Grannies I was back in a work routine, but a very different one from commuting to London every weekday.

Instead of a suit, I was in shorts, a t-shirt and flip-flops. Rather than an hour-long journey on the train and a walk over London Bridge into the city, the daily commute was a five-minute stroll from my room. When I was in the bank, I wished my days away and clock watched. Although I worked long days in Grannies, the time flew.

My day started at 8 am, after limited sleep. I got washed and dressed, had a quick breakfast and a chat with Sue in Tony's, before taking the short walk across the wasteland to the back of Grannies. Often, I arrived earlier than 9 am.

The first two hours before opening were always busy: clearing and washing glasses, sorting empty bottles, mopping the floor, stocking up, and my least favourite job – cleaning the toilets. We also sold t-shirts, so I had to make sure there was a good supply of the different sizes behind the bar from the stock kept in the storeroom.

At 11 am Mick, Pat or Graham joined me. They worked the lunchtime shift and then stayed on in the afternoon to work with Eduardo. On my Wednesdays off Mick came in early to do the cleaning. Even when they were not working in the bar, the others were busy shopping or organising bar-related business.

In the afternoons I tried to relax, either by having a siesta in my room or sunbathing at the pool or on the beach. Other times I met up with girls I had chatted up while working and spent time with them.

Evenings began again at 8 pm. We worked through until the early hours. It was the height of the season and we were rushed off our feet, but I enjoyed both the work and the socialising. The nights often ended up at El Cortijo.

Then at 8 am, it all started again.

* * *

On Wednesday I stayed in bed until midday. Margaret was working in the Red Lion when I arrived there mid-afternoon. We had a quick chat, and she handed me two letters, both from Alice. I took my bottle of San Miguel and sat at a table in the alley to read them.

Dear Fred,

I received your postcard today from the Monday after I left, which was ten days ago. It cheered me up as I thought you'd forgotten me. How are you anyway? Looking after yourself, I hope. I'm sorry you've still not found a job. How much longer do you think your money will last?

From the sound of it, your friends are proving to be quite a handful. I can't tell you off if you've been getting drunk with them, because I am ashamed to admit that last night, I got drunk.

I'd better explain. My friend Karen was 18 on Wednesday and to celebrate she held a party. I didn't go intending to get drunk, but Karen insisted. One drink seemed to lead to another until I was absolutely stoned. We left at 10:30 pm, rather different from Ibiza when I'd just be going out.

Two boys have asked me for a date, but I'm not interested. As I told you I regard them only as friends. But I will make an exception in your case. You know that don't you? Have you met any nice girls since I left? I suppose you must have. Are your friends going out with any girls? I expect you still go to the El Cortijo to round off the evening. It's strange but I miss that place. My favourite disco here has closed for redecoration.

At the moment I am watching Top of the Pops. Punk rock has taken over here. A group called the Sex Pistols are on and I've never seen anything like them in my life. Their speciality is being as coarse, vulgar, and obscene as they can. Their publicity stunts range from smashing up the hotels they stay in, to being sick over newspaper reporters and on stage whilst performing. If I were you, I'd stay in Ibiza because you are not missing much here.

Anyway, to contradict myself, when are you coming home to see me? Or shall I come back out to Ibiza? Don't tempt me, please.

In case you are interested, Paco did not telephone Jane as he promised. She is disappointed and unhappy. I hate him for what he has done to her. I've never seen her this way before. She has written to him, but I'm not sure he'll reply.

You may have gathered I've been suffering from the most diabolical hangover today. I don't know about me looking after you when you come home, you'll need to take care of me.

I'll go now because I want an early night.

Love and Best Wishes,

Alice

Dear Fred,

I received your second postcard today. It surprised me as I didn't expect to hear from you for a few weeks. Still, it was a very nice surprise.

I was glad you have a job, especially in Grannies as I liked it there. Do you work there in the evenings or the day as well? I presume this will enable you to stay in Ibiza until the end of the season. Did you get the job because someone left or because it's getting busier? Anyway, I hope you realise how lucky you are.

Are your mates enjoying themselves, although they must have gone home by now unless any of them stayed? If they did, I am sure neither you nor I would blame them. Jane and I both long to go back, but at least we have our other holiday soon.

When you next write will you make it a letter, please? Then you can keep me informed on the latest scandal without squeezing it on to a postcard. This time I had to use a magnifying glass. Your writing is terrible. Sorry, it's nice but I am long-sighted, and so is my mum. Even she has difficulty reading it.

The weather here is awful. It has been miserable and rainy every day. In fact, it's pouring with rain now. Don't tell me it's 100°F in Ibiza, in the shade. You must stop sunbathing because when you get home, I'll look anaemic standing next to you. I expect when you return your hair will be down to your waist.

I hope you've washed your hair since I left. I had mine cut last week, and it's shorter than I wanted. The man who did it talked me into having three inches off. By the time you come home, it will have grown, as I don't want to go out with someone with longer hair than me. Although I don't care if your hair is down to your ankles, provided you return in one piece and without bloodshot eyes.

I've noticed every sentence is about when you come home. I really do look forward to seeing you again. I hope the feeling is mutual.

Have you been out with any girls since I left? Do you think I'm nosey asking that? I don't intend to be, but I like to know what you are doing.

It is so frustrating only being able to write letters. I long to sit down and talk with you. Writing a letter isn't the same somehow.

Tomorrow is my day off as I must work on Saturday. Shall I pop over to Ibiza for the day? I've just remembered I can't as I have a driving lesson. Never mind, perhaps next week.

Jane is still pining away. Is there any news from Paco?

I will go now and look forward to hearing from you.

Lots of Love,

Alice

I read the letters a few times.

It was great to hear from Alice, and I longed to be with her. There was a real bond between us and I looked forward to seeing her again when I got back to England.

There was a spare aerogramme in my straw bag. I spent the next hour writing a proper letter to Alice to tell her how much I missed her, and that I wanted to spend time with her when I got back. I mentioned my haircut, which had happened since I wrote my second postcard. I wondered whether she would approve.

The erratic post Tich talked about had not affected the correspondence between me and Alice. Postcards had arrived with her within a week, and her letters only took a few days to arrive in Ibiza.

Because of that, it surprised me not to have got any post from Mother or Sarah. It was over three weeks since I had received anything.

The end of July was approaching, and I had been in Ibiza for close to four months.

46

Payday arrives

On Friday evening, the 18-30s arrived as normal, but Liz was not with them. Instead, a fresh-faced young man with short fair hair and a moustache accompanied the group.

The crowd were in a sombre mood, a complete contrast to the rowdy rabble we saw every 18-30 night. They spoke in whispered tones as they ordered drinks.

As they shuffled into the back room I glanced towards Mick, Pat and Graham to see if they had noticed something was wrong.

Pat came over. 'There's been some bad news, Fred. I only found out this afternoon and didn't get around to telling you. Mick and Graham know already.'

'What's happened, Pat – is it to do with Liz?'

'Yes, it's Liz. She collapsed in the early hours of yesterday morning in the Caribe's reception. The 18-30 crowd had been on a night out. As usual, there was plenty of partying and drinking. They think she was suffering from exhaustion and had a blackout.'

'Is she OK?'

'They rushed her to the hospital in Ibiza Town and put her on a drip. The news got back to the company's HQ in Peterborough. They flew a manager out yesterday afternoon as the situation was so serious. That's the guy with them this evening, Norman.'

I couldn't take it in.

Pat gave me a quick hug. 'Don't worry too much. Liz will be all right and make a full recovery, but she'll need time. Once she's stable enough, they'll fly her back to England to recuperate. They'll organise a replacement rep for the rest of the season.'

'What terrible news. I feel so sorry for her. She complained about the job and said it was getting too much for her, but this is awful.'

'I know. She often talked of resigning. I didn't realise how serious it was. She always put on such a brave face. It's a warning sign to all of us I suppose.'

We stood in silence for a moment, before Mick's shouts shook us away from our thoughts. It was busy, and they needed help serving customers.

* * *

Monday was August 1st and my first payday at Grannies. I worked the lunchtime shift with Graham, while Mick visited the bank in Santa Eulalia to organise cash for our wages.

He returned at 2:30 pm and went to the storeroom to work out the payments, then asked me to join him on the terrace, away from customers.

A wide smile spread across Mick's face. 'Thanks for your help, Fred. You've fitted in well. I hope you're enjoying the job.'

'Yes, it's great. I feel part of the team now.'

He showed me his calculations on a piece of paper. 'By my reckoning you've worked 22 days. At a rate of 600 a day, it comes to 13,200. If it's OK with you, I'll deduct your tab from that.'

I nodded in agreement and he continued, 'Although you get free drinks while you are working, there was an outstanding amount from before you started. You've also bought a lot of drinks for other people whilst behind the bar. Your total bill is 3620, so I can only give you 9580.'

He counted out the cash, and I slipped it into my money-belt. As I stood, Mick shook my hand and asked me to send Graham across.

Eduardo arrived just after 3 pm, and I handed over to him. He stood at the other end of the bar to Graham. There was, as always, a tense atmosphere between them. Mick left to go to the Cash and Carry and pick up more supplies.

I had two more tabs to settle, one at the Red Lion, and the other at Tony's.

Margaret was working in the Red Lion. She gave me a sweet smile. 'Hiya, Fred. How's it going?'

'It's going well, thanks. What about you?'

Her light green eyes twinkled. 'It's been very busy and we're having our best season yet. I hear you've settled into work at Grannies. Everyone says how well you are doing there.'

I averted my eyes in embarrassment. 'It's hard work, but I'm enjoying it. I've just got paid, so I'd better settle my tab.'

Margaret reached deep into the fridge and retrieved a bottle of beer, then leafed through the book to find out what I owed. 'It comes to 2780.'

She then surprised me by handing over two pieces of post. One was a postcard from Lesley, my platonic friend from Liverpool, that had arrived within five days. The other was a letter from Helen. It had taken longer.

I thanked Margaret and walked outside to my favourite table in the sunny corner of the alley. As I sipped on my beer, I read the card from Lesley.

Dear Fred,

I received your postcard today. I'm glad you're doing so well, keep it up (the work). You know you are always welcome to come to our house when you're in Liverpool.

I'm going to a wedding on Saturday, so I hope the weather keeps fine. It's been terrible ever since we came home. I wish I was back there in Ibiza. I don't half miss it and everyone.

Now you're earning, you can write a letter and not a postcard, thank you very much. When you come home in October, would you do me a favour? Bring a few packs of Lola cigs, and a Grannies t-shirt size 34 bust (you know what size I am now). I'll pay you for them because they are not cheap.

Oh, yea, could you get Bill's second name and address and I'll give his mum a message for him? Hey, I've just thought, Bill comes home in October too, so when you come to Liverpool the three of us can go out for a bevvy.

Look after yourself and write when you've got spare time, but don't forget will you?

Tara for now.

Lots of love,

Lesley

I opened the letter from Helen with trepidation.

Dear Fred.

Thanks for your postcard. It took 15 days to get here. You should have got my letter by now.

Liz told me you'd got a job (I said you would). That's great news.

I hope you don't mind me staying with you when I come out. You said I could when I was there, but I don't think you expected me to come out again this year. The money I've saved will last me for about six weeks. I've been doing evening work behind a bar to earn the extra cash.

The photos I took came out well, so I'll bring them with me. During a day off yesterday, I got a train to London to get my ticket. I'm leaving on Friday 5th August at 10:30 am so I should arrive at Ibiza airport at 1:15 pm (your time). I don't know how long it takes from the airport to Es Cana, so I'm not sure what time I'll get there.

Did your mates enjoy themselves when they were over?

Anyway, I must work now as I'm on my own today.

See you soon.

Lots of love,

Helen

P.S. I hope you <u>really</u> don't mind me staying with you and that it will not inconvenience you too much.

I sat in stunned silence. I read it again. It hadn't changed. Thoughts raced through my head. Had Liz phoned Helen? What would happen if she came? There was no way we could share my room. Why had I even suggested it?

　After ordering another beer I pondered my options.

* * *

Before working the evening shift, I stopped off at Tony's and had a meal of sausage, egg and chips. Tony handed me my bill for July, which came to 6015, half of it rent and the other half meals, drinks and laundry.

　I gave him the cash and realised my wages had all but evaporated. I had less than 1000 pesetas left from the money I had received only hours earlier. There was another 5000 in my money-belt, but that wasn't enough for the month. I'd have to change more travellers' cheques.

47

Funky moped

Helen dominated my thoughts.

I worried about what might happen if she arrived on Friday.

Pat worked with me on Tuesday lunchtime, so I checked with her about Liz. I thought of visiting her in hospital on my day off, to see how she was and whether she had spoken to Helen. It was too late. Pat told me they had already flown Liz back to England for further treatment and recuperation.

I needed to clear my mind.

On Wednesday, I hired a moped to tour different parts of the island. Although I owned a driving licence, I had never ridden one but figured it would be straightforward enough.

The hire shop was in the same street as Grannies and I arrived there at 9 am, keen to make the most of the day. They showed me a Honda Camino PA50. It looked almost brand new with white and yellow paintwork. The assistant explained it had a 49 cc two-stroke engine with automatic transmission. It could reach speeds of 48 kph (30 mph). As a deposit, I left my driving licence and 1500 pesetas. The cost of the hire was 75 an hour plus petrol and insurance, and I had to return it by 8 pm when they closed.

Out on the street, he showed me how it worked. With the moped on its stand, he inserted the key and turned on the ignition. He then rotated the pedals with his feet. It sprang into action. With the engine running, the stand flipped up as he moved the bike forward. They hadn't given me a helmet, and I only wore a t-shirt, shorts and flip-flops. I stowed sun cream, a towel, a map and a bottle of orange drink in a pannier on the side of the moped.

I weaved an unsteady path along the road to the east of Es Cana, but it wasn't long before I felt comfortable in the saddle. The rhythm of the bike was soothing as it jolted along the coast to Cala Nova and then La Joya to the north-east.

After a while, I turned inland and took the route to San Carlos. The sun beat down as it rose higher in the sky. I stopped by the side of the road and applied sun cream. I had a quick drink and started the bike again. There was thick forest to the left and olive groves to the right, which backed on to more forest. After a small settlement called Can Salvado, the views broadened, with lush green fields and whitewashed stone buildings either side. There was little traffic and before I knew it, I arrived in the village.

I came to a roundabout with roads leading off in three different directions. I stopped and looked at my map. The road to the left led back to Santa Eulalia, 6 km to the south-west. The one to the right went to the coastal resort of Figueral, 4 km away. I recognised the name as it was near to Agua Blanca. Instead, as it was still early, I headed straight ahead for the north-west coast of the island. On the map, I had spotted a place called Na Xamena, near to Port de Sant Miguel. The name sparked my interest. It was a ride of about 25 km.

As I passed through the village of San Carlos, groups of old men sat around at cafés playing games. They glanced up for a moment. There were women in traditional dress, black dresses with shawls and colourful headscarves, which helped reflect the heat of the sun to keep them cool.

The countryside passed by and I took in the sights as the moped sauntered along at a steady speed. Dusty paths ran through scrubland. Olive groves appeared on both sides of the narrow lane. Glimpses of white *fincas* and farm buildings were visible through the trees. Waist-high stone walls lined parts of the roadside. Pine-covered hills rose in the distance.

My mind cleared, and a weight lifted as I steered along the bumpy road. A warm breeze brushed against my face and through my short hair. The words of a chorus sprang to mind, and I sang it out loud. It was from the Jasper Carrot hit, *Funky Moped*.

The route skirted around the edge of wooded hillsides. Through openings in the trees, I saw several expensive new villas built for the rich and famous. There was more traffic along that stretch and the wind from passing lorries wobbled the bike. I struggled to keep upright as they roared past.

I crossed the main road between Ibiza Town in the south-west and Portinatx on the north coast. The track I joined was quieter but narrower and stonier. The moped skidded several times on the uneven surface, but I stayed in the saddle. Along the way, the countryside became more barren. I saw a typical Ibizan windmill, with its hexagonal spoked wheel atop a square stone building.

At a T-junction, I turned left on to a better-surfaced road. I passed through San Miguel and knew I was nearing my destination. From there, I headed north. Within a quarter of an hour, I looked out over a white sandy beach, in a small sheltered inlet. Steep cliffs rose on either side, topped with pine woodland and shrubs. This was Port de Sant Miguel, in times gone by a sleepy fishing village.

It was after midday and the sun was at its hottest. I located a *taberna* near the beach, parked up, and found a quiet spot to sit. Although I had only been on the moped for three hours, a wave of tiredness swept over me as I relaxed. I ordered a *carajillo* (coffee with brandy), *agua* (water) and a *bocadillo de jamon* (ham roll).

An hour or so later I resumed my tour and headed south out of Port de Sant Miguel, taking a narrow track that climbed towards Na Xamena.

I had to pedal on some uphill stretches to keep the momentum of the moped going. They had carved the roadway out of the side of a hill. The left-hand side comprised a wall of rock and compacted mud. Trees lined the route and provided welcome shade. Three-quarters of the way up, there were white stone entrance walls on either side of the road, with Na Xamena painted in large black letters.

As I reached the top, the views were spectacular. The turquoise waters of the Mediterranean stretched out in front of me from the high vantage point. I left the moped for a few minutes and walked to the edge of the clifftop. A wave of joy swept over me as I gazed along the pristine wooded coastline and appreciated its raw beauty.

On the way back down, I saw a sign to the Hacienda Na Xamena. Hidden behind trees, I discovered it was a large complex of upmarket holiday apartment rooms perched on an exclusive area of the clifftop. (Ten years later, it would become the only 5-star hotel in Ibiza and would hold that distinction for two decades.)

It was 4 pm and time to return. I retraced my route until I got to the main Portinatx road and joined the stream of traffic towards the turning for Santa Eulalia and then back home. There were hold-ups behind tractors and horse-drawn carts. The journey took an hour and a half, and my legs shook as I parked up and dismounted. It had been a long day, but accident-free. My outing achieved the purpose of clearing my mind and I loved the experience. They charged me for 9 hours, plus 275 pesetas for petrol and insurance, so I paid 950 in total. It was great value for a wonderful day out.

My gait was unsteady, my backside sore, and my throat parched. I stopped off at Grannies and downed three refreshing beers in a short space of time, as I leant against the bar and told Pat about my adventure. Then I returned to my room and had a bath to clean off the grime that covered my body, before heading to the Red Lion on the off chance another letter from Helen had arrived.

48

Anxious wait

There was no post from Helen. Two letters were waiting for me though, one from Janice (the landlord's daughter I had dated) and the other from Mother. There was nothing from Sarah and that concerned me. Had something happened to her?

Dear Fred,

I am glad to hear you are still enjoying yourself and hope the money situation doesn't become too desperate.

I started work on the 18th of this month and am working for a firm of loss adjusters called Toplis and Harding. The office is just the other side of London Bridge, opposite the Monument, so it's easy to get to. It's an interesting job. I have to go to Lloyds, the city document exchange and a variety of other places.

There is a Williams and Glyn's Bank in the same street as the exchange. Is that where you used to work? It's by the Commercial Union building.

I hope life won't be too boring for you over here after having lived it up over there for months. I suppose you'll return a lovely golden-brown colour. It doesn't seem like we'll get any summer here. It has been miserable.

Anyway, I look forward to seeing you again soon.

Lots of love,

Janice

My dear Robert,

Many thanks for your card and details of more work.

You must have thought there was a long gap between letters, but I was uncertain what you would be doing.

Chris and Sarah had their birthdays last week. Sarah was away for a week's holiday. Chris liked your present. She got cacti and indoor plants with the money. Alastair gave her a nice book on cacti, some darts and a Frisbee. Father and I bought her a bracelet.

Father's colleague Dave Adams is in America for a 4-month furlough. This means more responsibility for Father in preparing the radio programme. But he has been training regional representatives. They send in reports which he includes in the programmes, and that is a great help.

Tonight, Ali drove us and Kip to Reigate Hill. We went for a long walk along the top of Colley Hill. It was a lovely evening.

Ali needs as much driving practice as he can. His test is at the end of August. He is also having lessons with a driving school.

We send you all our love.

Mother

P.S. I have included letters from Chris and Ali.

Dear Robert,

Thank you very much for the birthday present. I bought lots of cacti which I've made into a beautiful indoor garden.

Oh yes, please remember to write to Sarah (SOON). And don't be too long coming home.

Love your little sis,

Chris

Dear Fred,

I shall join you in Ibiza on the 17th of August. My plan is to travel overland by minibus to Madrid and from there by public transport and plane.

I finish work at St. Lawrence's on the 31st of August.

One of these paragraphs is untrue. Guess which.

I do not have a place to stay when I go back to university as they have thrown me off campus. I may live in a tent for a while.

My driving test is on the 22nd of August at 9 am, and I've been having a few lessons. I do not expect to pass it the first time.

For Chris's birthday, I gave her a book on cacti and succulent plants, a Frisbee and a set of darts.

The strawberry season has just finished. We had a good crop in the garden.

Love From,

Ali

As always, it was great to get the news from home.

It was a coincidence Janice had landed a job in London near where I worked.

My sister's note was short, but it sounded as if Sarah had not received my most recent letter. Letters to England appeared to be taking longer than those coming to Ibiza.

* * *

After an early night, I woke up sore but refreshed on Thursday.

I threw myself into work and tried to put Helen's imminent arrival to the back of my mind.

At lunchtime, I worked with Graham. In between serving customers I talked to him about my problem and asked for his advice.

His smile vanished. 'Something similar happened the first season I was here. Like you, I only had a small room. I picked up a Scottish girl, Linda, halfway into her two-week holiday. We got on well and I spent my spare time with her. In a moment of weakness, I suggested she stay on and move in with me, never thinking she would. I saw her off and we said our sad farewells. She blew kisses through the window and tears streamed down her face. The coach set off, and I waved her goodbye. Then later in the day, I was working here collecting glasses. I glanced up the steps and saw a girl who looked like Linda coming down them. I realised it was Linda. She dropped her cases, ran over and threw her arms around my neck.'

I gave him a nervous glance. 'Bet you were shocked. Did she stay with you?'

Graham uttered a strangled laugh. 'She did, and it was terrible. We got on each other's nerves trying to share that small space. When I finished work at night, I wanted to sleep. She had other ideas on her mind. Even when I slept it was uncomfortable as we kept waking each other in my single bed. After a week I'd had enough and gave her an ultimatum, either find a room of your own or go home. She left two days later.'

'Thanks, mate. Not sure if that's meant to cheer me up or not.'

Shouts from the far end of the bar broke up our conversation. We rushed to serve the waiting customers.

* * *

I was a bag of nerves at work on Friday lunchtime and kept looking at my watch.

I was convinced Helen would arrive before I finished at 3 pm.

We were busy, and I worked with Mick. He knew of my situation but avoided mentioning it. The weather was hot with no breeze to cool us behind the bar. We took it in turns to go outside for a cigarette. It was cooler there and we collected glasses at the same time.

Eduardo arrived at 3 pm and joined Mick to work the afternoon shift. Helen was still not there, so I sat on the terrace with a beer and waited. As I chain-smoked, my nervous tension increased. I figured her plane was delayed but felt certain she would turn up soon.

I ordered another beer and then a third.

Mick looked concerned. 'Slow down, Fred. You won't be in a fit state to work tonight. Why don't you get yourself something to eat? If Helen arrives, I'll tell her to wait here until you get back.'

I nodded. After finishing my drink, I walked to Tony's where I had an omelette and a mug of tea.

At 5 pm I returned to Grannies and expected to see Helen waiting for me. She was not there.

The realisation dawned on me she might not be coming. I still could not relax.

Mick was serving a group of lads. He glanced over and smiled. 'Looks like you've had a lucky escape. A few people arrived this afternoon, and I checked with them. As far as they knew there were no delays from England today.'

I breathed a sigh of relief. 'Cheers, Mick. I'll have a quick siesta before work this evening. If she arrives in the meantime, could you ask her to go to Tony's?'

He grinned in acknowledgement.

* * *

I was restless and could not sleep.

At 7 pm I had a cold bath and put on fresh clothes. Back at Grannies, Eduardo had finished his shift, and Mick was off on a break. I joined Pat and Graham behind the bar. Another hectic night lay ahead, but I felt calmer.

I kept glancing at the steps, expecting to see Helen coming down them, but she never did.

49

Days fly by

Days and nights melted into one another.

The summer heat had reached a high point and topped 90°F (32°C) in the daytime. It was not much cooler at night.

This led to frayed tempers behind the bar at Grannies. Pat exploded at Mick several times. The mood darkened when that happened. Graham and I steered clear on those occasions. If things got out of hand though, Graham intervened.

The weather affected me too. I became more short-tempered, which was unlike me.

The bar was busy most of the day and night. Eduardo had adjusted to his afternoon sessions and attracted Spanish locals during otherwise quiet times. Pesetas were rolling in and Mick confided they were having their best season yet.

Since our visit to Agua Blanca, Graham had split up with his Spanish girlfriend, Margarita, and was making up for lost time. Girls often chatted us up at the bar. They hung around until we finished work, or we met up later at El Cortijo. This led to several flings and one-night stands.

Sleep became a rare commodity. On occasions, I spent the night with a girl and went straight from her hotel room to work. I tried to catch up with sleep in the afternoons.

The slimming tablets were still helping, but I needed to take more to get the same effect.

By the middle of August, my supply of pesetas had run out and on my day off I borrowed a bike from Grannies and cycled to Santa Eulalia. I changed another £60 and got 8750 pesetas at a rate of 147, less commission. That left me with £120 in travellers' cheques for the rest of the season, and to get back to England. The pay I got from Grannies would cover my month-end bills.

Upon returning to Es Cana in the afternoon, I visited the Red Lion to find letters from my platonic Liverpool friend, Lesley, and another from Alice.

Dear Fred,

Thanks for your letter. I am glad you plan to keep in touch.

I'm made up you're doing well and working again. Tell Bill to drop me a line.

So, you've had your hair cut eh (baldy rapper). I can't wait to see it and have a good laugh.

Remember I told you I was going to Rhyl in North Wales for a week. Well, I've been and I'm back now. I never stopped laughing the whole time I was there. It was great. The weather was brilliant, and we got dead brown again. We were out on the ale and visited clubs every night.

Don't be drinking and eating too much. Buy yourself some new clothes. Make something of yourself.

Write again soon.

Lots of love,

Lesley

Dear Fred,

How are you keeping?

It was Jane's birthday two days ago on Friday.

To celebrate, four of us girls went to Ragamuffins the night before. You must have heard of Ragamuffins. It's a great disco and nightclub in Camberley.

We arrived there dressed up and looking very glamorous, not knowing the embarrassment to follow. We marched in and got no further than the door. The reason being the age limit is 21. The bouncers, both of whom were 6-foot-tall and 6-foot-wide, did not believe we were 21, which none of us are. We are only 18.

So, we stood there holding up the queue for a quarter of an hour arguing. We lost. They said if we didn't have proof, we could not come in. We stormed off in a huff to the pub around the corner, had a drink and calmed down. One of our friends had a car, so we drove to Wokingham to the King of Clubs and spent a boring night there.

The main reason for writing this letter is to ask you a question. Will you still be in Ibiza in September? If so, what would you think if I said I might come back to Es Cana for a week? It won't be a package holiday thing though, because it's too expensive that way. Also, I wouldn't want to stay in a hotel on my own.

I have told Jane I am planning to go. She'd like to come too but does not think she can afford it. So, nothing is definite. There are so many details I am unsure about. I may not even be able to organise a flight, and for all I know, the thought of me coming back might horrify you.

It's all "ifs" and "buts" for now. So, if you could write as soon as you can and tell me what the verdict is. The problem is we are going on holiday again on August 11th, so please let me know before I go, if possible. By the time I return it will be too late to book a flight.

I'll put it this way, if you won't be in Ibiza in September or if the answer is "no" then you needn't bother to hurry and write. If it's "yes" then just drop me a line to say so, or even a telegram.

Whatever happens, I will see you when you get back to England.

I will end on that happy note.

Lots of Love,

Alice

There was also a brief note from Mother. My bank statements for the end of June had arrived and she gave me the state of my finances: deposit account £53.62, and current account £39.01. Father had bought her a second-hand Flymo, and she sent news and love from everyone.

The reminder about my finances was sobering. I hoped the £90 would tide me over until I found work when I returned home.

Alice's letter had taken over three weeks to arrive. She would already have left for her holiday. Even a telegram would not have reached her in time. There was no way Alice and Jane could have stayed with me, but it would have been nice to see them for a week. If the letter had arrived earlier, I might have been able to organise a room.

I would have to write to her and explain.

50

Meeting Angie

The following Saturday, two girls walked into Grannies at 9 pm. You couldn't miss them. Dressed in skimpy dresses with revealing tops, their eyes sparkled through their make-up, and beneath coiffured hair.

Graham and I spotted them at the same time. He got there first and served them rum and Cokes. Sat on stools at the bar, they soon became the centre of attention. All male heads in the vicinity turned in their direction.

It was another busy night, so we couldn't talk with them much, but they took a fancy to us two barmen and flirted throughout the evening. Their names were Angie and Lucy. They came from Essex and had arrived that afternoon for a week's holiday.

Angie was petite with ash blonde hair. Her bright amber eyes followed me up and down the bar as I worked.

Lucy was taller and bustier, with permed brown hair, and light hazel eyes. She focused her attention on Graham.

At 1 am we took a break from work. By then the girls were drunk and could not stop giggling. They had downed more than a bottle of rum between them, not realising the strength of Spanish measures. They were in danger of falling off their stools.

Graham glanced at me and smirked. 'There's not much chance with these two tonight, is there, mate?'

I grinned. 'No, but we'd better make sure they get to their hotel. Did you find out where they're staying?'

'Yes, Lucy said they're at the Panorama. We can't both leave but it's not far. I'll take them if that's OK with you. Let me check with Mick and Pat first.'

Mick and Pat agreed it was for the best.

It took a lot of persuasion to get the girls moving. They tottered and swayed on their high heels as Graham put his arms around their waists and guided them up the steps.

He returned twenty minutes later.

I was collecting glasses and called him over, 'Are you OK, mate? Did you get them back all right?'

He massaged his neck. 'I thought I was strong, but they were a dead weight by the time we got there. A Spanish guy who works at the Panorama, Jose, said he'd look after them.'

* * *

We did not see the girls again until Monday evening. Graham and I were working together alongside Pat. It was much quieter after a busy weekend.

Angie and Lucy had sheepish expressions as they sat at the bar. They wore shorts and t-shirts with less make-up than on Saturday, but they still turned heads.

I gave them a gentle smile. 'Evening ladies. How are you today?'

Angie's soft voice answered, 'Hi, Fred. We're OK now but felt dreadful yesterday. I can't believe how smashed we got. We don't remember much about leaving.'

Graham joined me and grinned at the girls. 'You're both looking better than last time I saw you. Did Jose take care of you after I left?'

Lucy replied with a nervous whisper, 'Thanks for getting us back to the hotel, Graham. Sorry, we must have been in a right state. Yes, Jose made sure we got to our room. The only problem is that he has now assumed the role of being our protector. He seems to have taken a real fancy to Angie and keeps asking her to go out with him.'

Angie averted her gaze. 'Yes, he won't give up, and keeps popping up wherever we are around the hotel.'

I gave her a concerned look. 'That's not good. I hope he gives up soon. Can I get you both a drink?'

They looked at each other, and Lucy smiled. 'I think we'll give the rum a miss. Can we have a beer each, please?'

I nodded and poured two beers.

We clicked our glasses against theirs. '¡Salud!'

By 1 am the bar had emptied, and Pat closed early, so Graham and I hooked up with Lucy and Angie who agreed to our suggestion of going to Cortijo's. We traipsed across the wasteland towards the disco. Graham led the way with Lucy, and they held hands. Angie and I followed behind. I put my arm around her shoulders. She cuddled into me.

John greeted us at the door, 'Good to see you all. There's not much happening tonight. It's always quiet on Mondays.'

We shook his hand and escorted the young ladies inside. The D.J. looked bored. He had moved on to slower music. The few couples on the dance floor were only interested in their partners.

We sat at a table in an alcove and Alan came over to take our order. Graham ordered a San Miguel, I asked for a vodka and orange, while the girls reverted to rum and Coke.

After the second round of drinks, Graham and Lucy moved to the dance floor. Angie and I relaxed into each other and had a long, lingering kiss.

Angie pulled back from our embrace and looked me in the eyes. 'Why don't we find somewhere else?'

I squeezed her hand. 'Sounds like a good idea. Where were you thinking?'

'Let's not go to the Panorama in case Jose's there. It might cause trouble. Can we go back to your room instead?'

I flinched. 'It's in a mess but if you don't mind then yes, let's do that.'

We finished our drinks. Angie interrupted Lucy to let her know where we were going. Graham glanced over and winked at me.

On the way out we said goodnight to Alan and John, who both gave me a knowing smile.

Once back in the room, I tidied up my belongings and was thankful I had the sheets laundered at the weekend. Angie flipped off her shoes and pushed me on to the bed. We lay side by side and kissed. Soon we were both naked. It was a hot night and perspiration covered our bodies as we explored each other. As morning light filtered through the windows, we fell asleep, exhausted, wrapped in one another's arms.

My alarm clock woke us at 8 am.

* * *

Angie was a fun girl to be with and I enjoyed spending time with her.

She often sat at the bar and waited for me until I finished work. Lucy accompanied her when Graham worked.

Graham spent his spare time with Lucy. At night they would go to the Panorama. Angie came to my place after the disco but would return to her hotel for breakfast when I went to work.

We had a day out as a foursome on the Wednesday. The girls wanted to visit the Hippy Market. I had the day off and Graham didn't have to work until 8 pm. He was in the Panorama reception area when I arrived at 10 am. I also got my first sight of Jose behind the reception desk. He was lanky, with short black hair and piercing brown eyes,

Angie and Lucy skipped down the stairs and threw their arms around us. Jose glared. He took an immediate dislike to me when he saw I was with Angie.

He came over and pulled Angie to one side. She resisted, and I told him to leave her alone. If looks could have killed, I would have been dead.

We made a swift exit and walked to Tony's for breakfast. Then we meandered along the dusty road to Punta Arabi. Passing the entrance to Tootsies, I realised I had not been back there since my dismissal. A young lady manned the t-shirt stall. I hoped she was being treated well.

We spent three hours wandering around the Hippy Market. It fascinated the girls, and they picked up a few tourist trinkets along the way. In addition, they paid for caricature drawings of us as couples, which they kept as souvenirs. None of us had cameras, so that was the closest memory they had of their holiday romances.

Afterwards, we decided to go to the Panorama pool. I returned to the room to get my straw bag and waited for the others in the reception area. Jose was still on duty. I felt his eyes boring into the back of my head as I ordered a coffee from the waiter.

We had a fun time swimming, splashing around in the pool, and sunbathing. The four of us got on well and enjoyed each other's company. The clock raced, and the afternoon was over too soon. Graham had to get ready for work. Lucy disappeared with him.

Angie and I had a romantic evening meal on the terrace of the Panorama Restaurant, trying to ignore the idea that Jose was lurking somewhere. We held hands over the table and shared secrets while drinking a jug of sangria after the meal. A slight breeze came off the sea. We watched mesmerised as the sun set and the stars appeared. The rising moon was almost full.

* * *

It was Saturday morning before we knew it, and the minibus to the airport was due at 7:30 am.

The girls had been with me and Graham the whole night. All evening they had sat at the bar in Grannies and we chatted with them when we could. Their alcohol consumption was moderate compared with the previous Saturday. At 2:30 am we had moved on to El Cortijo and Angie held me tight as we slow danced until the disco finished at 4 am. Graham and Lucy returned to the Panorama, while Angie and I walked along the beach. We pulled out a sunbed where we smooched under the full moon. We were in a reflective mood and promised to keep in touch.

Light crept over the horizon. The stars faded. I glanced at my watch. It was 6:15 am.

We rushed back to the Panorama, as Angie still needed to pack. Outside the hotel, we had another kiss and cuddle. Over Angie's shoulder, I saw Jose glaring at us from behind the reception desk. I thought it best not to go in with Angie, so I waited for her outside.

The minibus arrived as Graham appeared carrying the cases. Angie and Lucy looked flustered and upset. Graham told me later that Jose had shouted at Angie when they checked out.

After prolonged farewell hugs, the girls clambered on to the bus. They both waved and blew kisses in our direction as the driver raced away.

After Angie's departure, things deteriorated.

51

Fight night

That evening, as I walked to work, Jose appeared on the opposite side of the road with a group of Spanish lads. Their intentions were obvious as they stared, raised their fists and shouted at me across the street.

I stopped for a moment and considered my options. Then I raised my middle finger at them in defiance. It was foolish but satisfying. This angered them even more and they weaved between cars and dashed towards me.

Before they could catch me, I scampered up the road and escaped down the steps into Grannies. Their taunts rang in my ears as I headed for safety.

Graham, Pat and Mick stared in my direction as I dived behind the bar. There were loud shouts coming from outside. I was red-faced and frightened.

Graham took me to one side. 'Are you OK, mate?'

I gave a nervous laugh. 'Jose and his friends just chased me up the road. If I hadn't been so close to work, they would have caught me.'

'Be careful. You should be all right during the day while he works but take care at night. Make sure you're not on your own.'

'I'll do my best, mate.'

The bar was heaving, so I tried to forget Jose, and threw myself into work.

It was the busiest evening I could remember since starting at Grannies. Rushed off our feet, we had problems keeping up with orders, let alone collecting empty glasses. Two girls who had become regulars that week offered to help. They collected glasses and washed them in return for drinks.

A group of Pat's friends arrived at 1 am and she joined them. They became absorbed in conversation and drank copious amounts of cava, the Spanish sparkling wine.

Soon after, the crowds thinned. Mick, Graham, and I then had time for a drink ourselves. My thirst took over. I downed four vodka and oranges before we closed. By then any worries about Jose were at the back of my mind.

We closed the bar at 3 am. A group of us headed across the wasteland to El Cortijo for another drink and a dance. Graham and Mick accompanied me. Several Spanish lads hung around near the entrance.

The disco pulsed and the dance floor heaved. Lights from the disco ball flashed around writhing bodies as they cavorted to the sounds of Abba, Rod Stewart and Status Quo. We caught John's attention, and he passed us a bottle of San Miguel each.

Graham and Mick met up with the two girls who had helped in Grannies. Pat had gone back to the villa with her friends, so Mick was free for the night. Propped at the bar, I sipped my beer and relaxed after a hard night's work.

By instinct, I spun round to find Jose stood behind me. He glared at me and mouthed something. The music drowned out his words but he beckoned for me to come with him. Even though it was obvious he wanted a fight, I went. By the time I got outside, it was too late. The Spanish lads hanging around by the door were his friends.

My fighting skills were minimal. I had been bullied at school by two lads who pushed me around and sometimes thumped me. They wanted money, but I had none to give them. One time I gave in to their pressure and stole books for them from a sales exhibition held in the school hall. I never thought of fighting back. I didn't know how.

Now I stood on the dusty wasteland twenty yards away from the front entrance of El Cortijo. The full moon cast an eerie light over proceedings. Jose faced me, surrounded by his group of mates. It was a menacing atmosphere and none of my friends even knew I was there.

Jose screamed in broken English as he edged towards me, 'So, you silly man, what you say?'

I stumbled back. *'¿Qué pasa?* What's happening? What have I done wrong?'

I sweated in the heat of the August night and panic engulfed me.

He must have sensed my fear and moved closer.

The corner of his mouth curled upwards into a sneer. 'You took my girlfriend, English scum.'

'No, I didn't. Angie wanted to be with me, you arrogant pig.' I amazed myself with that response. The drink from earlier on gave me a false sense of courage.

My situation was dire and soon became worse.

Jose pushed me and I fell into a thorny bush. As I tried to extract myself, he towered over me. A cocky smirk crossed his face.

Scratches and traces of blood appeared on my arms and legs as I clambered out of the bush to get away from him. As I struggled to my feet, Jose swung his right fist toward my head. I ducked. There was a whoosh of air as he missed.

He turned and aimed another punch at me. This time his fist crunched into my jaw. I reeled backwards. Maybe I should have just gone to ground and admitted defeat. This time I fought back.

Well, *fought* might be too strong a word for it. I stumbled forward and made a dive for his midriff. Jose grabbed me by my shoulders and flung me to the dusty earth.

I spat out a mouthful of dust, before trying to get to my feet. Then I saw the flying shoes of Jose and his mates as they kicked me, connecting with my head, face and body. It became obvious they wanted to give me a severe beating.

In defence, I rolled into as tight a ball as possible, with my hands wrapped around my head. The kicks and punches continued, and my senses faded as a protection against the pain.

Then it stopped. Shouts came from the front door of Cortijo's. John, Alan, and two others screamed at the top of their voices to get them away from me. The Spanish lads scattered.

A German girl on her way to the disco had seen the scuffle and dived in to get help.

Worried faces peered at me as I uncurled myself. Although bruised and battered, there were no broken bones. I hauled myself to my feet. With support from my rescuers, I struggled back inside and collapsed in a chair near the bar.

There was a mirror on one of the nearby pillars and I saw my reflection. I looked a right mess: t-shirt and shorts covered in dirt, arms and legs scratched and discoloured, a nasty swollen jaw, bruises across my face, and blood matted in my hair.

John fetched me a large glass of neat brandy, which I sipped with gratitude. It helped calm the violent shaking that had overtaken my body.

Alan fetched the first-aid box. His Swedish girlfriend, Sonja, started the unenviable task of cleaning up my wounds.

She had a bowl of warm water and used swabs to clean off excess blood. That was soothing, but I cried out in pain as she pressed cotton wool soaked in antiseptic spirit against the wounds. She then applied iodine to the worst affected areas and used plasters to cover the bloodiest cuts on my legs and arms.

By the time Sonja had finished, the disco had closed and customers had left. Graham was by my side and helped me to my feet. Mick was also there to see how I was. He whispered something to Graham.

Then he turned to face me. 'Fred, you'll be in no fit state to work today. Why don't you take the day off and get some rest? Graham and I will cover your shifts. See how you feel this evening about working on Monday.'

My brows furrowed but even that hurt. 'I don't want to let you down, Mick. I'm sure I'll be OK to work. It was my fault I got beaten up. Graham warned me earlier. I still don't know why I followed Jose out there.'

Mick shook his head. 'Well, we can't change that now. If you try to work, you'll only make things worse. It's for the best if you take at least one day off to recover.'

I gave him a reluctant nod.

Alan and Sonja helped me back to Tony's, and I realised Mick was right. Every movement jarred my injuries, and I struggled to get down the steps leading to my room.

Sleep was elusive. I ached all over. Agonising pain shot through my body each time I tried to move.

52

Bundle of letters

Mick dropped by to check up on me early Sunday evening.

I was still in considerable discomfort and had not moved far from my bed. In the afternoon I had a bath. It was a struggle and left me exhausted.

Mick walked upstairs to Tony's and bought me a beer and a bowl of soup. I couldn't stomach anything else. My jaw was sore, which made eating difficult. As he left, Mick told me to take another day off and see how I felt by Monday evening.

I had a much better night's sleep on Sunday and didn't wake until midday.

It took a while to get moving as my body had stiffened overnight. I limped upstairs for a light meal. Roberto made me a bowl of porridge which I had with a mug of tea. He looked concerned as he served me.

I ventured out for a short walk and headed to the Red Lion, hoping there would be some letters to cheer me up. People gave me strange looks as I hobbled along the road.

Tich's face dropped as he saw me. 'You look terrible, Fred. Graham told me what happened. How are you doing?'

'Better than I was, but I'm getting there, and plan to go back to work tomorrow.'

'Well, take it easy. Mick would understand if you needed more time to recover.'

I tried to smile but it hurt.

Tich reached behind the bar and passed over a bundle of letters. 'Here you go, mate. There's quite a collection for you. Maybe they'll help you feel better. Did you want a beer?'

I took the bundle and gave him a thumbs-up. 'A San Miguel would be great.'

He handed me a cold bottle. I held it against my jaw to soothe it before taking a swig, then gave Tich a half-smile. 'Cheers, mate. I'll read them outside.'

'OK, let me know if you need anything else.'

I perched on the edge of the chair at my favourite table and sorted out the post. There were two postcards and three letters. I read the postcards first. There was one from Deb in Bristol, a girl I had a brief liaison with when I first worked in Grannies. The other came from Alice in Venice.

Dear Fred,

Thanks for your card. It was great to hear from you. I am glad you are still enjoying yourself. The weather over here is terrible. My suntan has faded already. I can't seem to get back to working in England. Also, the pubs shut so much earlier. I hope Mutts and Sam are getting on well with their jobs. When we were leaving our hotel, we almost missed the plane because we didn't wake up. I wish we had, as I could be over there now. Give my love to everyone. Hope to see you again.

Lots of Love,

Deb

Dear Fred,

Here we are in Italy this time, and what a contrast to Es Cana. Lido Di Jesolo is touristy but nice. Our hotel is tiny with rooms likewise. We are the only English here and the Italians pester us to death. We have not been to any discos as they warned us against it. So, we have been getting in early at night. The weather is in the 90s and the beach is beautiful.

Love,

Alice

I recognised the handwriting on two of the letters, so I opened them next. There was one from Mother.

My dear Robert,

Love to you from us in Dawn Cottage.

Chris is just talking about the next time you go abroad, and she comes with you.

Ali and I are fitting in lots of car practice. His test is next week, and he says he will fail.

Thinking towards the future. Dr Gibbons suggested something which might interest you. He mentioned that many big ships have banking facilities on board. He said you should contact the head office of, say, P&O to ask after one of these jobs aboard ship.

I haven't seen Sarah for a while. She was down at one point, but I trust this has passed now.

From your loving, Mother

The next was from Sarah written the previous Monday. It was the first I had received from her since the beginning of July – six weeks earlier.

Dear Fred,

Hope you are well and looking after yourself.

Your letter didn't arrive until the 11th. Sorry, I haven't written sooner, but I have been very busy. Last week I took time off. I went shopping and to the sea. Last night I saw your sister.

No, I've not lost any more weight, and I've got no photo of myself. If I get one, I will send it.

I got a lovely watch for my birthday from my parents.

My mum had to go into hospital last Sunday for tests, so I didn't have much of a holiday, what with cooking, cleaning, and keeping everything tidy. I have now vowed I shall not get married as it's too much hard work. It would have been much harder if I had been working.

What's the weather like with you? Ours is awful rain every day.

I shall close now but write again soon.

Love Sarah

I didn't recognise the handwriting on the final letter. It turned out to be from Annette, the girl Siv met while he was in Es Cana with the lads.

Dear Fred,

I got your address from Steve (Siv) as I wanted to let you know how things are here. Steve keeps saying he will write, but I know he won't, so I decided to instead.

Arrived home on the Friday night at 9:15 pm. We had a five-hour wait in Es Cana as bad weather delayed the incoming plane from New York. I should have been home by 3 pm.

Since being back I've seen your friends from Es Cana, and I've met Sam's dad in the club at Bletchingley. I went to The Crown in Nutfield with Steve. We've been out together three times. He said he'd pick me up on Friday night at 8:30, but he didn't turn up. That's Steve for you.

How are Mutts and Sam getting on with their jobs? They told me they were going to Germany to get a job when they finished in Ibiza. Are you still working hard?

Life in England is all work and no play, so make the most of life in Es Cana, Fred, and look after yourself.

Love,

Annette

Tich bought me two more beers as I sat re-reading the letters. They cheered me up, but I worried about Sarah. Mother mentioned she had been down, and her letter seemed quite abrupt. Sarah was concerned about her mum of course, but I had the impression she was upset with me and I blamed myself. Also, how could I have forgotten her birthday?

53

Back to work again

Late on Monday afternoon, I caught up with Mick in Grannies.

He took one look at me as I hobbled into the bar and told me it would be best if I had more time off to recover. I agreed to take the Tuesday and Wednesday, my normal day off, to recuperate and start work again on Thursday, which was 1st September.

The next two days I spent resting and relaxing on the beach under the shade of a parasol on a rented sunbed. I decided the Panorama pool was too risky, in case Jose had more revenge in mind. Instead, I swam in the warm sea. My wounds stung from the salt, but I felt the healing effect. The aches and pains lessened.

By Thursday morning I was much better and returned to work at Grannies. My jaw ached, and my head throbbed when I bent over, but I completed my tasks by 11 am when we opened.

Graham bounced down the steps and looked relieved to see me.

He shook my hand. 'Welcome back, mate. How are you?'

I touched my chin. 'Still stiff and sore in places, but I'm getting there.'

Lunchtime was busy, and I didn't have too much time to think. It was great to be working again. There were questions from customers regarding my cuts and bruises. I shrugged them off.

Mick returned from the bank at 2 pm. It was payday. After a few minutes in the storeroom, he called me over and we sat at the end table on the terrace.

His eyes checked me over. 'Well, you're looking better. How do you feel?'

'Much improved. Thanks, Mick. I'm still annoyed with how stupid I was, but I've learned something from the experience.'

'Be more careful in future. Life has a strange way of teaching us things sometimes. I'm just glad you're OK. It could have been much worse if that girl hadn't seen what was happening. You might have been recovering in the hospital instead.'

I winced. 'I know, I had a narrow escape.'

Mick gave me an awkward grin. 'I'm sorry, but I can't pay you for the three days you didn't work.' I gave him a slow nod. 'You worked 23 days, so your wages are 13,800. Your tab was 1675, so I can give you 12,125.'

He counted out the pesetas and pushed them across the table. I unzipped my money-belt and stashed the cash away. Although I'd lost a few days' pay my tab was lower than before, so it wasn't too bad.

Mick placed a gentle hand on my shoulder. 'Just one other thing. The season slows down this month and there won't be as many tourists. Grannies will stay open until the last weekend in September. After that, we'll only open in the evenings and I expect to close for the winter in late October. I can keep you on until the end of September, but we may have to reduce your hours. It depends on how busy we are.'

'That's great. I was thinking of heading back to England mid-October, anyway.'

Mick beamed and shook my hand. 'That's settled then. Could you send Graham over?'

* * *

In the afternoon I sorted out my other bills for the month. After paying Tony's and the Red Lion, I counted out the cash in my money-belt. There were just over 9000 pesetas. I figured if I was careful, that should last me the month, leaving my £120 in travellers' cheques intact.

I soon got into the routine again and it was more relaxed behind the bar as the stress of high summer had passed. We had time to talk to customers, and the atmosphere was more sociable.

Friday nights were also quieter. The numbers of 18-30 clubbers had lessened, and the partying was less manic. I met the new rep, a young man called Adam. It was his first year in the job. They had transferred him from Benidorm when Liz became ill.

Adam told me Liz had made a good recovery in England. She now worked in the Peterborough head office doing admin duties.

On Saturday evening, I saw Mutts and Sam for the first time in weeks. They were with Syd and Dave. Although sporting healthy tans, they looked worn out.

I strolled over to serve them. 'Evening lads, good to see you. It's been a while. How's it going?'

All four shook my hand and Mutts answered, 'We're OK but knackered. We finished the job in Santa Eulalia yesterday and are sleeping on the floor at Syd and Dave's place for the next couple of days.'

'Good, we'll see more of each other. Did you want a drink?'

They nodded. Sam asked, 'Can we have a round of whisky and Cokes?'

After scooping ice into four glasses, I poured in whisky until the ice floated and topped them up with Coke. Syd and Dave took theirs and headed off to the back room to play the pinball machines.

Mutts stared at my face. 'What happened to you, mate? You look like you've been in the wars.'

'That was a week ago. I didn't realise it still showed. I got on the wrong side of a Spanish guy. He and his friends beat me up.'

Sam leant forward. 'D'you want us to sort them out for you, Fred?'

I shook my head. 'No, that's OK. I don't want any more trouble.'

Mutts and Sam sipped their drinks.

I changed the subject, 'I got a letter from Annette, Siv's girlfriend, last week. She asked after you both and said she'd seen your dad in the club, Sam. Siv and Annette have been out together three times since they got back, but he stood her up the Friday before she wrote. What are your plans now you've finished work?'

Mutts gave me a broad smile. 'We're leaving on Tuesday and flying to Munich. A German couple we met in Santa Eulalia plan to stay here when their holiday ends. They arranged with the travel agent to have the return part of their tickets transferred into our names. We just had to pay the admin costs, which worked out at 800 pesetas each.'

'That's brilliant. Are you hoping to get work there?'

Sam sniggered. 'We might if there's any building work, but we've got enough money saved to last a few weeks. The *Oktoberfest* starts in the middle of September and runs to the start of October.'

'What's the *Oktoberfest*?'

They both threw their heads back with laughter.

'You've never heard of the *Oktoberfest*? It's only the largest beer festival in the world. We've both always wanted to go there, and this is the perfect opportunity. We'll find a cheap room and party for two weeks. It should be fantastic.'

232

'Sounds brilliant. Looks as though I'll get back to England before you. My work finishes here at the end of the month and I'll head home soon after. I must talk to everyone about the deposit I lost on the apartment.'

There was an awkward silence between us.

They finished their drinks and ordered another round, before joining Syd and Dave in the entertainments room.

* * *

I only saw Mutts and Sam once more before they left. They spent most of their time in the Red Lion with Tich.

Our farewell drink was on Monday night in Grannies. We promised to keep in touch back in England. Neither of them enjoyed writing letters. Instead, they gave me handwritten notes to pass on to people in Bletchingley when I returned.

Syd and Dave became regular customers again. They had a good laugh with Mick, Pat and Graham. Most of their conversations were about Leicester and what they wanted to do upon their return.

Their plan was to drive back to England in the middle of September. They had problems with the Cortina though. It kept breaking down, and they were unsure about the paperwork when they left the country. They discussed abandoning the car in Ibiza and making their way home from Barcelona hitch-hiking. Syd joked I should buy the number plates.

Mick arranged with a local mechanic to give the Cortina a service later in the week. He said he would get his lawyer to go through the paperwork and make sure it was in order.

54

Number plate incident

A group of lads from Manchester were in Grannies on Tuesday night. I got chatting to them and they invited me to join them on Wednesday afternoon. They had heard about a half-price drinks party at Tootsies. I hadn't been there since the end of June. This seemed a good opportunity to visit as a customer, and it sounded fun.

When I arrived at 2 pm, the lads were already there. Robbie had set up a special bar for the occasion at the rear of the garden area. I saw Gordon serving at tables in the distance, but I mingled with the crowd to avoid making eye contact.

One of the lads, Ian, explained there was a central kitty, and everyone had put in 300 pesetas. I handed over my contribution. The main drink on offer was Hierbas Ibicencas, an aniseed and herb-based green liqueur made on the island. Bottles of the stuff filled an entire table. Memories of drinking it the year before had faded, although I should have remembered its lethal effect.

I soon got involved with the rounds. Glass after glass of the strong, herbal, minty liquid slipped down my throat. I became giddy from its effect and sweated from the warm September sunshine.

I knew I should have stopped but got swept up in the crowd's mood and kept drinking. Everybody around me got more and more drunk. I tried to convince myself I was OK but became aware I was slurring as I talked to Robbie. My grasp on reality slipped away as the afternoon passed.

I didn't remember leaving Tootsies.

* * *

The next morning, my alarm clock jolted me awake.

My memory of the evening was a blank. I trawled through my mind to find any trace of where I had been after Tootsies, or how I got back to my room.

As I struggled out of bed, I still felt drunk. Brushing my teeth only made it worse.

I had cuts on the palms of my hands and noticed fresh bruising to my knees. I figured I had fallen over as I tried to get home.

In Tony's, I sat sipping on a hot mug of tea. Sue commented on how rough I looked.

Work was a nightmare. Everything became an effort, and I threw up as I cleaned the toilets.

I was still stocking the bottle shelves when Mick arrived.

He noticed the state I was in straight away. 'You look awful, Fred. What's happened?'

I pushed myself up from the floor and leant against the bar. 'Sorry, Mick. I got drunk on Hierbas with the Manchester lads yesterday afternoon. I can't remember how I made it back to my room or anything.'

He smirked. 'Hierbas can be a killer. How much did you drink?'

'I don't know. We knocked it back all day.'

'Be careful with that stuff. I learned my lesson the hard way my first summer here, and I've not touched a drop since. Are you able to work?'

I massaged my forehead. 'Yes, I should be OK. Have you got any aspirin?'

'There's a bottle in the first-aid cupboard in the storeroom. Take a couple.'

* * *

The lunchtime session dragged, and the hangover grew worse as each minute passed.

Mick gave me worried glances as I struggled to remember orders and add up prices. I just wanted to get back to my bed for a siesta.

It was 1:15 pm when we heard shouts from the street.

It sounded like Dave. 'Syd, stop, don't be an idiot, it can't be him.'

Then again, this time closer. 'Don't be stupid Syd, stop for Christ's sake, stop.'

With a loud clatter, Syd raced down the steps and came straight for me. He grabbed my t-shirt and dragged me across the bar. I felt the material rip with the force.

With his face close to mine he screamed, 'What the hell have you done with the number plate, you bastard?'

By then Dave had caught up with him. Red-faced and out of breath, he tried to grab Syd by the shoulders and pull him away from me.

235

Mick reacted and leapt over the bar to restrain Syd, who was still fuming.

As Syd let go, I fell back against the fridge.

I was shaking from the shock of what had just happened.

Dave and Mick restrained Syd and sat him on a stool at the bar. They talked to him for several minutes to calm him. Astonished punters returned to their drinks and conversations, after the brief but dramatic distraction.

There were two customers waiting for a beer. I tried to serve them but shook so much that the beer spilt on the counter.

Mick came back behind the bar and sat me on a chair in the corner to recover. He completed the order and found me a new Grannies t-shirt to wear.

In the commotion, I forgot my hangover. Adrenaline raced through my body and I was sick to the stomach. My mind raced. What had I done to deserve Syd's anger? In the state I was in, could I have done something that stupid?

Mick poured four beers, one each for Dave, Syd, him and me. He called us together and tried to understand what had happened.

Syd's eyes were still full of fire, so Dave explained. 'We visited the Hippy Market yesterday afternoon and parked the car there. Early evening, we drove back and saw Fred staggering along the road. We offered him a lift, but he refused, slurring that he needed the fresh air.'

He glanced at me, sipped his beer, and continued, 'We left the car behind Tony's, and came here for a few drinks, before going to bed. After breakfast this morning, we planned to take the car for a drive along the coast. Only then did we notice the missing front number plate. Straight away, Syd assumed it was Fred, as his initials are on the plates.'

Mick argued my case, 'I'm sure Fred wouldn't have done something that stupid. Besides, he was in a right state after getting drunk at Tootsies.'

I stood open-mouthed. I couldn't believe what was happening.

With a shaky voice, I asked Dave, 'Are you sure it happened at Tony's? Could somebody have taken it while you were at the Hippy Market?'

Syd stared at me and shouted, 'But why would anyone do that? You're the only person with a reason to steal it.'

I was stunned into silence. Three pairs of eyes looked in my direction.

236

I shrugged my shoulders. 'If I find the number plate, I'll let you know, but I didn't take it. Besides, it would have needed a lot of effort to remove it. I wasn't in any state to do that.'

Syd didn't look convinced.

Mick consoled him, 'I'll have a word with the mechanic. I'm sure he can knock up a replacement for you when he does the service tomorrow.'

Syd gave a slow nod. 'OK, Mick. If I ever find out it was you, Fred, I'll throttle you.'

My stomach turned over at the thought.

Syd and Dave sank the rest of their beers and headed up the steps.

I worked for a while longer but when Mick told me to get some rest, I didn't argue. The bar had quietened down, and he said he could cope on his own until Eduardo arrived.

* * *

My brain was whirring, and I struggled to sleep.

Fragments of the evening pierced my dreams. My mind tried to piece together what had happened. I woke with a scream late in the afternoon, just as Syd caught me after a long chase and throttled me.

I lay in a pool of sweat, as sunlight streamed through the windows and hit the far wall. Something attracted my attention out of the corner of my eye. There was a glint as the sun reflected off a metallic object hidden behind the back of the wardrobe.

My heart sank as I realised what it might be. I clambered off the bed and pulled out the offending article. It was the number plate. I stared at it in horror as the initials and numbers RJF 97C came into view.

Thoughts raced through my head.

Fuck, what have I done? I can't admit to taking the number plate. Syd will kill me. If anyone else finds out, I'll lose my job, and everyone will hate me. I must get rid of it. Now.

I saw the world around me collapse and I panicked.

In total confusion, I grabbed the metal plate and bent it in half. Then I bent it again, and again until it was an eighth of the original size. It took a huge effort. Then I stamped on it to squash it as much as possible.

I slipped the piece of metal down the front of my shorts behind my money-belt. It scraped against my stomach as I dashed out of the door and upstairs.

There was nobody around, so I headed across the wasteland towards trees at the far edge. I kept glancing behind me to make sure no-one followed. My stomach churned, and I heaved.

Once in the wood's shade, I smelled the overpowering aroma of pine. It soothed me a little. My pace slowed, as I walked deeper under the cover of the trees.

After ten minutes I located the ideal place. It was away from the trodden paths, in a hollow, and pine needles covered the whole area.

I found a spot behind a tree and dug with my bare hands. They were raw by the time I had removed six inches of hard soil. I placed the squashed piece of metal at the bottom.

The accusing twitter of birds surrounded me as I refilled the hole. When I had finished, I dragged pine needles across with my feet to cover the earth.

It was only when I got back to my room that I breathed easier.

Maybe I had got away with it.

55

Meeting Penny

For the next two days, I was in a subdued mood.

My guilt about the number plate incident weighed me down. Every time I saw Syd and Dave, I felt they knew what I had done.

That changed on Saturday night when I got picked up by Penny. She was very different from any of the girls I had been out with over the summer.

Penny was on an 18-30 holiday with her friend Pippa. They had arrived the previous weekend and lived in Kent. I talked to them when they were in Grannies with the 18-30 crowd.

You could not help noticing Penny. She was a big girl with a raucous laugh, a boisterous personality, and she loved her drink.

At 2:30 am we were trying to get closed. Penny, Pippa, and six of their friends occupied the last tables that needed clearing. They were drunk and refused to move. After collecting their empty glasses, I wagged my finger at them and shouted it was time to go.

Penny pointed her camera at me and took a photo. That did not impress me at all.

She grabbed my hand and pulled me on to her lap. 'Come on, kid. Stay cool, we're just having fun. Why don't you join us, we're going to the disco in a minute?'

I struggled to free myself from Penny's grasp. She planted a sloppy kiss on my lips and hugged me tight against her voluptuous breasts. Despite myself, I got aroused. Something about her attracted me.

As I freed myself, she stroked my groin, and squealed, 'Ooh, I think it likes me.'

'Give me ten minutes to finish up and I'll come with you.'

She pushed back her permed brown hair and gave me a drunken grin. 'You won't regret it, kid.'

The rest of her crowd headed off to Cortijo's, while Penny waited for me.

Graham had spotted my encounter and smirked. 'You'll have your hands full with that one, Fred. Enjoy yourself.'

Two minutes away from Grannies, in a secluded alleyway, we snogged with an urgency that surprised me. My hands massaged her breasts, and she rubbed me through my jeans. Lust took over and nothing around us mattered.

She freed me from my jeans. I grunted as she pulled me off. Then I lifted her flimsy dress. My fingers eased into her knickers and explored the wetness between her chunky legs. Shrieks pierced the night as she came.

We straightened our clothing and Penny dragged me over the wasteland to her room at the Caribe.

Our lovemaking moved to the next stage. The bed creaked as I surfed over her perspiring body. She threw her legs wide open and arched her back as I slid inside her. My hands skidded across her sweaty breasts as I tried to gain purchase. She grabbed my buttocks and pulled me right into her and we rocked back and forth. Loud screeches followed, accompanied by groans of satisfaction, as we bounced around on the squeaking bed.

A while later we lay exhausted in each other's arms.

Penny purred, 'Well, kid. Was that what you expected?'

I gasped for breath. 'I wasn't expecting that. You don't hold back, do you?'

'What's the point, I've learnt to grab every opportunity you can in life, and I love sex. You were up for it too. I could tell in Grannies the way you reacted to me.'

She stroked me again to see if I was ready for more. I responded, and she heaved herself on top of me. With legs astride, she lowered herself over my erection and gyrated her body as she held me tight. It was painful as her hips dug into mine, but her actions stirred me, and I thrust back into her. Only when she lay forward across my chest did her weight become too much. I pleaded with her to get off.

As Penny slid on to the bed, she whispered, 'Sorry, kid. I forget how heavy I am sometimes. Did you enjoy it though?'

I gave a gentle nod. 'Yes, it was fantastic. I just couldn't breathe during the last part.'

She pulled my head into her breasts and I sucked her nipples.

* * *

Over the next few days, Penny and I found out more about each other.

If she was not out on an 18-30 activity, she met me for the afternoon. Pippa and her Scottish boyfriend, Sandy, joined us on two occasions. We spent time on the beach, sat in the shade, and had a few drinks. We laughed non-stop, and Penny could not keep her hands off me.

I learned Penny was a snob at heart. She referred to people she considered being below her class as common. She had attended the Langley Park School for Girls. As I had gone to Reigate Grammar School for Boys, she thought of me as her equal.

Her school motto had been "*Ad Rem Mox Nox*", which they translated as "Time is short, get to work". A more literal translation was "Get it done before nightfall". She seemed to have taken that to heart, as she always lived for the moment.

When Penny discovered my real name, she started calling me Robert or Bertie. Her favourite affectation remained "kid" though. She refused to call me Fred from the start, as she considered it was common.

She joked about the way I spoke, suggesting I had two ways of talking. One being my posh voice, and the other my common voice, which I adopted if I got annoyed or talked to ordinary people.

Penny referred to her parents as Mummy and Daddy, which I found odd. She pointed out, it was just as strange for me to refer to mine as Mother and Father.

* * *

I had very little sleep with Penny around and relied on the slimming tablets to keep me going.

She was always there at the end of the night when I finished work, often inebriated. Penny had an incredible capacity for drinking but stayed in control. She dragged me along to Cortijo's and we danced the nights away.

That first night in her room was the only occasion we spent much time together there. Pippa and Sandy often returned before us anyway, but I also discovered Penny loved having sex outdoors. She enjoyed the risk-taking involved. We made love in different spots around Es Cana during the early morning hours before it got light.

The nights were cooler in mid-September and I had reverted to wearing jeans, a shirt and my denim jacket. These, along with Penny's dress, provided protection against the ground (or sand) wherever we ended up having our impromptu sex sessions.

* * *

Penny's departure was early on the Sunday morning of the 18th.

The 18-30 crowd had their farewell party in Grannies on Saturday night. Penny, Pippa and their friends were as boisterous and drunk as ever. Mick and Graham went over several times to ask them to quieten down.

At 2 am the 18-30 stragglers drifted off to the disco, but Penny had other ideas for our last night together. When I finished work, she grabbed my hand and dragged me along the road. She had found a spot behind the beach she wanted to try out.

Sheltered by the trees, we stripped and lay on our clothes. There was a sense of urgency as Penny pulled me on top of her, and we humped away as though the world was ending.

There was a sudden shriek as she shot up and pushed me off her. My elbow bashed against a rock and I howled with pain. She started jumping up and down. Her hands swept across her shaking body.

She clutched at my arm and screamed, 'I'm covered in ants. Get them off me, kid.'

It took a moment for me to realise what had happened. The spot we had chosen was above an ants' nest. As I had been on top, only a few of the pesky creatures were on me. I brushed them away with ease. I grabbed my jacket and swatted at her to remove the insects from her body. That only made matters worse as the denim was swarming with them.

'Run for the water!' I shouted.

It was a comical sight as she raced across the sand flailing at her body with her arms. Within a few seconds, she reached the water's edge and splashed herself all over to wash away the biting insects.

I picked up our clothes and gave them a vigorous shake, before laying them on a nearby sunbed to allow the ants to disperse.

Then I joined Penny, and we lay together in the shallow water to soothe her.

After recovering from the shock, we sat on the sunbed and let our bodies dry. We checked our clothing and removed any remaining ants before getting dressed. I'd never seen Penny so subdued.

Still stunned, she croaked, 'I'll go back to the hotel and try to get some sleep before we leave.'

'OK, if that's what you want,' I replied, 'is it worth it though, it's after 4 am?'

She nodded, and we plodded across the road towards the wasteland.

56

Stormy weather

The week with Penny had exhausted me. Once I finished the lunchtime shift, I returned to my room to catch up on sleep. The skies were deep blue, and it was another hot day. The afternoon sunshine streamed across my bed as I dozed.

By the time I returned for my evening session, though, the air had become humid. A warm wind blew over the wasteland. It was gloomier than normal as the moon hid behind darkening clouds.

I worked with Graham. As it was quiet, we had a few drinks and chatted. He laughed when I told him about the ants' nest incident.

He told me about some recent news. The *Guardia Civil* (Civil Guard) had arrested fifty nudists on several beaches around the island. They handed the culprits over to the authorities, who charged them with immorality and creating a public scandal. There was uncertainty regarding their nationalities and if their cases had reached court yet. The *Guardia Civil* had since set up a permanent guard on those beaches that attracted nudists. This included Agua Blanca, the one we visited.

We closed at 1 am. Neither of us wanted to go anywhere else, so we locked up and went our separate ways. The wind picked up and squalls of rain blew across the wasteland as I rushed home for more sleep.

* * *

Loud claps of thunder woke me in the early hours. Flashes of lightning lit the area.

Then the downpour started. It was torrential, and I pulled the windows closed to prevent water from pouring into my room.

I flipped the light switch, but nothing happened. There had been a power cut. I dressed in a pair of shorts, a t-shirt, and my flip-flops, before edging along the corridor in the dark. At the top of the stairs, I looked out at the sheets of rain hitting the ground and forming large puddles.

There were still distant rumbles of thunder and occasional lightning flashes, but they receded as the intensity of the deluge increased.

I glanced at my watch. It showed 5:15 am. There was nothing I could do, so I returned to bed. I drifted off to the sound of heavy rain slamming against the closed windows.

* * *

Rain still hammered down when I woke again at 7:30 am, and the power remained out.

After dressing and brushing my teeth, I headed upstairs in the gloomy light. Small lakes formed across the wasteland and streams poured past Tony's Bar. Waves lapped over the edge of the step leading to the stairs and corridor where I stayed.

I rushed back to my room and moved everything at floor level and in my wardrobe to the bed. As I headed upstairs again, water flooded down the steps. I hoped my possessions would remain dry.

Tony's Bar was well above ground level. Although water streamed around the outside walls, the inside was safe. As I entered, I saw Sue with Tony, Roberto and Pedro at a table deep in conversation.

I walked over. 'Morning all, this is an amazing storm isn't it? Did you know the rooms downstairs are flooding? I've just moved my gear on to the bed to keep it dry.'

The Spanish lads looked shocked and leapt up with exclamations of, '¡Mierda!' – Shit. They rushed past me to rescue their possessions.

Sue gave me a grim smile. 'Thanks for letting us know. We were discussing what to do about opening. The restaurant and bar are OK, but there's knee-deep water in the cellar. We've brought as much as we can up to the kitchen but have lost some stock. With no power, we can't cook anything, so we'll stay closed and try to clear up once the rain stops.'

Tony sat with his head in hands. He looked up at me. 'This is terrible, Fred. I've never seen anything like this before. Do you think Grannies will be all right?'

'I'm not sure. I'd better get over and check.'

'Let us know if you need any help.'

The route across the wasteland was muddy where I tried to avoid the larger pools. The rain continued to pour, and I got drenched.

I reached the back door of Grannies. Even before I unlocked it, I saw there was a problem as water streamed through the gaps from the inside. As I pulled the door open, a rush of floodwater poured out and almost bowled me over.

My plimsolls were sopping wet, so I took them off and rolled my jeans up to the knees. I then waded along the dark corridor, trying not to slip on the greasy surface. I peered into the stockroom but saw little, apart from a slight glistening off the water.

As I waded to the bar, an eerie light reflected through the windows of the shutter doors. I saw more of the damage and destruction the storm had caused. The floor was six inches deep in grimy water and I noticed floods out on the terrace. Floodwater streamed down the steps through the bars of the gate at the top.

With a huge effort, I pulled one shutter aside. Water washed around me and created waves as I stumbled toward the entrance. I gripped the railings and dragged myself up the steps against the flow. As I unlocked the gate, a fresh influx of muddy floodwater rushed past me.

I stood at the front of the pub and gazed out in horror. The main road had become a river. Water lapped up over the edges and flooded properties on either side. It was fortunate the entrance to Grannies lay well above the street in the middle of a row of shops. Otherwise, the damage would have been much worse.

The force of the flood lifted cars and floated them along the road towards the seafront. Debris littered the thrashing torrent. The rain continued to fall but lessened in intensity. Other people stood nearby, open-mouthed at what had overtaken us.

There was little I could do until the floods subsided, so I sat under the entrance arch and took a Ducados from a sealed pack I had in my pocket. The lighter sparked to life after many attempts. I inhaled on the harsh taste and pondered what I should tackle first.

At 9:15 am the rain stopped. The skies cleared and were soon blue and cloudless. The sun shone as though nothing had happened. Water still streamed down the road, but the strength of the torrent lessened. Within half an hour the tarmac was visible again. Steam rose off the drying surfaces.

Graham arrived not long afterwards. 'Hi, Fred. Sorry, I couldn't get here any earlier. My apartment is over near the Miami. The roads were so flooded, there was no way I could walk through until now. Is there much damage?'

I stood and shook his hand. 'It's knee-deep in places. We've got a hell of a cleaning job ahead of us. Shall we make a start?'

'Yes, I suppose we'd better. I'm not sure when Mick and Pat will be here. The flooding in the countryside near their villa must be bad too. Maybe Steady Eddy will turn up to help, but I doubt it.' That was his name for Eduardo.

We struggled downstairs to inspect the damage. A stream still flowed out of the back door. A pool had formed in the cage containing the barrels of beer and bottled drinks.

The power remained off. Graham found a torch and we looked in the storeroom. Most of the stock was safe as the shelves were high up and remained dry. Only the boxes on the floor had any damage.

The entertainments room was another story. Water had poured in with nowhere to escape. Cushions from the settees floated in the murky filth. We made the pinball machines safe by unplugging them.

Next, we lifted the wooden boards from behind the bar and stood them outside on the terrace to dry. Then we set about clearing the water.

First, we tried to sweep it along the passageway out of the door, but it kept swilling back. Instead, we resorted to filling buckets. It was a laborious job as we scooped up the filthy liquid and emptied it beyond the rear of the pub.

Mick and Pat arrived at 2:30 pm. Eduardo was with them.

They looked around in horror at the damage.

Pat called Graham and me over. She pointed to a bench on the terrace. 'Why don't you have a rest. You look tired out. I've brought some sandwiches my mum made. Dig in.'

Mick gave us both drinks of vodka and orange (no ice). 'Here you go, this should give you a boost. I'd have pulled you a beer but need to make sure it's OK first.'

After a short break, we returned to the job of clearing up the mess.

The power came back on at 4:30 pm but only lasted a few minutes. There was an almighty flash and a bang as the fuses blew. Mick walked over to check the state of the fuse boxes.

He returned with a grim look on his face. 'I must get Jim to inspect the electricity. There's a lot of damage and I don't want to risk blowing us to smithereens. Let's take a break and come back later?'

We agreed to return at 7 pm. Mick locked the place and drove off with Pat to fetch Jim.

Graham and I took a walk towards the seafront to survey the destruction.

There was chaos everywhere you looked. Cars blocked the street and lay at jaunty angles. Rubbish littered the pavements and road. There were frantic efforts underway to clear up the mess.

Further along, we walked past the entrance to Restaurante Es Cana and turned to look at the beach.

It was gone.

Where a perfect sandy strip of sand lined the curving bay the day before, there was nothing. The storm had stripped the whole area bare and restored it to its natural formation of rocky outcrops.

It was only then I realised it had been man-made. There would be no sunbathing there for the rest of the season.

We stared in disbelief at the transformation.

* * *

By the time I got back to my place, they had scrubbed the floors in the rooms and corridor.

My possessions were dry, and the power was on again.

Jim had sorted out the electricity at Grannies. It took us Monday evening and Tuesday to finish cleaning. The pub opened again Wednesday lunchtime. I worked both shifts, even though it was my day off, as Mick and Pat needed to clean up at their villa.

We heard later that two people died in the floods. There was extensive damage across the island. Ten inches of rain had flooded hotels and businesses, destroyed crops, and swept away facilities at several beaches.

57

Finishing work

The missing beach was a constant reminder of the floods.

Preparations were being made to replace the sand during the winter months.

Life in Es Cana returned to normal over the next few days. The weather was warm, but there was an end of season feel about the place. Tourists were still arriving, but not in the droves we experienced in July and August.

As I had worked on Wednesday, Mick gave me Thursday off. Early afternoon I visited the Red Lion. Tich grinned and handed me a San Miguel. 'Hi, mate. Good to see you. Sounds like you had a rough time with the floods at Grannies.'

'It was a nightmare cleaning the place. Did you have any damage here?'

'No, we were very lucky. The surrounding buildings provided shelter on three sides, so the water missed us. Tony's got hit too didn't it?'

'Their cellar was knee-deep, and they lost some stock. The basement rooms flooded. Everything's OK now though.'

Tich reached behind the bar. 'There are more letters for you. Here you go.'

'Cheers, Tich. It's been great having them sent here. I'm finishing a week on Friday and plan to return to England a few days after. Is there any way you can send me the post which arrives after then?'

He scratched his head. 'It shouldn't be a problem. Give me your address before you leave.'

There were four letters. I read the one from Alice first.

Dear Fred,

I will not be coming out to Ibiza this month as there were no available flights, which I guessed would happen.

The weather is glorious here today, but friends tell us while we were away, it was the usual miserable drizzle. So, you have that to look forward to when you get back.

Jane and I had a fantastic holiday. I loved Italy, although it differs from Ibiza. We were the only English people in the whole resort. They translate nothing into English, and few spoke it. If we wanted to communicate it had to be in French.

Jane did not fall in love with anyone, which made leaving easier than last time. This brings me round to the subject of Paco from Hotel Caribe. He has written to Jane twice, but the letters are in Spanish, so we haven't got a clue what they say. But I found someone who will translate them for her. Paco has also telephoned her. So, what will happen between them I do not know. I only hope it does not affect our plans for next year, although we are still undecided where we are going.

I forgot to say. We travelled to Yugoslavia for two days, crossing from Italy. It is a beautiful, unspoilt place. There are two drawbacks: the language – they speak six different ones, and that it's a communist country. You discover this as soon as you reach the border and see the guards with loaded machine guns. Our courier told us they have no hesitation in using them. I went quiet when he mentioned that.

Looking over your letter I did not realise you were working so much. Until what time? And are you eating enough?

Did Liz get her postcard? I must admit I am disappointed at not being able to visit this month, still never mind, perhaps next year. Maybe I could come out and drive you up the wall if you are out there again.

I don't know if I told you, but Jane passed her driving test four weeks ago. So, we are getting out and about, but that does not stop the yearning to go abroad again.

See you soon.

Love and Best Wishes,

Alice

The next one was from Sarah.

Dear Fred,

I was pleased to get your news.

My mum is much better now.

Last Tuesday I did Christine's hair, so I saw your mum who is very well.

I am going out with a fella, but it's nothing serious.

Friends invited me to a wedding on Saturday. The reception was at the Skylane and the food was nice. The ceremony was at 3 pm and the party finished at midnight.

We have had atrocious weather here apart from the bank holiday when it was sunny.

Pat is still with her boyfriend, so I don't spend time with her anymore. I've made a lot of new friends, male and female.

I hope you are keeping well and looking after yourself.

Well, I must go.

Lots of Love,

Sarah

Angie had written also.

Dear Fred,

I was both pleased and surprised to hear from you. Sorry about the trouble you had with Jose. I can't help blaming myself.

I am glad you are still enjoying yourself though, and the weather is hot, although that's like rubbing salt into the wound, as it's awful here. Still, I shouldn't complain as we had a fantastic holiday, and the weather was great too.

Since we have been home, we haven't been out much as the nightlife here leaves a lot to be desired. On Friday, we went up Sweeny's. Lucy and I latched on to a stag-night crowd. Boy, did we get drunk. Can't remember how I got home. Reminds me of our first night in Ibiza.

Hope to hear from you soon.

Love Angie

The last one was from Mother.

My dear Rob,

I hope this will reach you as I am not sure when the end of the season is. Some said August, some say this month, and some say October.

Life here has moved on so fast we feel almost breathless. So just a few jottings to keep you in touch.

Alastair returned to Stirling last Friday, pack on back and bike carried in one hand up Euston Station steps. There is a special British Rail offer for push-bikes until September 30th and they travel free with their owner. Before his next semester starting September 19th, he is touring the northernmost part of Scotland for a week.

September 19th seems an important day here.

Chris had news from her Community Service Volunteers and she travels north to Liverpool on the 19th. She is going to a day centre for the handicapped and will find out more when she gets there.

I am having the week of the 19th off from work to tidy up the garden before the winter.

There is a "bread strike" in England at present and lots of people queue for hours to get a loaf. Not me though.

Last Saturday, I set the shed on fire with a bonfire. We managed to put it out.

Chris wishes she could see you before she leaves, but we doubt it. She has been sewing for High Beech and so your bedroom was a workroom. It is nice sitting by your window in the early evening when the sun is shining in. I may take on her job for a while if they agree. Without the Elf (car) it is long-winded when I go to the surgery by train. So, I hope to drop the evening work soon.

Another crisis last Saturday. They told us late at night that the tape for Sunday's "First Day" had not reached Monte Carlo. Father booked a high-frequency telephone line at 7 am on Sunday. For the first time, he had brought home a cassette of the programme. He put his recorder by the telephone mouthpiece and sent the whole programme to Monte Carlo that way. They broadcast it at 9 am. Not the usual high standard of clarity, but easy to hear.

Surgery is hectic this week with two away on holiday. We have a new doctor, Dr Ferguson. He is young, quiet and the patients are appreciating him. Dr Gibbons retires this month.

That's everything for now and we send our love. Don't drink too much (friends worry in case you do).

My fondest love,

Mother

Reading the news from home made me realise how soon I would be back there.

Letters had been my lifeline all season and kept me in touch with friends and family.

Why was I jealous when Sarah mentioned she was going out with someone? It shouldn't have surprised me. I had not been loyal to her.

* * *

My time working in Grannies was coming to an end, and I started to plan for my departure from Ibiza in October.

Mick asked me to stay on full-time until the end of the month, rather than reducing my shifts. I also worked my Wednesday off, giving him and Pat the opportunity to take time for themselves. Graham and I took over the lunchtime and evening sessions, while Eduardo paired up with either Mick or Pat during the afternoons. I got my last wage packet on the afternoon of Friday 30th. Mick paid me for 27 days. After deducting my tab, I received 14,850.

The final night was a sad one for me. I had enjoyed working at Grannies.

I said my goodbyes to Eduardo when he finished at 8 pm, and I took over. He stayed for a drink but left soon afterwards. I think he was glad to get away from Graham.

There was a steady flow of customers during the evening. It was not an official closing party, as Grannies would open in the evenings during October, but a celebratory atmosphere prevailed. Alcohol flowed, and we had a laugh remembering what had happened during the season.

We closed at 2 am and sat with drinks at the bar for another hour.

Pat gave me a hug. 'Thanks for your help, Fred. It's been a pleasure working with you. What are you planning to do next year?'

'Not sure yet. I'd love to come back here, but I might spend two or three months hitch-hiking around Europe first. It depends on whether I can earn enough money over the winter in England.'

Mick put his arm across my shoulder. 'You've always got a job here if you want one, Fred. It could work out well if you returned early in July. If no rooms are available, you could sleep in the back. What do you think?'

I gave him a broad smile. 'That would be fantastic. Thanks for the offer. I'll let you know nearer the time.'

Graham winked. 'It would be brilliant if you came back. We've made a great team.'

I welled up inside and struggled to hold back the tears. 'Thanks, guys. You don't realise how much that means to me.'

58

Letters from Penny

I slept until late on Saturday.

Tony and Sue were working in the restaurant. Pedro and Roberto had returned to the mainland.

Sue came over and gave me a hug. 'Afternoon, Fred. How are things? I hear you've finished at Grannies.'

Tony shook my hand.

'Would you like something to eat?' Sue asked.

'I'd love a full English and a mug of tea, please.'

She disappeared into the kitchen to make my breakfast.

Tony handed over my tab for September. 'Here you go. Once we sort this out, I've got a proposition for you.'

I glanced at him with interest, before reviewing what I owed, which as usual put a dent into my earnings. After handing over the cash, I enquired, 'So what's this proposal then, Tony?'

'I wasn't sure when you planned to leave. The other rooms downstairs are unoccupied now. I need a hand clearing them out. Could you help? In exchange, I'll give you free board and lodgings until you go.'

I nodded with enthusiasm. 'Sounds like a great idea. My plan is to leave within the next two weeks. When do you want me to start?'

'How about Monday morning?'

We shook hands just as Sue brought out my food.

* * *

Margaret was working the afternoon session in the Red Lion. She looked tired.

I waved as I approached the bar. 'Hiya, how are you?'

'Oh, I'm OK. It's been a tough season but rewarding. We're looking forward to getting back to England to visit family and friends.'

'Will you have to work again this winter?'

Her face broke into a smile. 'No, we shouldn't need to this year. We've made enough money to see us through and have put a deposit on an apartment we plan to buy. We intend to move out here for good in January.'

'Great news, I hope it works out for you. Is there any post for me? Oh, and I'd better pay my tab.'

Margaret leafed through the notebook and totted up my bill. 'It comes to 1425, Fred.'

I counted out the money and she gave me the change, before reaching under the bar and handing me a small bundle. 'Three letters in the same handwriting. The last one arrived this morning. The postmark's from Wednesday, so it got here fast.'

I took my post and a bottle of San Miguel outside to my favourite table and opened them in date order. They were from Penny.

Dear Robert,

I thought how lonely you must be, now I am out of your life, and realised how excited you'd be to receive a letter from me.

Well, you'll be glad to know I arrived home in one piece. Let me bore you with what happened.

When I left you (as tears stream down the author's face) I staggered back to the hotel (keeping a close lookout for any men in the bushes who might attack me). I sat in a nice comfy chair to doze, but I heard voices upstairs and realised half my luggage was still in someone's bedroom. I had to creep around and fetch it, so I had no sleep (OK – so you were right).

When we arrived at the airport, they announced our flight straight away. Pippa and I thought we'd be home soon. How foolish we were. We sat on the plane for an hour. It was so hot it was unbearable. As we waited in a queue with other planes to take off the Captain (who sounded drunk) told us to disembark. We were called again at 9:50 am and took off just after 10.

In the middle of the flight, the Captain said he'd got bad news, that we'd have to land at Luton (instead of Gatwick). We laughed at his sense of humour until we realised it was no joke.

The worst part of flying is landing. I was sitting there terrified, as we circled. People kept telling me Dan Air doesn't fly to Luton, so the pilot didn't know where we were and was circling around looking for the airport. We seemed to be too low as we came in to land. All I could see were trees. I thought we'd had it. I'll sail next time.

The coach journey to Gatwick took two hours, and we arrived at 3 pm. I was home by 5 pm and went straight to bed.

At 2:20 am I awoke, not knowing where I was. I'll tell you what woke me up – bloody ant bites – itching like mad. I'm covered in the damn things. It's not your fault, but I know full well where I got them.

Today I started my new job. I had to get up at 6:45 am. That killed me. It was fortunate Daddy took me in, as I didn't have to worry about buses. It's not a bad place but the people are so common (I knew that would amuse you).

Pippa is here now. She's just read the start of your letter. She is writing to Sandy, the Scottish fella she met. Her delays were at least two hours longer than mine. She's after his sympathy.

The weather is lousy. It won't be long until I'm back in my duffel coat. I'm a real turn-on in that.

It's now 7:45 pm. You're just getting prepared for your evening shift, and I'm ready for bed – but then I always was.

Pippa took our photos into a 48-hour place today. When they are developed, I'll order re-prints to send you.

Hey, I forgot to mention. When I arrived home yesterday Mummy looked at my head in shock.

Mummy: "What on earth is that in your hair?"

Penny: "What?"

Mummy: "That"

Penny: "What?"

Well, it turned out I'd got an ants' nest in my head, and the ants had laid eggs in my scalp. So, I've had my head shaved and my brain removed as they'd eaten into it. But it's OK now. I just get a headache when I try to think.

Pippa has told me I can't send you the last paragraph, but I know you're so gullible you'll believe it.

I've written enough for this time.

This is the last bit and has to be the best, so I got rid of Pippa so I can concentrate.

OK, so it was only a holiday, but I feel a lot for you (in my legs).

Please write soon.

Take care of yourself.

Lots of love,

Penny

Dear Bertie,

I'm pissed off, so I hope you don't mind me writing to you again. The novelty will wear off soon.

I'm being morbid because I've been watching a programme called "Marc". It is a series Marc Bolan was recording before he died. It's sad... well I think so anyway. When Elvis died, his record topped the charts. Marc Bolan's record is doing very well now too. It seems you have to die to be a success these days.

I haven't told you yet why I'm so pissed off. I had a bloody awful day at work. The woman in charge of the kitchen used to do the job I'm now doing, and so she resents me for being there. She's been a real bitch today, by being awkward, and unhelpful. I got depressed and wanted to sit in a corner and cry. If you've ever felt that way, you'd understand what I mean, but then being a fella, you wouldn't.

Mummy has just told me about the floods in Ibiza, so I'm worried about you now, are you OK?

Pippa should get the photos back today. How exciting. I'd better post this before I see your photo. Otherwise, I might change my mind, as I was drunk every time I was with you. It's OK kid I'm only joking. I can still remember those penetrating blue eyes.

We are going for a booze-up tonight, with our photos, so we can sit and reminisce over those wonderful times we spent in sunny Ibiza. You might even get a mention.

I met the girl I know who lives in Outwood. She said Nutfield was a nice place, and the chances are you've got a large, expensive house. So, I was wondering if you'd like to marry me (if the rumour is untrue, please ignore this offer).

I'm annoyed now because Pippa has just rung and said she didn't go to work today (she's got a poorly tooth). So, she hasn't got the photos back, and I was so looking forward to a laugh.

Sorry, but I can't write anymore, I'm getting depressed as the prospect of another day's work tomorrow. Why didn't you let me stay and miss that damn plane?

Well kid, take care of yourself. Maybe next time I'll be happier. I hope so, or you may find me penniless on your doorstep one morning... you should be so lucky.

Now, remember, the last bit is always the best. I must think of something nice... through these hard times I am having, it's the memories of the good times that keep me going.

STAY COOL.

Lots of love and

Affectionate Hugs,

Penny

Dear Robert,

Yet another letter from me, even though I've not received one from you yet. I'll blame it on the post for another two days. If I still haven't got one by then, I'll cross you off my Christmas card list, not to mention the other lists I keep.

My week in Croydon got me down. So, they transferred me to St. Mary Cray (Have you heard of it? It's one big council estate, and very rough. You might like it). I am there this week, cleaning vending machines, drying up and clearing tables. Wow, I'm glad I spent three years at College.

I had a boring weekend. Pippa has been in bed since Wednesday with bronchitis, so I was with her on Friday night playing the sympathetic friend.

Yesterday evening Daddy and I fixed up my 21st. I wanted it on Saturday 12th Nov (MY BIRTHDAY IS ON THE 13TH), but everywhere was booked, so I had to have it for Friday. A friend of mine is a D.J. and he said he'd do the disco. Oh, I'm so excited. I'll send you an invitation to your home address. Make sure you're free that night.

I took my negatives into the chemist to get re-prints. They should be back any day, so I'll forward the copies to you.

I've just found an old school report. The music teacher described me as "noisy, and disruptive influence in the class". What a bloody cheek. That's upset me now.

Are my letters boring? I'm running out of things to say – and I'm tiring – too much hard work.

Last bit: - I miss you.

Lots of love,

Penny

In fact, the letters were longer than this; these are edited versions. By the time I'd read through Penny's post several times, my head was spinning.

59

Last days in Es Cana

I walked back to my room to freshen up.

It seemed strange to think I was the only person remaining in the basement. Even stranger that I never met three of my former roommates. The only ones I'd known were Pedro and Roberto.

I counted the cash I had in my money-belt. There were 9200 pesetas. I figured that would last me until I left. I still had the £120 of travellers' cheques in reserve and to get me home.

After a bath and a change of clothes, I went for a walk along the seafront.

Restaurante Es Cana was open, so I sat on the veranda and looked out over the sea. I ordered a San Miguel and a Spanish omelette. There was a chill breeze and wispy fishtail clouds streaked the sky. As the light faded, there was an eerie feel to the curved bay where rocks now made up the landscape instead of the sandy beach.

My mind drifted back over the past six months as I sipped on another beer. So much had happened, and I knew my life would never be the same again. When I first came to Ibiza, I took a huge risk. I didn't know if I'd find work and how long my money would last. Doubts had played on my mind. Would I have to return to England, admit defeat and find a steady job again? As the months progressed my self-confidence increased. My outlook changed too as I went out with different girls and found a job I enjoyed. I realised I could achieve whatever I set my heart on. Travel plans evolved as I thought about hitch-hiking around Europe and other places I might visit. Work would no longer be career-orientated but provide the means to travel further afield. I felt sure I would remember this summer as the one that changed my life.

At 8:30 pm I strolled up the road to Grannies.

It was odd descending those steps as a customer. I looked around. There were a few people on the terrace. Others sat inside at tables and the bar. Graham and Mick were working. They both smiled as I approached.

I pulled up a stool and Graham came over to serve me. 'How's it going, mate? What can I get you?'

'Good, thanks. It feels strange being in here as an ordinary punter again. Could I have a vodka and orange?'

Within seconds the drink was in front of me and I took a large gulp. 'Cheers, Graham. How are things with you? What are your plans once you finish here?'

'I'm going to Switzerland at the end of the month.'

'Interesting. Have you been there before?'

'Yes, I spent last winter in Zermatt, working behind a bar. They offered me a job for this coming season, so I jumped at the chance. The money's good and it's a fantastic atmosphere. I love it there.'

'Sounds great. It must be cold though. Do you have time to ski?'

He flashed me a huge grin. 'I don't mind the cold. It makes a refreshing change after the summer here. They give me two days off a week, so I learned to ski last winter. I'm not that good yet, but it's fun. I get my ski passes free.'

'What a brilliant combination. You've got life sorted, haven't you? Can you save money there?'

'I've been lucky. The cost of living is high in Switzerland, but so are the wages. I spend very little while I work, so I put most of it away. My plan is to buy a small apartment here. I should have enough saved for a deposit when I come back next year.'

'That's fantastic. Well done.'

John and Alan from Cortijo's joined me at the bar. There were handshakes all round.

John bought us drinks. As we clinked glasses, he explained, 'Tonight's the last night at El Cortijo, so we're having a closing party. Entrance is free, so spread the word.'

Graham nodded. 'We'll let customers know during the evening. I'm sure Mick and I will be there once we close. Pat and her friends should be around later, so I'll tell them.'

I turned to John. 'I'll come along in a while. Have you had a good season?'

'Yes, it's been our best yet, but it's quieter now. Tootsies had their closing party this afternoon, and the hotels are winding down for the winter. Club 18-30 and Cosmos still have a few tourists arriving, but not enough to justify us staying open.'

Alan chipped in, 'Will you be back next summer, Fred?'

'I hope so, but maybe later in the season. I want to get the money together in England and hitch-hike around Europe first. What about you, Alan? Are you going to Scotland for the winter?'

'I might go for Christmas and New Year, but the rest of the time I'll be here.'

He glanced at John, before continuing, 'There's improvement work needs doing at El Cortijo, so John has asked me to help him. I'm fed up with Scottish winters, so it will be nice to stay here.'

'Hope it goes well for you. Look forward to seeing you again next year.'

'Yes, that would be great.'

Alan looked at his watch. 'I suppose we'd better open, John.'

They finished their beers, and with a cheery 'See you later', headed out of the door.

I asked for another drink and sat watching Mick and Graham in action behind the bar. I missed being involved.

The voice of a young lady by my side shook me away from my thoughts. She was trying to attract attention. I called Graham across to serve her.

I noticed her foreign accent as she ordered two rum and Cokes.

She placed her hand on mine. 'Thank you.'

I smiled back at her. 'You're welcome. I couldn't help noticing your accent. Where are you from?'

Her shy smile was delightful. 'I live near Frankfurt in Germany and am on a week's holiday with my friend. This is our last night. We fly home tomorrow morning. My name is Rita. What is yours?'

'Hi, I'm Fred. Pleased to meet you. Where are you sitting? Do you mind if I join you?'

She hesitated and looked embarrassed. 'That would be nice. We are outside on the terrace.'

I picked up my drink and followed her.

Rita was shorter than me. Plump but well-proportioned, she had shoulder-length brown, wavy hair and brown eyes. Her friend was petite and fair-haired, with dark blue eyes. I noticed scars on her face.

Rita introduced me to Heidi, and the three of us fell into conversation. Both spoke good English, and I found their accents enchanting. We talked a lot about our lives. It fascinated them how I had left my job in England to come to Ibiza for the season. The girls worked together in a printing company on the outskirts of Frankfurt.

Heidi explained she had been in a car accident the previous year. It had been serious, and she had to have her lower left leg amputated. They had fitted her with a prosthetic limb in August and she was still getting used to it.

After two more rounds of drinks, I invited them to join me at Cortijo's. As it was after midnight they declined. Heidi wanted to get some sleep before the taxi picked them up at 9:30 am. Rita asked me back to their rented apartment for another drink instead.

We walked for twenty minutes, before reaching the building on the outskirts of Es Cana. I worried about Heidi as she limped along the road, but she struggled on and waved away any efforts to help. Rita was close by my side and linked arms.

The apartment was spacious, with a lounge, kitchen, bathroom, and two bedrooms. I sat in a chair while Rita poured us a generous glass of chilled Henkell Sekt, the German equivalent of champagne.

The girls raised their glasses. *'Prost.'*

I clinked my glass against theirs. 'Cheers.'

After a few sips, Heidi made her excuses and retired to bed.

In the lounge, Rita and I settled back on the comfortable sofa. We relaxed into each other as we drank more Sekt. My head spun from the bubbles, and we both became aroused as we kissed.

After a while, Rita stood up, turned out the lights, and led me to her bedroom. She changed into a nightdress while I stripped to my underwear.

We clambered into bed. The kissing and cuddling resumed, and our touching was sensual. There were limits though. If my hands wandered too far, she would move them back to more acceptable areas. It was still a wonderful experience.

We awoke wrapped in each other's arms as it got light.

The girls prepared a breakfast of rolls, cold meats, orange juice and coffee. It was delicious.

Rita and I swapped addresses. She made me promise to visit her when I came to Germany. She lived on the top floor of her parents' house in a small village in the Taunus mountains outside of Frankfurt.

I felt lightheaded as I walked along the road through Es Cana to my room.

* * *

On Monday morning, I met up with Tony. After breakfast, he showed me what needed doing in the five basement rooms.

He explained that a French guy had occupied the room next to mine. He worked as a chef in the Miami Hotel. They had not seen him for six weeks and he owed two month's rent. His possessions were scattered across the floor and bed. Some were damaged from the flood. The plan was to store them until he returned to pay his outstanding bill.

My initial job was to box up the belongings and carry them to a storeroom at the rear of the building. Then I moved the bed and wardrobe to the centre of the room, before covering them with sheets.

The flooding had stained the walls, so Tony wanted them and the ceiling whitewashed. I also had to scrub the floor clean. The plan was to do that with all five rooms. Mine would be done after I left.

By 4:30 pm I had finished the first room and splattered myself in whitewash into the bargain. It was fortunate I had worn an old pair of shorts and a t-shirt. I made sure I used those on the following days too.

On Tuesday, I speeded up and completed two more of the rooms by late afternoon. By Wednesday, I got into a proper rhythm and finished the rest by 3:00 pm.

Tony inspected the results. He appeared to be satisfied.

I had a bath and scrubbed myself clean.

* * *

Later, I sat in Tony's and enjoyed a plate of shepherd's pie Sue had prepared, accompanied by a San Miguel, then joined Sue at the bar. The restaurant was empty, apart from one family in the far corner.

Tony handed me another bottle of beer. 'Thanks for your help, Fred. You've done a good job. When do you plan to leave?'

'I'm thinking early next week. Do you know if the ferries to Barcelona still sail daily in October?'

Tony turned to Sue. 'Not sure, what about you, Sue?'

She swept back her long brown hair. 'I think they do, but why not get a flight instead? They're inexpensive this time of year. It could work out cheaper than travelling by ferry and bus, and faster of course.'

'I hadn't thought of that. Where would be the best place to book?'

263

'Have a word with the 18-30 rep, Adam. The Dan Air flights to Gatwick are half empty in October, and he might organise a deal for you.'

'Brilliant. Thanks, Sue. I'll go over to the Caribe later and see if I can catch up with him.'

60

Leaving Ibiza

It was Friday before I tracked Adam down.

I sat with him at his desk in the Caribe while he made a phone call to the Club 18-30 headquarters in the UK to check about a flight.

After a few minutes' discussion, he held his hand over the mouthpiece and asked, 'How does Wednesday 12th at 10:00 am sound? The best price they can do is £35.'

I nodded and replied, 'I'll take it. Can I pay with travellers' cheques?'

He grinned. 'Yes, no problem, we'll sort it out in a minute.'

Adam confirmed the details, then took me to the hotel cashier. I signed over £40 of my travellers' cheques: £35 for the ticket and £5 to cover the phone call and admin.

I would arrive home six months to the day after I had left.

* * *

I started to make my preparations for leaving.

There was not much to pack. I had less to take back than I brought with me. I had given away the tent to Sam. I returned the straw bag to Sue in case anyone else could use it. The only extra items were two beach towels, and three t-shirts from Grannies.

Mick offered to drive me to the airport.

The weekend went by in a flash. I spent my time in Tony's and the Red Lion during the day and Grannies in the evening. There was a sense of relief everywhere that the season had almost ended. Now was the time for well-deserved relaxation and celebration.

I picked up my ticket from Adam on Monday afternoon.

Tuesday was a day of goodbyes and it became emotional. Roger and Margaret were in the Red Lion. Tich had the day off but left a message that he would meet me in Grannies for a farewell drink in the evening. Two letters awaited me.

The first was from Penny.

Dear Robert,

I hope this letter reaches you before you leave for home.

These are the photos I took. You look better when you're not annoyed.

Thanks for your postcard. I got it on Thursday. You should start receiving the first of my letters in Ibiza (as I write this), so I know it won't be long before I receive a long letter from you.

It's cold here. Pippa and I started our Badminton classes on Thursday. For an hour we learnt how to serve. It was boring but we will persevere.

We saw the James Bond film "The Spy Who Loved Me" last night. It wasn't too bad but very far-fetched. The cinema is almost next door to McDonald's, so we visited there afterwards. We're real pigs, but we'll go on a diet next week. I will be so skinny.

I got a letter last week from Sandy (the Scottish bloke Pippa paired up with in Ibiza). They had to wait 1½ days before they got their flight home. I hope your journey isn't that bad.

It's "football day" today. The rest of the family are watching The Eagles (Crystal Palace in case you're not up in these matters). All I want to eat are the hot crumpets for tea, and I'm tired of waiting. I must sound like the compulsive eater that I am.

A lot later:

I got waylaid, with my crumpets, very sorry. I've had great fun writing out birthday invitations. Last night was pub night. Pippa and I bored everyone with our holiday photos.

Sundays are so boring, nothing to do, apart from thinking about work tomorrow. I have to report to St. Mary Cray again to find out where I'll be working next week. I'm hoping for Brixton. It must be hot there because they all seem to have good suntans.

Hope to hear from you soon.

Take Care Kid.

Lots of love,

Penny

The second was from Sarah.

Two of the three photos Penny sent were all right. I was not so sure about the first. I felt guilty about only writing the postcard. Maybe I could go to her 21st party and catch up then.

The future with Sarah seemed uncertain. Was she still going out with that fella? How would we get on together after six months apart? Time would tell.

I sat at the bar and chatted to Roger. He was in a buoyant mood and told me about their plans of migrating to Ibiza for good. We drank several bottles of San Miguel as we talked. I settled my tab of 2630 pesetas. We shook hands and wished each other well.

Margaret gave me a massive hug and claimed she knew I would be back in 1978. 'Once you get Ibiza fever,' she said, 'you never lose it.'

As I strolled along the alleyway, my heart sank. Pablo's stocky figure headed towards me. He still thought I owed him 4000 pesetas for the damage to his apartment. A scowl was fixed to his face, but his eyes were focused on the ground. He walked straight past me. I breathed a huge sigh of relief.

* * *

My final evening in Grannies became a haze.

Pat and Graham worked behind the bar. It was Robbie's last night too, and he had a flight booked for Hamburg the following afternoon. Alan and John were able to stay for the evening now El Cortijo had closed. Tich sat

268

next to me at the bar. Tony and Sue popped in later. The two reps, Cosmos Bill and 18-30s Adam, also appeared with a few of their clients.

The air was full of reminiscences and talk of the season just gone. There was excitement all around, and the alcohol flowed. Around midnight I ordered drinks for my friends. Shouts of 'Cheers' and *'¡Salud!'* resounded as we clinked glasses.

People started to drift off at 1 am. There was much hugging and shaking of hands.

I settled my tab of 2700, before saying goodbye to Pat and Graham. As I hugged Pat, there were tears in her eyes. I welled up too.

* * *

I did not sleep well, worried I would oversleep.

At 6:45 am, packed and ready to leave, I checked my money. I had 850 pesetas left in cash and £80 in travellers' cheques, which could go towards my next trip.

After a final look around the room, I wandered upstairs with my black duffel bag. Sue brought me a mug of tea and a round of toast. We sat in silence, not knowing what to say.

Mick arrived on time. Sue and I hugged. We promised to keep in touch over the winter. Tony gave me a vigorous handshake and wished me all the best.

Soon we were on our way. There was not much conversation as Mick concentrated on the road ahead. A warm breeze ruffled my hair through the open window. There was a freshness to the air as we drove through the now-familiar countryside scenes: dusty red paths, pine trees and white buildings.

We arrived at the airport at 8:30 am. Mick shook hands and gave me a quick hug. 'Take care, Fred. Have a good flight home. Hope to see you again next year.'

I gave him a broad smile. 'Don't worry, Mick, I'll be back. Thanks for everything you've done for me this year.'

I checked in, handed over my bag, and strolled through passport control. While I waited for the flight, I ordered a draught Estrella and a ham roll.

An announcement came over the tannoy. They had delayed the scheduled departure by an hour. The inbound plane from Gatwick was late because of bad weather in England.

I bought another beer and climbed up to the outside viewing gallery to watch the plane land. It arrived forty-five minutes later, and passengers were soon walking down the steps at the rear of the aircraft, a Dan Air Comet. As the pale-faced newcomers trailed across the tarmac and entered the arrivals building, the boarding announcement boomed over the tannoy.

I clambered up the steps on to the plane. A strong smell of fuel pervaded the air. My window seat was towards the front on the right-hand side.

My stomach lurched as we took off. The plane rose in a steady path towards the south-west and the land below us disappeared as we headed out to sea.

As the aircraft turned to head north, I started to catch glimpses of the island. We continued to ascend, and I could make out the beaches and hotels of San Antonio dwindling below.

Soon the window framed the entire magical island. It became smaller and smaller as we flew higher. Then it disappeared behind the wispy clouds. All I could see was the sparkling blue sea.

A feeling of loneliness and sadness swept over me. I was missing Ibiza already.

In that moment I mouthed a solemn promise.

I will be back, dear Ibiza, whatever it takes, I will be back.

What happened next?

My return to England was a shock to the system.

It was great to see Mother again, and even Father welcomed me back. They both commented on how much weight I had lost.

For the first few days, I caught up on sleep. The weather was miserable, and I felt the same way. I missed Ibiza and the slimming tablets.

Only while researching this book did I discover the over-the-counter pills I took contained amphetamine (speed) – this was commonplace in the 1970s. That explains why I felt the way I did while taking them, and the withdrawals I suffered when I stopped.

After a week at home, I was more positive about life again. I met up with friends at the Station, The Crown and the Prince Albert. It was great to see everyone and catch up with the gossip. I saw the Bletchingley lads. Mutts and Sam had just returned from Germany. We discussed the deposit money, but they were all short of cash, so I did not pursue it.

I also caught up with Sarah, and we enjoyed an evening out together. The spark between us had disappeared though. She had a new boyfriend, and my feelings for her had diminished. We promised to stay friends and keep in touch.

Getting a job weighed heavily on my mind as reserves ran low, and I wanted to save money for the next summer. My intention remained to hitch-hike around Europe.

I picked up a copy of the local newspaper, the *Surrey Mirror*, and scanned the Jobs Vacant columns.

There was a vacancy at a company called Doeflex, a plastics factory on an industrial estate in Merstham, three miles from where we lived. Despite their reservations about how long I would stay, they offered me a job to start on October 31st. It involved five 12-hour shifts, days and nights for alternate weeks. The day shift ran from 6 am to 6 pm and the night shift from 6 pm to 6 am.

Before starting, I travelled up to Liverpool to visit my sister, Chris, for a few days and celebrate my 22nd birthday on the 27th. It was great to see her. She loved her community work in a home for handicapped children. While there, I met up with Lesley and Bill from Ibiza for a bevvy.

* * *

The factory work became monotonous, but they paid well.

Most of the time I spent at the end of a production line, packing pieces of plastic sheeting. They used these as the basis for mouldings. Other times I stood at the grinder, wearing ear protectors, re-cycling plastic sheets that had failed quality control. The most stressful job was making sure we kept the hoppers filled with the correct mix of granules for the plastic being produced.

For the day shift I walked to work, setting out at 4:30 am. The route involved a trek up the hill from South Nutfield, through top Nutfield, across Nutfield Marsh and into Merstham. It was a cold winter. Many of those days became tough as I trudged the three miles through snow and ice. All other times I could get the train.

During the winter I received letters from some of the girls I met in Ibiza. Alice, Angie, Penny and Rita were the most frequent writers. I tried to reply when I could, but time was short because of work. The dream of getting together with Alice faded, although we spoke several times on the phone.

Work limited my social life, but I tried to go out most weekends.

* * *

By April 1978 I had saved enough money (£500) and started to make plans to leave in early May. I bought a framed rucksack, a sleeping bag, a tent and a small camping stove. My bible was Ken Welsh's *Hitch-hiker's Guide to Europe.* I absorbed its contents and advice.

On the morning of Tuesday, May 9th, I set out by train to Harwich, a port on the Essex coast. From there I travelled across by ferry to the Hook of Holland, in the southwestern corner of the Netherlands.

My new adventure had begun.

From the moment I got the first lift, I was hooked on hitch-hiking. Sometimes it was frustrating when I waited hours for a car or lorry to stop. Other times someone picked me up within minutes.

I had a Youth Hostels Association (YHA) membership card which entitled me to stay in their hostels around Europe at cheap rates, below £5 per night. My *Hitch-hiker's Guide* proved invaluable in planning my routes and finding inexpensive accommodation and places to eat. On occasions, I pitched my tent and saved on the cost of an overnight stay.

My journey took me south through Germany. I stayed for two nights at the youth hostel in Frankfurt, on the Main River. I phoned Rita, and we met up for my second evening. She showed me around Sachsenhausen, a nearby area full of bars and restaurants. We enjoyed a fabulous time and I was sorry when I had to return to the hostel before it closed at midnight. Rita told me she planned to be in Es Cana in September for a week's holiday. I promised to be there too.

From Frankfurt, I kept heading south, through Austria, and down the coast of Yugoslavia, before arriving in Greece on Wednesday, June 7th. I spent three weeks there, two days in Athens, and then exploring several islands. The one which made the biggest impression on me was Santorini, where I stayed for five days.

After that, I caught a ferry from Patras on the west coast of Greece to Brindisi in Italy.

My hitch-hiking took me northwards through Italy and westwards across the border into southern France. I remember a scary night spent sleeping rough in Marseilles.

By Tuesday, July 4th, I had arrived on the Spanish border at La Junquera. The next day I was in Es Cana once more.

The eight weeks travelling around Europe cost me an average of £40 a week. That left me with £180 to last the rest of the season.

While in Greece, I had sent a postcard to Grannies to let them know I would return early in July. Mick, Pat and Graham welcomed me with open arms. They let me stay in the back room at Grannies, so I had no rent to pay. The day after I arrived, I resumed working for them.

It did not take long to get into the rhythm again.

My solemn promise to return to Ibiza had been fulfilled.

Contact the Author

Hi, it's Fred here.

Thank you so much for taking the time to read my book. I hope you enjoyed it. If you did, I would be grateful if you could leave a review on Amazon, even if it is only a few words. Reviews are important in getting an author's work noticed. I also enjoy reading them.

If you want to get in touch, please e-mail me at fd81@assl.co.uk

You can follow me here:

Facebook: www.facebook.com/fredsdiary1981

Twitter: @fredsdiary1981

Amazon: www.amazon.co.uk/Robert-Fear/e/B005CN2OL8

Website: www.fd81.net

If you love reading memoirs and are on Facebook, I recommend you join the We Love Memoirs group (if you haven't already). It is known as the friendliest group on Facebook, and for good reason. Follow this link and tell them Fred sent you: www.facebook.com/groups/welovememoirs

You can also follow them on Twitter: @welovememoirs

More about the Author

Robert Fear has lived in Eastbourne on the south coast of the UK for half his life. He moved there to be with Lynn, his future wife, and is still there with her thirty years later. As cat-lovers, they have taken on several rescue cats over the years and are owned by three now.

For his day job, Robert works as a self-employed software consultant. In his spare time, he writes, edits, and self-publishes books.

Robert's interest in travel goes back to his twenties when he spent most of his time abroad. His experiences included: a summer in Ibiza, hitch-hiking around Europe, and touring the USA and Canada. His most eventful trip was in 1981 when he travelled through Asia.

Born into a religious sect known as the Exclusive Brethren, his father, John, took the brave step of leaving it with his young family when Robert was nine years old. Robert never saw his grandparents again but is thankful for being able to grow up outside this restrictive group. His life has been full of adventures he would never have experienced otherwise.

Other books published by Robert Fear

Fred's Diary 1981: Travels in Asia

Have you ever wanted to read someone else's diary?

Would you like to experience travelling in Asia without leaving home?

Then this book could be for you.

Fred's Diary 1981 is a fascinating insight into a young man's travels around Asia in the early 1980s.

Follow Fred throughout his extensive travels to Hong Kong, Thailand, India and Nepal.

Word of warning: This book is what it says, a diary. It follows Fred's daily highs and lows as he travels through Asia. If you are expecting a similar format to *Summer of '77*, then you will be disappointed. Also, be warned there is extensive drug use throughout the book. If that is likely to offend you then this diary is not for you. Otherwise, enjoy the book for what it is – 158 days of Fred's journey through Asia in 1981, recording his thoughts and actions as they happened.

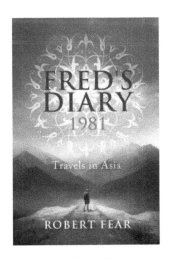

getBook.at/FredsDiary1981

279

Exclusive Pedigree: My life in and out of the Brethren

John Fear was born into a religious sect known as the Exclusive Brethren. This sheltered him from the outside world as he grew up but could not hide him from its influences. A struggle began in his mind that led him to leave the Brethren, along with his young family.

During his later life, John prepared a lot of the book, along with notes for chapters he knew would not be completed. It is only now, over twenty years later, that the memoir has been published, introduced and edited by his eldest son, Robert, as a tribute to his father's amazing life. It contains original content written by John, along with diary notes, letters and magazine articles. The final chapters are written by his second eldest son, Alastair.

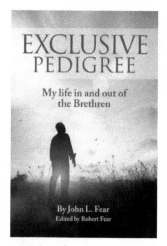

getBook.at/ExclusivePedigree

Travel Stories and Highlights: 2017 Edition

50 stories from a variety of authors take you on journeys through Australia, Borneo, Brazil, Chile, England, France, French Polynesia, Germany, Hawaii, India, Ireland, Israel, Japan, Kenya, Lithuania, Nepal, Peru, Scotland, Siberia, South Africa, Spain, Sumatra, Tasmania, Thailand, Tunisia, Uruguay and USA.

50 highlights engage you in more amazing experiences from around the globe.

Travel through time, sail across oceans, fly through the skies and navigate land by public transport, car and foot.

This is an absorbing book that will live on in your memory.

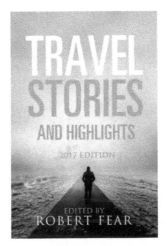

getBook.at/TravelStories2017

Travel Stories and Highlights: 2018 Edition

60 compelling Travel Stories and 40 absorbing Travel Highlights from 44 authors, writers and poets.

An enthralling mix of travel experiences that will let you explore different parts of the world from the comfort of your own home. A book you can just pick up and enjoy whenever you have a spare minute.

Travel from the Australian outback to the wilds of North Borneo. Spend time rafting in Bosnia, trekking in the Himalayas and on a road trip through Europe. Experience living as an illegal immigrant in Mexico. Encounter a shark and swim with dolphins. Enjoy the ambience of Paris and a miracle at Lourdes. Marvel at Bedouin hospitality. Travel by train across India and meet a prince along the way.

Immerse yourself in these and many more wonderful recollections.

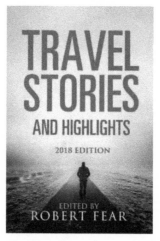

getBook.at/TravelStories2018

Travel Stories and Highlights: 2019 Edition

This anthology showcases the talents of 55 authors, writers and poets. Among them are well-known travel memoirists, experienced travel writers and rising stars in the travel writing world.

A compilation of 66 short stories and 66 highlights, this collection will transport you around the globe from the comfort of your own home. It is a book you can enjoy whenever you have a spare moment.

See the world through the eyes of a Dominican man on his first trip abroad. Travel across the outback to the most remote roadhouse in Australia. Teeter on the edge of a cliff on the Adriatic coast as the bus loses control. Chill out on a Flotel in the remote Amazon tributaries of Bolivia. Find Christ in the high Andean passes between Chile and Argentina. Experience terror in the Egyptian desert at the hands of armed soldiers. Swim as nature intended with reef sharks in the warm waters of the Maldives.

Enjoy these and many more fascinating insights.

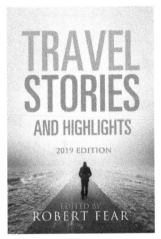

getBook.at/TravelStories2019

283

Acknowledgements

The many people I met and worked with in Ibiza.

Julie Haigh and Frank Kusy, for encouraging and supporting me throughout the writing of this book.

Luis Fernando Pareja Valdés for his help with the Spanish.

Ida at Amygdala Design for another wonderful cover.

Jennifer Barclay for her superb editing skills and advice.

Fellow-authors and beta readers at We Love Memoirs for their support and suggestions.

Last, but not least – you, the reader, for taking the time to read my memoir and leave a review.

Heartfelt thanks to you all.

CPSIA information can be obtained
at www.ICGtesting.com
Printed in the USA
LVHW042207281019
635548LV00002B/252

9 781692 936549